JUST IMMIGRATION

Just Immigration

American Policy in Christian Perspective

Mark R. Amstutz

WILLIAM B. EERDMANS PUBLISHING COMPANY
GRAND RAPIDS, MICHIGAN

Wm. B. Eerdmans Publishing Co.
2140 Oak Industrial Drive NE, Grand Rapids, Michigan 49505
www.eerdmans.com

23 22 21 20 19 18 17   1 2 3 4 5 6 7

ISBN 978-0-8028-7484-9

Library of Congress Cataloging-in-Publication Data

Names: Amstutz, Mark R., author.
Title: Just immigration : American policy in Christian perspective /
    Mark R. Amstutz.
Description: Grand Rapids : Eerdmans Publishing Co., 2017. |
    Includes bibliographical references and index.
Identifiers: LCCN 2016058806 | ISBN 9780802874849 (pbk. : alk. paper)
Subjects: LCSH: Church and state—United States. | Emigration and immigration—
    Religious aspects—Christianity. | United States—Emigration and immigration—
    Government policy.
Classification: LCC BR516 .A535 2017 | DDC 322/.10973—dc23
    LC record available at https://lccn.loc.gov/2016058806

For my students
past and present

Contents

Preface

Traveling with a group of religious leaders to the US-Mexico border near Douglas, Arizona, in March 2015, I witnessed aliens entering the United States unlawfully on two occasions. We stopped our vehicles on a hill where the border fence ended and where iron barriers had been placed to prevent vehicles, but not people, from entering the United States. As the sun was setting, two people darted across the border and ran into the Arizona desert. Soon after that, two Border Patrol all-terrain vehicles rushed to the vicinity where the two individuals had entered US territory, and within minutes of the border crossing, I saw the two individuals being walked back to the ATVs. On another occasion, I was traveling with a Border Patrol agent in the vicinity of Nogales, Arizona, when his radio alerted him to the fact that someone had scaled the eighteen-foot iron fence and run into the Arizona desert. Within a short time, that alien was found hiding in the dense brush and was taken away by another BP agent. Once the man was detained, I asked him in Spanish whether this was the first time he had entered the United States unlawfully. He responded that he had worked periodically as a roofer in Tucson and that this was his seventh illegal border crossing.

Although the United States has an elaborate immigration system to regulate entry into the country, my trip to the Mexican-American border in the Southwest certainly reinforced the belief that not everyone is following the established government rules. Getting permission to enter the United States from developed countries in the West—temporarily for business or tourist purposes—is relatively easy. However, getting a tourist visa from a low-income country or an unfriendly regime can be especially difficult. Securing a long-term (immigrant) visa is even more difficult, with delays ranging from five to twenty years. The concerns with border security are only one small dimension of a very complex and multidimensional policy concern: namely, what should be the policy toward foreigners who wish to come to work and live in the United States? Should the United States welcome an unlimited number of immigrants? If not, what should the annual admission ceiling be? And what should be the policy toward those who have entered the country unlawfully or have entered lawfully as tourists but have decided to remain in the United States?

My interest in US immigration policy was first sparked by the growing cry from American churches and Christian organizations for comprehensive immigration reform, including the legalization of migrants living in the United States without official authorization. Their impassioned advocacy made me want to understand the factors behind it: Why do they believe that the immigration system is unjust? Why do they believe that they have a unique contribution to make to the policy debate over immigration? More specifically, are the problems with the US immigration system due to the policies themselves, or do they arise from inadequate, inconsistent, and unpredictable enforcement of existing laws? Is the entire system bankrupt, or could modest, piecemeal reforms help to resolve some of the system's major shortcomings? Why are many Christian denominations and religious organizations advocating for comprehensive immigration reform? Finally, what explains the churches' interest in this public-policy issue, and why do they overwhelmingly support a more liberal policy, including amnesty for those who have entered the country unlawfully? The effort to answer these and other questions led me to carry out an extensive, multiyear investigation involving scholarly research, immigration court visits, interviews with government officials and human rights activists, and visits to the Mexican border in the American Southwest.

This book is the result of my investigation. Since I am a scholar in the discipline of international relations, I write from the perspective of one who seeks to understand the nature and role of international migration from the perspective of the existing international political system of nation-states. And because of my previous work in international ethics, I am deeply concerned about the moral dimensions of transnational migration. Finally, because I am a Christian, I seek to understand how Christian perspectives help to structure the analysis of international migration.

The Plan of This Book

Therefore, this book describes and assesses the US immigration system from a Christian perspective. It examines the values and biblical perspectives espoused by Roman Catholic, Mainline Protestant, and Evangelical churches, and it assesses how these values and perspectives are applied in the ongoing debate about immigration reform. Since Christianity proclaims that all humans are created in God's image and thus entitled to dignity and respect, Christian groups typically emphasize the fundamental rights of all persons, regardless of legal status, and call for compassionate and hospitable treatment of all migrants. But hospitality to strangers and compassion for migrants are inadequate pillars on which to build immigration policy.

Although Christian groups tend to acknowledge the decentralized nature of the contemporary world, the prevailing approach to immigration among Christian groups is a cosmopolitan perspective that highlights human welfare and de-emphasizes the regulatory policies of sovereign states. While biblical and theological norms are important in structuring the moral analysis of immigration policy, the task of applied ethics is not simply to set forth ideals but to illuminate how morality can contribute to a more humane and just world in general—and greater public justice within nation-states. Therefore, the analysis of this study begins by accepting the structure of a global society that is rooted in state sovereignty. In particular, it seeks to examine immigration in light of both the universal bonds affirmed by cosmopolitanism and the national loyalties of communitarianism.

This study explores the contributions and the limits of Christian ethics in the immigration debate. It examines how Christian norms can help structure the analysis and application of immigration reform in the United States. Since Scripture does not offer policy prescriptions on migration, I argue that Christian ethics provides a method for approaching the complex task of making and implementing immigration policy. At a minimum, a credible framework must involve: (1) competent knowledge of the problem; (2) an understanding of fundamental biblical/theological norms relevant to the issue; (3) a sophisticated integration of biblical morality with the issue; and (4) humility in advancing proposed analyses and recommendations.

I begin by describing and assessing the current US immigration system in the first chapter. Chapter 2 highlights key laws and institutions involved in the US immigration system, and chapter 3 assesses the system's effectiveness, emphasizing some of its major strengths and weaknesses. Chapter 4 describes the two dominant international-relations paradigms used in analyzing global affairs and illuminates how these different perspectives influence conceptions of international migration. In addition, the fourth chapter examines these alternative immigration perspectives from a Christian perspective. Chapter 5 illuminates how Christians approach social and political concerns: it highlights key elements of Catholic social thought and Protestant political ethics before examining how Christians have historically used Scripture to address social and political issues, including international migration. Chapters 6, 7, and 8 describe and assess how Catholics, Evangelicals, and Mainline Protestants have addressed US immigration. The final chapter offers suggestions for strengthening Christian political engagement in promoting a just and effective US immigration system.

Since immigration terminology is contested terrain, a brief description of key terms is in order. According to US statutes, an *alien* is any person who is not a citizen or national of the United States. In official usage, an *immigrant* is an alien who comes to live permanently in the United States. The US government distinguishes between *nonimmigrants*, who come to visit or work temporarily, and *immigrants*, who are admitted lawfully to live and work permanently in the country. Immigrants are legal permanent residents (LPRs) and are granted "green cards," which allow them to work and receive benefits. LPRs, however, are not allowed vote or serve on juries. In short, a lawfully admitted alien can be a legal permanent resident (immigrant), a temporary resident (nonimmigrant), or a refugee—that is, an alien who has fled his homeland because of war or fear of persecution.

According to the US Code, Title 8, an illegal alien is one who has entered the United States without inspection or one who has entered legally as a nonimmigrant but remained after his or her temporary visa (permit) expired. There is little consensus on how to refer to such aliens. Pro- and anti-immigration groups define unlawful residents differently. Human rights groups tend to refer to aliens who have overstayed their visas or who have crossed the border unofficially as "undocumented immigrants." Although this term is widely used by pro-advocacy groups, it fails to provide an accurate description of unauthorized aliens, since nearly all of them possess "a spectrum of valid and fraudulent papers." By contrast, groups that emphasize border enforcement refer to undocumented migrants as "illegal aliens" or simply "illegals." Although I use "undocumented alien," "unauthorized alien," "illegal alien," and "irregular migrant" interchangeably, most of the time in the following pages I shall refer to such migrants as "unauthorized aliens" because this is the most common way US government agencies refer to such persons.

Acknowledgments

In writing this book I have benefited from the assistance of many individuals. First, I thank Wheaton College, the Christian liberal arts college where I have taught for more than four decades, for granting me a semester's sabbatical leave in the spring of 2015. The leave allowed me to give undivided attention to carrying out research and writing and to interviewing church leaders, government officials, and policy experts. The leave also facilitated two trips to the Southwest border of the United States to meet with Border Patrol agents and policy activists. Second, I have been blessed with the outstanding help of three teaching assistants who provided helpful support. Annie Dehnel contributed early on in gathering relevant data, providing suggestions on important organizations and websites, and later reviewing portions of the emerging manuscript. Ariana Schmidt reviewed all the draft chapters and gave helpful substantive and editorial suggestions that contributed to the clarity of some of the book's key themes. Amy Wills provided invaluable assistance during the production phase by fact-checking and helping with the index. Third, Dee Netzel, who many years ago was my teaching assistant but now works as a freelance professional editor, reviewed the manuscript and provided invaluable editorial suggestions. Finally, I thank students in my International Politics and Ethics and Foreign Policy courses for raising important questions and concerns when addressing contemporary challenges posed by international migration. It is to those current and former students that I dedicate this book.

« 1 »

Morality, Law, and US Immigration Policy

As with most complex public-policy issues, the subject of immigration gives rise to a variety of views and perspectives. For some, regulating immigration is an important task of government as a means of building communal solidarity by giving priority to the assimilation of immigrants into the new community. For others, border control is a means to give priority to the interests and preferences of citizens. But for critics of such an approach, immigration control is a way by which citizens in stable, prosperous societies give precedence to their own needs over those of people from foreign states. In effect, immigration regulations allow states to justify global inequality. For business interests, the unimpeded movement of workers across territorial boundaries is assumed to be desirable to foster economic growth. According to this view, since domestic labor mobility is important in maximizing economic efficiency, unimpeded transnational labor mobility is also important to advancing global economic growth. For others, regulation of international migration is an impediment to the affirmation of universal human rights because the division of the world into sovereign nations legitimates radical inequalities among states. Immigration concerns arise only because the international community has been divided into nation-states.

In her book *Undocumented*, Aviva Chomsky captures this latter perspective when she writes, "Immigration simply should not be illegal."[1] In her view, immigrants should be accorded the same rights and privileges as citizens: "Immigrants are human beings who have arbitrarily been classified as having a different legal status from the rest of the United

---

1. Aviva Chomsky, *Undocumented: How Immigration Became Illegal* (Boston: Beacon, 2014), ix.

1

States' inhabitants. The only thing that makes immigrants different from anybody else is the fact that they are denied basic rights that the rest of us have. There is simply no humanly acceptable reason to define a group of people as different and deny them rights."[2]

I do not accept Chomsky's premise that the existing global order of nation-states is morally illegitimate. Rather, the analysis of immigration that I set forth in this book is based on the existing global order of nation-states. This does not mean that sovereign states can disregard the interests and concerns of peoples from other nations. Rather, the challenge of advancing justice in the international community—and, more specifically, the task of devising morally just immigration practices—must begin with the recognition that nation-states are the fundamental units of the contemporary global order. Under the world's constitutional order, enshrined in the United Nations Charter, states are responsible for the affairs within their territorial boundaries. This means that sovereign governments are responsible for maintaining social order, protecting human rights, and promoting prosperity. Since states are ultimately responsible for domestic economic and social life, regulating borders is an important task of sovereign governments. The worldwide acceptance of sovereignty and border regulation is evident by the widespread use of passports and visas that facilitate governmental control of transnational migration. As Cheryl Shanks notes, sovereignty is a fundamental norm of the political architecture of the world. "Controlling access to citizenship," she writes, "helps states stay sovereign in the face of globalization."[3]

Citizens have the right to leave their homeland without official permission, but they do not have a right to enter another country. That decision is in the hands of the host state. The asymmetrical relationship between emigration and immigration is a source of enormous humanitarian challenges in the modern world. Such challenges have become especially difficult in the post–Cold War era because of globalization and the collapse of states. The first development is important because technological modernization has fostered increased economic and social integration, resulting in increased knowledge about foreign societies and dramatically lower costs in transnational migration. The second development, the rise of failed states, is a byproduct of the decline of sovereign authority coupled with increasing ethnic, tribal, and religious conflicts.

2. Chomsky, *Undocumented*, ix.

3. Cheryl Shanks, *Immigration and the Politics of American Sovereignty, 1890-1990* (Ann Arbor: University of Michigan Press, 2001), 1.

In some countries, such as Somalia, Afghanistan, Iraq, Libya, Rwanda, Syria, and the former Yugoslavia, civil wars have resulted in enormous human suffering, leading to millions of refugees and displaced peoples. In 2015, the United Nations High Commissioner for Refugees (UNHCR) estimated that there were nearly 20 million refugees and about 40 million internally displaced people.[4] When more than half a million Syrian refugees sought entry into Europe in 2015, it precipitated a crisis within the European Union (EU).

Since most EU member states allow free movement among its members, the entry of large numbers of refugees into Greece led some countries, such as Hungary and Macedonia, to establish border security in order to restrict the flow of refugees. Even Sweden and Denmark, which have maintained liberal migration policies, established tighter border controls to curb the influx of asylum seekers.[5] As of early 2016, it was estimated that more than one million refugees, nearly half of them from Syria, had sought asylum in Germany alone.[6]

Since the United States is protected by the Atlantic Ocean on its eastern coast and by the Pacific Ocean on its western coast, it has not had to face massive flows of refugees, such as those entering Europe from the Middle East.[7] Instead, the United States has been faced with millions of aliens who have entered the country unlawfully through its porous southwest border with Mexico. Furthermore, because of lax enforcement of laws governing visitors, students, and temporary workers, many aliens who arrive lawfully decide to remain in the country even after their visas have expired. It is estimated that of the 11 million aliens living in the United States without authorization, about 40 percent arrived legally but have overstayed their visas.[8]

Immigration policy has two dimensions. First, a government must

4. UNHCR Mid-Year Trends, 2015. Available at: http://www.unhcr.org/56701b969.html.

5. Charles Duxbury, "Sweden, Denmark Tighten Borders," *The Wall Street Journal*, January 5, 2016, A7.

6. Andrea Thomas, "Germany Took in 1.1 Million Migrants in 2015," *The Wall Street Journal*, January 7, 2016, A8.

7. It did allow some 100,000 Vietnamese refugees to enter the country in the aftermath of the communist takeover of South Vietnam in 1975. It also accepted some 125,000 Cubans in the spring and summer of 1980, when Fidel Castro allowed Cubans to leave the island.

8. Bryan Roberts, Edward Alden, and John Whitley, *Managing Illegal Immigration in the United States: How Effective Is Enforcement?* (New York: Council on Foreign Relations, 2013), 32.

determine the total level of new migrants it wishes to admit. This task involves not only determining the number of immigrants and refugees who are accepted for resettlement but also determining the number, if any, of temporary or guest workers. Second, the government must establish the criteria used in admitting immigrants. Currently, the United States grants visas to roughly 800,000 immigrants per year, but the total number of people who are accepted as legal permanent residents (LPRs) is about a million per year. The number of new LPRs is higher than the number of newly admitted immigrants because the total also involves persons admitted as refugees and those seeking asylum, as well as persons who already live in the United States and whose legal status is adjusted by the government. This second policy task, establishing admissions criteria, is especially difficult because it involves setting priorities in the face of competing and conflicting political demands.

Because of the perceived limitations in the current US immigration system, political leaders have undertaken numerous initiatives in the new millennium to reform current policies. For example, President George W. Bush sought to advance immigration reforms but was unable to get the Congress to adopt the proposed changes. Subsequently, President Obama called for broad changes in immigration policy, but he, too, was unable to garner sufficient legislative support to advance comprehensive reforms. The most recent significant legislative initiative has been the bipartisan US Senate Bill 744, titled "Border Security, Economic Opportunity, and Immigration Modernization Act." The bill, a massive document of more than a thousand pages, calls for, among other things, strengthening border security, legalizing undocumented aliens, and increasing the number of employment-based visas. Although the US Senate passed that bill in June 2013, the House of Representatives refused to take up the measure. As of 2016, no major immigration initiatives are pending in Congress. But while immigration reform was dormant in 2015 in Washington, DC, the topic was featured prominently among some presidential candidates during the 2016 election campaign. Given the continuing demands for low-wage workers, the growing size and influence of the Latino population, and the desire to resolve the status of illegal aliens, immigration reform will likely surface again with a new administration in 2017.

The Need for Immigration Reform

There is widespread agreement that the design and implementation of US immigration policies suffer from major limitations. Many of the policy shortcomings are the result of competing, if not irreconcilable, political interests. These competing pressures and tensions include the excessive demand for immigrant visas beyond the number that the US government is legally authorized to supply; the challenge of being compassionate to unauthorized migrants while also seeking to maintain the rule of law; the desire for having high-skilled and low-wage workers while also maintaining a restrictive policy on employment-based migration; and the demand to enforce employment laws without implementing an effective identification system to facilitate this task. Besides the shortcomings in the laws themselves, the US immigration system also suffers from inadequate and inconsistent implementation. Given the broad and complex nature of immigration policies and the limited resources available to implement them, government agencies rely on executive discretion in channeling resources to enforce concerns that are regarded as a priority.

The following diverse cases illustrate some of the challenges and contradictions that present themselves when one attempts to maintain a credible, humane immigration system.

1. In 1996, the US Congress passed the Illegal Immigration Reform and Immigrant Responsibility Act (IIRIRA) to reduce the number of illegal immigrants. The law sought to do this by forcing those living in the United States without authorization to return to their own countries to secure a visa at a US consulate. The problem with this initiative is that aliens who have lived in the United States unlawfully are prohibited from returning immediately because the law imposes a heavy penalty of three to ten years for "unlawful presence." Since many unauthorized aliens have lived in the United States for many years, have families there, and have established roots in local communities, being separated from spouses, children, neighbors, and friends for several years makes legalization extraordinarily difficult. Thus, instead of encouraging unlawful aliens to seek to normalize their status by securing a visa, the current system motivates aliens to "live in the shadows." As with other government initiatives, immigration policies often result in unintended consequences; that is, good intentions do not necessarily lead to desired outcomes.

2. In 2014, tens of thousands of unaccompanied children, mostly from El Salvador, Guatemala, and Honduras, entered the United States unlawfully. The dramatic and sudden increase in the number of children

entering the country through the southwest border was not a random development. Rather, it reflected families' decisions to use children, aided by smugglers, to enter the country with the knowledge that they would be treated differently than adults. Since US law requires that children entering without authorization must be processed quickly and separately from adults, the sudden increase in children led the government to construct several shelters to care for their needs while they were being processed. The effort to address the unexpected arrival of unaccompanied children resulted in shifting resources from established refugee programs to the needs of children. Here again, the unintended result of compassion-driven policy toward children forced the American government to withdraw support from another sector of society in need of care. Competing interests are not always between economic and humane concerns; sometimes they involve making a hard choice between competing moral values.

3. My frequent visits to the Immigration Court in Chicago during 2015 illuminated the uncertain, complex, and time-consuming action of processing immigration hearings. Immigration Courts, which are supervised by the US Department of Justice, hear deportation cases initiated by Immigration and Customs Enforcement (ICE). During my court visits, a large number of cases were heard from respondents in prison via tele-video. Those individuals had committed crimes and had thus come under the scrutiny of ICE. In one case, the unauthorized alien had been imprisoned for driving under the influence of alcohol (DUI) and using false documents. Since he was not married and had no US relatives, the judge issued a deportation order. He also told the respondent that returning to the US unlawfully would be a felony, subject to a longer prison sentence. In another tele-video case, the unauthorized alien had been arrested and convicted of DUI. Although he had twice been returned to his Mexican homeland under voluntary departure, he was currently in detention for entering the country unlawfully. He had a job, and his employer indicated that he was an effective worker. He had a girlfriend and three children who were born in the United States. Since his original conviction for DUI, he had converted to Christianity, and the judge noted that the respondent showed evidence of rehabilitation. He lowered the $10,000 bond to $2,500 so that he could live at home and work. He gave the respondent a new hearing date so that he could seek relief from deportation.

In a third case, a Mexican alien had entered the United States illegally and was convicted of making a false claim that he was a US citizen.

He posted a $25,000 bond. Supported by his wife and children in court, he was seeking the cancellation of his removal. The judge set a new hearing date in 2018—three years in the future!

Court cases such as these illuminate the complex task faced by immigration judges in determining the extent to which humanitarian concerns should mitigate strict legal enforcement. Since living in the United States without legal authorization is a misdemeanor, it does not lead automatically to deportation. The many immigration court cases that I observed were being heard because aliens had committed offenses after entering the United States. The task of the judge was to address the offense of unlawful presence while taking into account factors that might mitigate the need for deportation.

4. In March 2015, federal agents executed search warrants at several southern California sites that were allegedly involved in "birth-tourism"—that is, promoting temporary visits to the United States by pregnant women. According to press reports, several businesses were providing assistance in coordinating travel, lodging, and medical care to help mothers deliver so-called "anchor babies." The centers that were raided catered to wealthy Chinese women, who paid a broker fee of close to $50,000, excluding medical expenses.[9] Since a child born in the United States is a US citizen regardless of the nationality or legal status of the mother, some immigrants desire to have their children gain a foothold in the United States so that they will become eligible for public services and later, after turning twenty-one years of age, be able legally to sponsor family members as immigrants to the United States. Although some legislators and political leaders have denounced birth-tourism, it is difficult to prosecute individuals for seeking to give birth in the United States because it is not illegal for a pregnant woman to travel to the United States on a tourist visa. Although some American observers find the birth-tourism phenomenon troubling, the practice of coming to the United States to have a child illuminates the high value that some foreigners place on having formal citizenship ties in the United States. It also shows the extent to which some aliens will seek temporary entry for reasons other than tourism or work. Therefore, in issuing tourist visas, American consular officers have the additional complex responsibility of determining applicants' true intentions.

Cases such as these exemplify the challenges that US government

9. Miriam Jordan, "Birth-Tourism Spots Raided," *The Wall Street Journal*, March 4, 2015.

officials face in seeking to establish a humane and just immigration system and to ensure that its rules are enforced impartially and consistently. This is a difficult task in a world where millions of people from foreign countries—especially Asia and Latin America—would love to come to the United States to work, settle, and become citizens. The US government has established a highly complex immigration system involving many different types of visas, each with its own requirements, coupled with annual caps for each visa category as well as annual country ceilings. Because of the complexity of the policies and the excessive demand for immigrant visas, a large number of people seek to enter the United States unlawfully or to enter lawfully with a tourist visa and then remain in the country without authorization. To explore US immigration policy is to raise profound moral questions about human rights, the rights and responsibilities of sovereign states, and the rule of law within constitutional democracies.

Historical Roots of America's Ambivalent Immigration Policy

The limitations and problems in current US immigration policy are not recent developments; they are rooted in the tensions, ambiguities, and inconsistencies in the diverse and conflicting goals that emerged when the US government first began trying to regulate immigration in the early nineteenth century.

Unlike many other nation-states, the United States and its populace resulted from the departure of foreign peoples from their homelands for economic and religious reasons. Although some scholars suggest that the United States is a land of immigrants, Samuel Huntington claims, legitimately, that the first Europeans to arrive in the New England were not immigrants but settlers. Settlers, he writes, are those who leave their homeland in order to create a new community. They arrived in the new land not as individuals but as groups that were guided by a sense of collective purpose. Immigrants, by contrast, do not seek to create a new society. Instead, they move from one society to another to advance their personal interests.[10]

---

10. Samuel P. Huntington, *Who Are We? The Challenges to America's National Identity* (New York: Simon and Schuster, 2004), 38–40. It is important to emphasize that the English settlers did not arrive in unclaimed territory—or what international lawyers call *terra nullius*. As a result, in establishing new communities in Virginia, Massachusetts,

According to Huntington, America's early settlers established the moral and political foundation of a new political order. The basis of the new nation was a shared moral-cultural system based on the Christian religion, Protestant values, a work ethic, the English language, and British traditions of law, justice, and the limits of governmental power. From this shared Anglo-Protestant culture, the settlers developed a set of political beliefs (or a creed) to inspire and structure the politics of American society. According to Huntington, this American creed is rooted in principles of liberty, equality, individualism, representative government, and private property.[11]

Once the settlers had established the new nation by declaring political independence from Britain and devised a constitution to regulate governmental power, immigrants began arriving in the late eighteenth century. Early on, American leaders were unsure whether the states or the national government should bear responsibility for regulating immigration. As a result, for the first one hundred years, immigration was largely unrestricted. Even though a growing number of efforts were made to control immigration, especially immigrants from China, roughly ten million persons immigrated to America between 1820 and 1880.[12] In response to the increasing pace of immigration in the late nineteenth century, the US government sought to institutionalize immigration policy by creating the Bureau of Immigration in 1891. This new federal agency—the forerunner of the Immigration and Naturalization Service (INS) and later Citizenship and Immigration Services (CIS)—was charged with regulating immigration.

Immigration increased rapidly in the late nineteenth century. Total immigration in the 1880s and 1890s was estimated at 5.2 million and 3.6 million, respectively. In the first decade of the twentieth century it peaked at 8.8 million; however, World War I led to a dramatic collapse in new migration. Furthermore, where earlier immigrants had come from northern and western Europe, at the turn of the twentieth century, immigrants were arriving from southern and eastern Europe. As a result of the changing origins of immigrants, American public opinion shifted from managing total immigration to an emphasis on keeping some ethnic groups out.

Rhode Island, and elsewhere, settlers had to contend with opposition from indigenous peoples, conflicts that resulted in the death of some settlers and many Native Americans.

11. Huntington, *Who Are We?*, 41.

12. David Weissbrodt and Laura Danielson, *Immigration Law and Procedure in a Nutshell*, 6th ed. (Minneapolis: West Publishing Co., 2011), 4–5.

The first major effort to restrict Asian immigrants was adopted in 1882, when the Chinese Exclusion Act was enacted. This act, which halted all immigration of Chinese laborers for ten years, was later extended and made permanent. The law was not repealed until 1943. In addition to the efforts to restrict Asians, Congress also sought to limit immigrants from eastern and southern Europe. In 1917, for example, Congress passed an immigration law that established a literacy test as an entrance requirement; this was designed to limit the less-educated immigrants from southern and eastern Europe. Four years later, Congress adopted a quota law based on a person's national origins, which capped new European immigrants at 3 percent of the number of foreign-born persons of that nationality residing in the United States in the 1910 census. (This formula was amended in 1924, and again in 1929.)[13] Of the 150,000 immigrant visas granted in 1929, the law allocated 85 percent to persons from northern and western Europe and 15 percent to persons from southern and eastern Europe.

Ironically, the efforts to expand border regulation spawned increased illegal immigration. This was especially the case during the 1940s and 1950s, when American farmers, especially those in California, began hiring more Mexican agricultural workers. To address significant labor shortages during World War II, the Mexican and US governments established a seasonal bilateral guest-worker program (known as the *bracero* program), which was operational from 1942 until it was terminated in 1964 due to alleged migrant exploitation and opposition from organized labor. Although some 4 million Hispanic workers participated in the *bracero* program, the demand for low-wage labor far outstripped the availability of official permits to work in the United States.[14] As a result, the number of unauthorized migrant workers continued to expand during the 1940s and 1950s. Indeed, by the mid-1950s, there were more unauthorized migrant workers than *bracero* guest workers. To confront the crisis of illegality, US authorities deported about one million migrants in the mid-1950s.[15] Even after the crackdown on "wetbacks" (the so-called unauthorized workers who supposedly "got wet" crossing the Rio Grande), opposition to guest workers persisted.

13. Three years later, Congress further restricted immigration by reducing the number of immigrants to 2 percent of the foreign-born under the 1890 census. In 1929, Congress further changed the basis for calculating the "national origins formula" by using the ethnic background of the entire US population.

14. Chomsky, *Undocumented*, 11.

15. Chomsky, *Undocumented*, 58.

In 1952, Congress passed the Immigration and Nationality Act (INA), which consolidated previous immigration laws into one statute. The INA, which has served as the foundation for all subsequent immigration reforms, retained the national origins quota and established admission preferences. Despite increasing apprehensions by the Border Patrol, immigration increased significantly in the 1950s and 1960s. It is estimated that 2.5 million people immigrated to the United States in the 1950s and more than 3.3 million in the 1960s.[16] In 1965, Congress abolished the national origins quota formula with the adoption of the Hart-Cellar Immigration Act, which divided the world into the Eastern and Western Hemispheres and placed an overall limit of 170,000 annual immigrants from Europe and 120,000 from Latin America. More important, the new law revised the preference system, giving priority to families over workers. Since 1965, the INA has been amended several times; in each case the aim has been either to make adjustments in total admissions and preferences or to address a specific problem, such as refugee admissions, illegal immigration, or the need for seasonal workers. (Chapter 2 describes key features of the most important immigration statutes adopted since 1965.)

This brief historical overview reveals how immigration policy continues to evolve in response to changing domestic and international conditions and the shifting values and attitudes of the American people. Americans have welcomed migrants, but they have also sought to restrict their entry. Because of this American ambivalence, Aristide Zolberg argues that developing a coherent immigration policy has been an elusive quest. On the one hand, the US government has tried to establish a "front door" policy for legal immigration but has tolerated a "back door" policy for unauthorized entry to meet the demand for low-wage workers. It has also maintained a "side door" policy to admit refugees, especially those from areas threatened by communist regimes, such as Vietnam and Cuba.[17] For legal scholar Philip Kretsedemas, the US immigration system has involved ambiguous, paradoxical policies that encourage some migration as well as some restraint. He declares, "The implicit message being sent by these [US government] policy decisions is that immigration may not be desirable but it is most certainly necessary." Because of the variability

---

16. Weissbrodt and Danielson, *Immigration Law*, 16-17.

17. Aristide R. Zolberg, *A Nation by Design: Immigration Policy and the Fashioning of America* (Cambridge, MA: Harvard University Press, 2006), chap. 10.

and inconsistency in US immigration policy, he suggests, the American immigration system is best defined as "institutionalized irregularity."[18]

Peter Skerry observes that Americans express special ambivalence toward immigrants who have arrived or remained unlawfully. "Americans do not, by and large," he writes, "approve of those who reside here without permission, yet we implicitly invite them to do so and only reluctantly crack down on their employers. Just as the circumstances faced by illegal immigrants in our country are simultaneously threatening and encouraging, so the nation's attitude toward illegals has long been at once hostile and welcoming."[19] Yuval Levin similarly concludes that the root source of illegal immigration is the people's ambivalent attitudes toward immigration. "The United States," he writes, "has invited them in even as it has pushed them away."[20] Robert Suro expresses the legacy of ambivalence as follows: "It was illegal for these immigrants to be here, but no one made them leave."[21]

Christian Ethics and Immigration

Immigration policy concerns the movement of persons across territorial boundaries of nation-states. From an ethical perspective, who has the right to decide who should be admitted into a country? How many migrants should be allowed in, and what criteria should be used in the admissions process? What should be done with those migrants who have violated the law by overstaying their visas, or who have crossed the border unlawfully? How many refugees should be admitted? And how should the claims of refugees be weighed against the businesses and families who are sponsoring immigrants? Should immigration policies simply reflect the interests of its citizens, or should morality also play a role in determining immigration practices? In order to address such issues, we need not only to understand the domestic laws and institutions regulating migration but also to know the political ar-

18. Philip Kretsedemas, *The Immigration Crucible: Transforming Race, Nation, and the Limits of the Law* (New York: Columbia University Press, 2012), 4, 19.

19. Peter Skerry, "Splitting the Difference on Illegal Immigration," *National Affairs* 14 (Winter 2013): 11-12.

20. Yuval Levin, "The Immigrant Middle Ground," *National Review Online*, August 14, 2014.

21. Robert Suro, *Watching America's Door: The Immigration Backlash and the New Policy Debate* (New York: Twentieth Century Fund, 1996), 33.

chitecture of the international community and the shared values and interests of states.

The international community is made up of nearly two hundred sovereign nation-states, each of which is regarded as autonomous and legally equal. Since each state is sovereign, it is responsible for affairs within its borders. This means that states are responsible for managing immigration—that is, determining the number and criteria for admitting migrants. Typically, a country's foreign policy, including migration, is designed to advance the goals of its citizens. This view is captured in the final report of the US Commission on Immigration Reform, released in September 1997, when it declared, "It is both a right and a responsibility of a democratic society to manage immigration so that it serves the national interest."[22]

To a significant degree, people's beliefs about migration will be based on how they conceive of the international community. International-relations scholars have developed a variety of paradigms by which to assess global politics. Two of the most influential theories are *cosmopolitanism* and *communitarianism*. The first views the world as a unitary global society in which the individual rights of people take precedence over the sovereign rights of territorial states. The second views the world as a society of nation-states in which the primary responsibility of such states is to protect and enhance the rights and well-being of its own people while also caring for all people.

These two perspectives give rise to different conceptions of migration.[23] Since cosmopolitans view the nation-state as an impediment to global justice and the promotion of human rights, they favor an open-borders approach to migration. For them, freedom of international movement is a basic human right. In their view, people should have the right to migrate to whatever country they wish to. Communitarians, by contrast, believe that sovereign states can only maintain social solidarity by regulating borders. For them, the state must give priority to the needs of its own people before it addresses the needs of peoples in foreign societies. Following international law, communitarians believe that people have a right to emigrate, but the decision whether to be admitted is a responsibility of the host state.

22. US Commission on Immigration Reform, "Becoming an American: Immigration and Immigrant Policy." Available at: https://www.utexas.edu/lbj/uscir/becoming/ex-summary.pdf.

23. For a discussion of how these two international-relations paradigms influence conceptions of migration, see my article "Two Theories of Immigration," *First Things* (Dec. 2015): 37–42.

How should Christians approach immigration issues? More generally, how should they view the international community and its member states? Is there a Christian perspective on global order? On the rights and obligations of citizens? On the right to migrate? The Bible is not a manual for social and political life, nor does it serve as a direct guide to public policy. It does not provide direct guidance on the policies that governments should pursue in addressing concerns such as poverty reduction, climate change, or migration. Rather, Scripture provides principles and perspectives that can help guide thought and action on the morality of important public-policy issues. In his book *Foreign Policy in Christian Perspective*, theologian John C. Bennett argues that while the Christian faith does not provide specific policy guidance, it does offer "ultimate perspectives, broad criteria, motives, inspirations, sensitivities, warnings, and moral limits" that can help structure the analysis of public affairs and inspire and guide action.[24]

This book seeks to illuminate a Christian approach to the challenge of international migration—and particularly the immigration concerns facing the United States. Since major Christian denominations have sought to influence the policy debate on immigration in the new millennium, this book describes and assesses their analyses and advocacy. An important aim of this study is to examine and critique the churches' immigration work in order to provide recommendations for strengthening their moral contribution to the policy debate. I believe that churches and religious groups can make an important contribution to the moral analysis of immigration by illuminating important biblical and moral principles. They can also contribute to the ethical analysis of immigration by confronting tradeoffs between competing moral norms, such as the rights of citizens versus the rights of migrants, the claims of families versus the claims of employers, the desires of economic migrants versus the rights of refugees, and the protection of human rights versus honoring border security.

Since politics involves power and competition, it inevitably results in conflict and divisiveness. As a result, when churches become directly involved in advancing political goals, they risk diluting and even undermining their transcendent mission. Alexis de Tocqueville long ago called attention to the dangers that would result from political action by religious actors. In *Democracy in America* he says, "The church cannot share

24. John C. Bennett, *Foreign Policy in Christian Perspective* (New York: Charles Scribner's Sons, 1966), 36.

the temporal power of the state without being the object of a portion of that animosity which the latter excites."[25] In view of the dangers of a politicized religion, I wish to examine in this book the ways Christian denominations have sought to address one temporal public policy concern: immigration.

This book is not concerned with abstract theorizing about how the world should be reconfigured or what a perfectly just immigration policy might look like. Aaron Wildavsky, a noted scholar of public policy, observes that the challenge in crafting effective policies is less about the realization of ideal goals than about their transformation. Policy analysis, he argues, is less about pursuing established preferences than about reconfiguring those preferences in light of environmental and political constraints. "A policy that is marginally preferable has much to commend it," he suggests, "compared to one that is perfectly impossible."[26] Following Wildavsky's admonition, this study examines US immigration policy not from an idealistic, cosmopolitan worldview but rather from a communitarian perspective that accepts nation-states as normative. It explores how Christian values and perspectives can help structure the analysis of immigration in order to advance a just immigration policy in light of domestic and international political constraints.

25. Alexis de Tocqueville, *Democracy in America*, trans. Henry Reeve (New York: Appleton, 1904), 1:334.

26. Aaron Wildavsky, *Speaking Truth to Power: The Art and Craft of Policy Analysis* (New Brunswick, NJ: Transaction, 1987), 404-8.

« 2 »

The Rules of the Game

A sovereign nation-state is responsible for the welfare and security of all people living within its territorial boundaries. Under the United Nations (UN) constitutional order, a sovereign state has ultimate authority over its own domestic affairs and its international relations with other states. Because freedom is a basic human right, people are free to leave their homeland, but they do not have an inalienable right to enter another country. Citizens are free to emigrate, but they do not have the right to immigrate. Whether a person is allowed to enter a foreign country is decided by officials of the receiving state. "People have a right to leave," writes Cheryl Shanks, "but not a right to enter."[1]

The imbalance between leaving and entering communities is not unique to global society; it is a widely shared practice in most human communities. The decision of whether one can join a business firm, for example, is up to the leaders of that business enterprise. Similarly, students who seek a college education must be granted admission by the specific institution they choose. In the liberal arts college where I teach, prospective students complete a detailed application form, and only months later are they notified whether they have been accepted. College enrollment, in short, is carefully regulated, with the demand for admission far outstripping the availability of openings in prestigious universities and colleges.

All nation-states, including the United States, regulate migration. This means that entering a foreign state requires the permission of that receiving country. To facilitate international travel, nationals must pos-

---

1. Cheryl Shanks, *Immigration and the Politics of American Sovereignty, 1890-1990* (Ann Arbor: University of Michigan Press, 2001), 3.

sess an official identity document (typically a passport) that identifies a person's nationality. When citizens of one country seek to enter a foreign country, a government official will inspect their passport at an entry post and then stamp it, thereby acknowledging official admission. Upon a person's departure, the passport once again is stamped to acknowledge departure. Some people may seek to bypass established government procedures by either entering legally and then failing to leave in accordance with visa requirements or by entering illegally, thus bypassing official inspection. In the United States, it is estimated, roughly 40 percent of unauthorized aliens are those who have overstayed their visas.

Each nation-state must decide the number and background of persons it wishes to admit. Some countries, like Japan, admit few migrants; other nations, like Australia, Canada, and the United States, admit a relatively large number of aliens. A few countries, such as Kuwait, Qatar, the United Arab Emirates, and other Middle Eastern oil-producing nations, admit a large number of guest workers who are given temporary work permits but are barred from permanent residency. Some countries, such as Canada and the United States, offer a limited number of work permits to unskilled agricultural and nonagricultural workers, but these laborers are similarly prohibited from establishing permanent ties to the host society. Because of the inherent challenges involved in protecting migrant human rights, most liberal democracies, especially in Western Europe, have refrained from using migrant labor. Countries like West Germany discovered that guest workers quickly established bonds to the host economy and were reluctant to return to their homeland, especially if their families had established social and cultural ties in the host society.[2]

There are two major types of international migration: temporary and permanent. People in the first type—called "nonimmigrants"—are by far the largest in number and include millions of temporary visitors, tourists, students, business travelers, and guest workers. The second group involves "immigrants": these are people who seek permanent settlement in a new country. In 2012, the US government admitted about 165.5 million nonimmigrants, while the number of immigrant admissions was a little over one million.[3]

---

2. In the early 1970s and 1980s, West Germany welcomed workers from Turkey in order to meet its labor needs, but it then discovered that workers who established roots in the host society were reluctant to return home.

3. Alberto R. Gonzales and David N. Strange, *A Conservative and Compassionate Approach to Immigration Reform: Perspectives from a Former US Attorney General* (Lubbock: Texas Tech University Press, 2014), 3.

Typically, the US government issues immigrant visas to roughly 675,000 persons annually. More than two-thirds of these visas are granted to facilitate family unification; only 140,000 visas are granted for employment purposes. Individuals admitted as immigrants are classified as legal permanent residents (LPRs) and given a so-called green card, which officially entitles them to work and to travel abroad. In addition to the admission of immigrants, however, each year a large number of nonimmigrants already living and working in the United States are allowed to adjust their status to LPR. All told, roughly one million aliens are added permanently to the population of the United States each year.

The Basic Elements of US Immigration Law

The backbone of US immigration law is the Immigration and Nationality Act (INA) of 1952. This law, also called the McCarran-Walter Act for its two sponsors, Senator Pat McCarran (R–NV) and Congressman Francis Walter (D–PA), is important because it consolidates previous laws governing immigration into one statute, thereby establishing the foundation for contemporary immigration policy. The law retains and codifies the National Origins Quota System (first established in 1924) by continuing to give preferential treatment to individuals from northern and western Europe. While the law repealed existing measures that excluded Asian immigrants on the basis of nationality (e.g., Chinese), it nevertheless continued to discriminate against Asians on the basis of race. It is worth noting that countries from the Western Hemisphere were exempted from the quota system. Finally, and most significantly, the INA established a system of preferences to prioritize visa applications. The law created three preference groups: those with special skills; those who had immediate family (spouses, children, or parents) who were US citizens; and those who were considered "average" immigrants. Immigrants in the second group were to be admitted without restrictions, while the number of "average" immigrants was not to exceed 270,000 per year. In addition, the law provided for the admission of refugees as a distinct group.[4]

Since adopting the INA, Congress has passed more than 140 laws

4. Refugees—"forced migrants"—are persons who flee their homeland because of war, persecution, or natural disasters. According to international law, refugees are persons who seek safety in a foreign land because of a "well-founded" fear of persecution for reasons of race, religion, nationality, membership in a particular social group, or political opinion.

that have modified this statute. The most important revisions are the following.

- The Immigration and Nationality Act of 1965 (Hart-Cellar Act), which abolished the national-origins quotas and replaced them with preferences based on family ties and employment needs. The law placed an overall cap of 170,000 immigrants from the Eastern Hemisphere and a cap of 120,000 from the Western Hemisphere; in addition, it set a 20,000-per-country limit for Eastern Hemisphere countries, a cap that was extended to Western Hemisphere countries in 1976.
- The Refugee Act of 1980, which separated asylum seekers and refugees from the general immigration policies. While the original annual ceiling for refugee admissions was set at 50,000, it gave the President, in consultation with Congress, the authority to adjust that cap in light of global humanitarian needs.
- The Immigration Reform and Control Act (IRCA) of 1986 (Simpson-Mazzoli Act), which addressed the growth of illegal immigration. The law called for greater border enforcement, sanctions against employers who knowingly hired unauthorized workers, and legalization of unlawful aliens who had been living continuously in the United States for four years (i.e., since January 1, 1982). The amnesty, which was conditional on payment of a fine and back taxes and a criminal background check, resulted in nearly three million aliens being given LPR status.
- The Immigration Act of 1990, which increased the ceiling for annual immigration to 700,000 (later reduced to 675,000) and strengthened skills-based immigration with the establishment of five preference categories. The number of employment-based immigrant visas tripled. Additionally, the law created a "diversity" visa program to allow people from underrepresented countries to apply for an immigration visa through an annual lottery known as the "diversity visa lottery." In 2015, close to 9.4 million qualified applicants registered for the lottery. The 1990 law established the following annual immigration ceilings, which remained valid fifteen years later (2015): 465,000 visas for family preferences, 140,000 for workers, and 55,000 for diversity.
- The Illegal Immigration Reform and Immigration Responsibility Act (IIRIRA) of 1996, which sought to reduce unauthorized migration by strengthening border control and imposing stiffer sanctions on ille-

gal aliens, stricter employer sanctions, and greater ease in deporting unauthorized aliens, especially those who have committed crimes. One of the important measures of this statute is the three- and ten-year bar for unauthorized aliens. According to this provision, aliens who have been in the United States unlawfully for more than 180 days but less than one year must remain outside the United States for at least three years before they can apply for a visa, while those who have been in the United States unlawfully for more than a year must remain outside the United States for at least ten years before they can apply for a visa to return to the United States.[5] In addition, the law mandated the detention and deportation of those noncitizens (LPRs and unauthorized immigrants alike) who had been convicted of an "aggravated felony." The law also expanded the offenses that qualified as "aggravated felonies" (e.g., tax evasion and receipt of stolen property) and applied this new standard retroactively to crimes committed in past years. Finally, the law restricted judicial review of immigration officials' decision to deny admission.

- The Homeland Security Act of 2002, which abolished the Immigration and Naturalization Service and transferred most of its functions to the Department of Homeland Security (DHS). Under the new law, immigration tasks are now handled by three bureaus: the Citizenship and Immigration Services (CIS), which processes immigrant and nonimmigrant petitions, naturalizations, asylum, and other related matters; the US Customs and Border Protection (CBP), which is responsible for inspection at ports of entry; and the US Immigration and Customs Enforcement (ICE), which enforces immigration laws within the country.

Despite the many changes in the INA, the 1952 statute remains the basic building block for US immigration policy. The INA is a large, complex document that is divided into titles, chapters, and sections.[6] In the following, I describe some of the most important principles and guidelines of the US immigration system by focusing on: (1) nonimmigrant admissions; (2) immigrant admissions; (3) family-based preferences;

5. Unauthorized aliens can seek relief from these provisions in an immigration court if these measures impose significant hardship on family members who are US citizens.

6. The INA is also contained in the United States Code, which is a collection of all laws of the United States. The Code is arranged in fifty subject titles, with "Aliens and Nationality" listed as Title 8.

(4) employment-based preferences; (5) diversity visas; and (6) refugees and asylum seekers.

Admission of Nonimmigrants

As I have noted above, a nonimmigrant is an alien who seeks to enter the United States temporarily for business, pleasure, academic or vocational study, or temporary employment. Such a person is a resident of a foreign state who is committed to remain a national of that state. To be eligible for admission, a foreign national must meet the following criteria: establish that the visit is temporary; agree to depart at the end of the authorized visit; possess a valid passport; maintain a foreign residence (i.e., country of origin); be admissible; and abide by the terms of admission.

Ordinarily, admission requires a visa that is secured by way of an application and an interview at a US embassy or consulate. To be admitted at airports and seaports, visitors must complete Form I-94, which records their arrival. Canadian and Mexican nationals with a border-crossing card are exempted from these requirements. In addition, some thirty-six countries participate in a Visa Waiver Program, which allows nationals of designated countries to travel to the United States as tourists or business travelers without a visa.[7] In 2013, the leading countries for nonimmigrant admissions were Mexico (29 percent), the United Kingdom (7.5 percent), Canada (7.3 percent), and Japan (7 percent).[8]

According to the Department of Homeland Security, in 2013 the United States granted 173 million admissions, most of them for commuting aliens who cross the border frequently on business. About 35 percent of these admissions are for temporary business and pleasure travel that involve an I-94 form.

The US government maintains a wide variety of visa categories to meet the needs and desires of its citizens and those of foreign nationals. The three major types are:

1. *B visa.* Two types are available: B-1 is for temporary business

---

7. The waiver program, which specifies entries as WB (waiver business) and WT (waiver tourist), accounts for roughly 45 percent of all nonimmigrant visas issued annually.

8. Katie Foreman and Randall Monger, "Nonimmigrant Admissions to the United States: 2013," Annual Flow Report, July 2014, Office of Immigration Statistics, US Department of Homeland Security.

purposes, and B-2 is for temporary leisure travel. B visas account for roughly 42 percent of all nonimmigrant visas.[9]

2. *F visa.* These are reserved for aliens who seek to pursue education at an accredited academic institution. The F visa accounts for about 3 percent of nonimmigrant visas.[10]

3. *H visa.* This type is for aliens carrying out short-term work.[11] The two main classes of H visas are for temporary skilled work (H-1B) and for temporary unskilled work (H-2). The H-2A visa is for seasonal agricultural work, and the H-2B is for temporary nonagricultural work. The H-1B visa, which is capped at 65,000 per fiscal year, is valid for a maximum of six years. H-2A and H-2B visas, which are capped at 66,000 per fiscal year, are generally valid for up to one year but may be extended for a maximum of three years, after which the temporary worker must leave the United States for at least ninety days.[12]

Other important types of visas include the L visa, which is available to businesses for intracompany transfers; the R visa, which is reserved for religious workers; the T visa, which is available to victims of severe human trafficking; and the U visa, which is available to an alien who has suffered substantial abuse and possesses information on criminal activity that would contribute to an offender's prosecution.

Admission of Immigrants

According to the INA, total annual immigration to the United States is capped at 675,000. Of this worldwide total, 480,000 is allocated for

9. Gonzales and Strange, 137.

10. Gonzales and Strange, 139.

11. H visas account for roughly 2 percent of nonimmigrant admissions annually. Spouses and unmarried minor children of temporary workers (H visas) are eligible to apply for H-4 nonimmigrant visas. These family visas account for 16 percent of all H-visa admissions. See Gonzales and Strange, 141.

12. To secure temporary foreign workers, an employer must apply for a temporary labor certificate (TLC) from the US Department of Labor. To be eligible for a TLC, an employer must demonstrate that there are not enough workers who are qualified and willing to do the work. Additionally, the employer must show that the use of foreign workers will not depress the wages of native workers and agree to pay temporary laborers the same wage that local workers receive. Once the TLC is approved, the employer petitions the CIS for a visa. After the employer's petition has been approved, the prospective worker applies for a temporary worker visa at a US embassy or consulate.

family reunification, 140,000 is for employment, and 55,000 is to advance diversity—that is, to promote the admission of underrepresented groups of people. In addition, the United States admits other aliens not subject to a global ceiling, such as refugees and asylum seekers. The annual ceiling for refugee admissions is established by joint collaboration between the President and the Congress. In addition, US law limits immigrant admissions from any country to 7 percent of the worldwide total in order to inhibit overconcentration from some nations.[13] The per-country ceiling is an entitlement rather than a limit to prevent monopolization. Furthermore, the per-country ceiling is important because, as economist Paul Collier has argued, there is a propensity for immigration from particular countries to accelerate as the size of the diaspora increases in the host state.[14] Notwithstanding this provision, however, recent immigration to the United States has been dominated by a small group of countries, including Mexico, China, India, and the Philippines.[15]

All persons admitted as immigrants are automatically legal permanent residents (LPRs), or "green card" recipients. This status allows immigrants to live and work permanently in the United States and to participate in the social, economic, and cultural life of the nation. LPRs, however, are not allowed to vote and are barred from receiving most welfare services. After several years of permanent residence, an LPR can pursue naturalization, a process that culminates in citizenship. In recent years, about one million aliens have been accepted annually as LPRs. This means that the total number of new legal residents is much greater than immigrant admissions. The reason for this is that every year the US allows hundreds of thousands of nonimmigrants in the United States to adjust their legal status. In 2013, for example, of the nearly one million aliens receiving LPR status, a majority (53.6 percent) of the applications were based on change in status, while a minority (46.4 percent) were for new arrivals.[16]

13. In determining immigration quotas per country, persons who immigrate to the United States are allocated to the foreign state in which they were born.

14. See Paul Collier, *Exodus: How Migration Is Changing Our World* (New York: Oxford University Press, 2013), 27–53.

15. According to the DHS, of the nearly one million aliens granted permanent legal residence in 2013, Mexico accounted for 13.6 percent, China for 7.2 percent, India for 6.9 percent, and the Philippines for 5.5 percent. See Randall Monger and James Yankay, "US Lawful Permanent Residents: 2013," Office of Immigration Statistics, Department of Homeland Security, May 2014, 4.

16. Monger and Yankay, 2.

Based on the INA guidelines, four major principles govern permanent immigrant admissions: the reunification of families; a priority for workers with needed skills; the protection of refugees; and the promotion of diversity by country of origin. Below I briefly highlight key features of each of these four categories of immigration.

Family-based immigration

Unlike most advanced democracies, the United States is unique in that almost two-thirds of its permanent immigrant admissions are based on family ties. This policy was first institutionalized with the Hart-Cellar Act of 1965. Developed democracies that support modest increases in immigration, such as Australia and Canada, give priority to skilled workers over family reunification. Family-based immigration is a result of petitions of citizens or legal permanent residents already in the United States. The most important element of family-based immigration is the inclusion of immediate family members—that is, spouses, minor children, and parents.[17] In addition, citizens and LPRs can sponsor other relatives using four preference categories. Although immediate family members are not subject to a numerical limit, the additional family preferences are each subject to quotas.

The four family-preference categories are as follows.

1. *First preference* applies to unmarried adult sons and daughters of US citizens and has an annual cap of 23,400, plus any visas not required for the fourth preference.
2. *Second preference* allows LPRs to sponsor spouses and minor children and unmarried sons and daughters. The ceiling for these two subgroups is capped at 114,200 and visas not required for the first preference. In addition, at least 77 percent of the admissions must be allocated to the first subgroup.
3. *Third preference* allows citizens to sponsor married sons and daughters and has an annual ceiling of 23,400, plus visas not required for the first or second preference.

17. To be able to sponsor an immediate family member, the US citizen must be at least twenty-one years old. The age stipulation is important for children born in the United States to unauthorized parents because such children are automatically US citizens. The age requirement thus prevents minors from sponsoring immediate family members until they reach adulthood.

4. *Fourth preference* allows US citizens to sponsor brothers and sisters and has an annual cap of 65,000, plus visas not required for the first, second, or third preferences.

According to the INA, total immigration from the four family preferences must be at least 226,000 per year. According to the Department of Homeland Security, the total number of LPR admissions in 2013 was 990,553, of which 439,460 (44.4 percent) were accounted for by immediate relatives and 210,303 (21.2 percent) by family-sponsored preferences.[18]

Employment-based immigration

Employment-sponsored immigration permits persons with needed skills, professional qualifications, or educational credentials to immigrate in order to meet the needs of an enterprise. The INA, which has established an annual quota of at least 140,000 employment-based visas per fiscal year, specifies five preference categories, each with a numerical limit: "priority workers"—that is, persons with extraordinary abilities in the arts, education, business, science, or athletics; professionals with advanced degrees; skilled workers, professionals, and other workers; special immigrants, such as religious workers; and entrepreneurs who are willing to start a new business venture by investing at least a million dollars. Each of the first three preferences is limited to 28.6 percent of the total employment-based annual quota; the fourth and fifth preferences are limited to 7.1 percent of the annual quota.[19]

Diversity immigration

The diversity visa program, which was established by the Immigration Act of 1990 in order to promote greater global representation, allocates 55,000 visas annually through a lottery. Fifty thousand of these visas are selected randomly, while the remaining five thousand are allocated to Nicaragua or other Central American nationals under the Nicaraguan and Central American Relief Act of 1997. The program, which is run by

18. Monger and Yankay, 3.

19. Ruth Ellen Wasem, "US Immigration Policy on Permanent Admissions," Congressional Research Service (March 13, 2012), 4.

the Department of State, allows aliens from eligible countries to enter the annual lottery. Those who are chosen in the lottery can then apply for a diversity visa. Besides currently living in an eligible country, applicants must have at least a high school degree or have two years of work experience in an occupation that requires a minimum of two years of training within the past five years. In the 2014 lottery, close to 11.4 million persons registered to participate. In recent years, several immigration reform bills, including the 2013 Senate bill 744, have called for the elimination of the diversity program. They have done so in the belief that the diversity initiative detracts from the more fundamental goals of facilitating family unification and bolstering a skilled workforce. According to DHS Office of Immigration Statistics, of the 45,618 diversity visas allocated in 2013, Africa received 40.7 percent, Asia 32.8 percent, and Europe 22.2 percent; South America received only 1.4 percent. The countries with the largest number of "lottery" immigrants were Iran (3,447), Nepal (3,210), Uzbekistan (2,944), Nigeria (2,778), and Ethiopia (2,255).[20]

Refugees and asylees

Although distinct from the formal US immigration system, the United States maintains a program to care for refugees—that is, persons who have been persecuted or have a well-founded fear of persecution in their home country. To be eligible for refugee status, an applicant must meet the definition set forth in the INA (101 [a][42]): someone who is unable or unwilling to return to his or her country of origin because of persecution or a well-founded fear of persecution on account of *race, religion, nationality, membership in a particular social group*, or *political opinion*. Refugees are aliens who apply for protection outside of the United States. Asylees, by contrast, are aliens who apply for protection after arriving in the United States.[21]

20. Department of Homeland Security, Yearbook of Immigration Statistics, 2013, Table 10. Available at: https://www.dhs.gov/sites/default/files/publications/ois_yb_2013_0.pdf.

21. Asylum status can be pursued affirmatively through an asylum officer of the US Citizenship and Immigration Services (USCIS) or defensively before an immigration judge of the Department of Justice's Executive Office for Immigration Review. Aliens who pursue the affirmative process have arrived in the United States with a valid visa, while those pursuing the defense process are in removal proceedings because they have arrived unlawfully or have violated another law.

In the aftermath of World War II, the US government implemented a number of initiatives to respond to the plight of persons fleeing severe oppression and violence. Many of those requesting asylum were fleeing totalitarian oppression in communist countries such as Hungary and Cuba. To develop a more institutionalized approach to the intermittent but growing suffering of refugees, the US Congress adopted the Refugee Act of 1980. In 1967 the United States ratified the 1951 Refugee Convention and undertook the passage of the 1980 act to further institutionalize the nation's commitment to refugee concerns and to demonstrate its commitment to international norms concerning the status of refugees. This new law created a program to process refugee admissions and to set an annual refugee quota that was to be established by the President in consultation with Congress. While the refugee quota was first set at 50,000, in recent decades it has varied between 60,000 and 80,000 per year in the new millennium. In 2016, the refugee admissions ceiling was increased by 15,000 to 85,000.[22]

According to the Department of Homeland Security, the United States admitted 69,909 refugees in 2013. The leading countries from which people sought refuge were Iraq (19,487), Burma (16,299), Bhutan (9,134), Somalia (7,608), and Cuba (4,205). The total number of persons who were granted asylum in 2013 was 25,199, with China accounting for 35 percent of the total and Egypt accounting for 13.5 percent.[23] The rise of failed states and civil wars has resulted in a significant rise in the total number of refugees and internally displaced persons (IDPs) in the world. According to the United Nations Refugee Agency (UNHCR), 11.7 million refugees were under its care at the end of 2013.[24] A year later, the total number had increased to 14.4 million, a 23 percent increase. Of the total, three countries accounted for more than half of all new refugees: Syria, with 3.88 million; Afghanistan, with 2.59 million; and Somalia, with 1.1 million.[25] The rise in

22. Proposed Regional allocations were as follows: Africa—25,000; East Asia—13,000; Europe/Central Asia—4,000; Latin America/Caribbean—3,000; Near East/South Asia—34,000; and unallocated reserve—6,000. Source: US Department of State, "Proposed Refugee Admissions for Fiscal Year 2016," Table 1. Available at: http://www.state.gov/documents/organization/247982.pdf.

23. Daniel C. Martin and James E. Yankay, "Refugees and Asylees: 2013," Office of Immigration Statistics, Department of Homeland Security, August 2014, 3.

24. UNHCR, "Statistical Yearbook 2013," 28. Available at: http://www.unhcr.org/54cf987d9.html.

25. UNHCR, "Global Trends, 2014." Available at: http://www.unhcr.org/556725e69.html.

the number of refugees, especially from Syria, has resulted in hundreds of thousands of people risking dangerous journeys by land and sea in search of a safe haven.[26] As of 2015, the United States had admitted fewer than two thousand Syrian refugees. In light of the humanitarian crisis posed by Syria, US government officials announced that the United States would welcome as many as 10,000 Syrian refugees in 2016.

Miscellaneous immigration

In addition to family-based, employment-based, and diversity-based immigration, the INA also provides other avenues for aliens to become LPRs. One way is for the attorney general to parole an unauthorized alien, who in time can apply for an adjustment of status. In addition, certain nonimmigrants may be allowed, based on extreme personal hardship, to remain permanently in the United States through a process known as "cancellation of removal." Finally, and most significantly, refugees and asylees are given the opportunity to adjust their status to LPR. According to one estimate, miscellaneous immigration accounts for roughly 15 percent of all annual LPR admissions.[27]

US Government Agencies Involved in Immigration

Historically, the major agency responsible for immigration has been the Immigration and Naturalization Service (INS), which was established in 1933. Prior to that time, immigration issues were the responsibility of the Immigration Bureau, housed in the Department of Labor. In 1940, President Franklin Roosevelt shifted the INS from the Department of Labor to the Department of Justice because of growing security concerns about aliens living in the United States. The INS remained within the Department of Justice until 2003, when it was replaced by the Citizenship and Immigration Services (CIS), which became housed in the newly

26. Because of the generous benefits and economic prospects available in Europe, more than a half million migrants have sought entry there. Since the EU has a common policy on refugees and because movement among member states has few constraints, the great number of refugees have presented a major challenge in how to distribute the social and economic burden involved in caring for them. As of late 2015, European countries had been unable to devise a collective strategy to the crisis.

27. Monger and Yankay, 3.

created Department of Homeland Security. The new organization was established in the aftermath of the terrorist attacks of 9/11 in order to strengthen national security with improved border control and more effective monitoring of immigration.

Although numerous departments are involved in immigration affairs, the chief agency responsible for implementing the INA is the Department of Homeland Security (DHS). Its importance stems from the fact that it is responsible for preventing terrorist attacks and ensuring the security of the homeland, administering and enforcing immigration laws, and securing the country's borders. With more than 200,000 employees, DHS is the third-largest cabinet department in the US government. Although DHS has many different organizations that are involved in domestic security, three agencies are directly involved in regulating the entry of people and goods into the United States: the Citizenship and Immigration Services (CIS), which reviews petitions for immigration, adjustment of status, and naturalization and ensures that people working in the United States are legally authorized to do so; the US Customs and Border Protection (CBP), which regulates the entrance of all goods and people into the United States; and the Immigration and Customs Enforcement (ICE), which is responsible for enforcing immigration laws within the country.[28]

The Departments of Justice and of State, and, to a lesser degree, the Departments of Labor and of Health and Human Services also play pivotal roles in immigration policy implementation. In the following I describe the work of the three key agencies of the Department of Homeland Security and briefly discuss the role of the other departments.

Citizenship and Immigration Services (CIS)

Most of the work carried out by CIS is the processing of forms for aliens who desire to immigrate to the United States, to adjust their legal status from nonimmigrant to immigrant, to receive authorization to work temporarily in the country, or to change their legal status from LPR to citizen (or other related requests). In processing these applications, CIS seeks to ensure the accuracy and reliability of an alien's information and to determine the merits of each application. For example, eligible LPRs

---

28. Other important agencies of the DHS include the Coast Guard, the Secret Service, the Transportation Security Administration (TSA), and the Federal Emergency Management Agency (FEMA).

who seek citizenship must complete a naturalization application (Form N-400), demonstrate basic knowledge of English and American history and government, and undergo an interview.

CIS also plays an important role in processing refugee applications and asylum petitions. To qualify for refugee resettlement in the United States, the alien must meet the internationally accepted standards for refugees, be of special humanitarian concern to the American people, and meet the criteria for admissibility. Further, the alien must meet the criteria of the US Refugee Admissions Program (USRAP), which establishes the priorities for refugee admissions.[29] After receiving a referral from the admissions program, the applicant is interviewed by a CIS officer overseas to determine eligibility for resettlement. If the application is approved, the alien (along with family members) is given a medical exam, cultural orientation, and assistance in making travel plans. Upon arrival, the responsibility for the refugee's adjustment and well-being is given to the Department of Health and Human Services' Office of Refugee Resettlement.

Two types of asylum petitions are available: affirmative asylum, which involves a petition with the CIS, and defensive asylum, which involves a request before an immigration judge. Typically, the affirmative petitions are initiated by nonimmigrants who are in the United States lawfully and who seek to remain in the United States because of a well-founded fear of persecution if they were to return to their own country. Defensive asylum petitions, which are initiated by unauthorized aliens after they have been placed in removal proceedings, represent requests to remain in the United States because of a fear of persecution in their homeland. The defensive asylum request is made in court to an immigration judge. Both types of asylum seekers must complete an application form that details the threats that the applicants are likely to face if they return. A CIS asylum officer then interviews the applicant. If the officer approves the petition, the case goes to an immigration judge, who makes the final determination. In 2013 there were 21,717 defensive asylum applications, and 30 percent of them were approved. At the same time there were 14,957 affirmative applications, of which 74 percent were approved.[30]

29. Each year the President, in consultation with Congress, issues a Presidential Determination on Refugees, which establishes overall admissions levels and regional allocations. Those eligible for refugee resettlement must fit into the established government admissions priorities and geographical distributions.

30. Executive Office for Immigration Review, *FY 2013: Statistics Yearbook*, Office of Planning, Analysis, and Technology, April 2014, K3.

CIS also plays an important role in processing work-authorization forms and verifying a worker's employment status. Since every non-citizen who seeks to work in the United States must be authorized by CIS, aliens must complete and submit the Application for Employment Authorization (I-765). If the applicant is approved, CIS issues an employment-authorization document, which is usually valid for one year. Because employers are required to verify the status of workers, they do so by reviewing the Employment Verification Form (Form I-9) in light of corroborating documents submitted by the employee. While the completion of Form I-9 is mandatory for all employers, its value has been questioned because of the ease of documentation forgery; in addition, the I-9 Form does not require a Social Security number or a photograph. To improve the credibility of employment verification, CIS has developed a computer-based program called E-Verify, which verifies an employee's data against government records. If E-Verify fails to corroborate the data, the employer must take additional steps to ensure the legality of the employee's status or, failing that, terminate the laborer's employment. Even though the completion of E-Verify is still voluntary as of 2015, it is nonetheless used by more than 560,000 businesses and organizations.

Customs and Border Protection (CBP)

CBP, the largest federal law enforcement agency in the United States, is responsible for monitoring and controlling the entry of people and goods into the United States. It carries out its mission by inspecting travelers and cargo at 324 ports of entry and by patrolling some six thousand miles of land border and nearly two thousand miles of coastal waters surrounding Florida and Puerto Rico.[31] In carrying out its border surveillance, the Border Patrol relies on electronic monitoring, video monitoring, night-vision scopes, drones, helicopters, and boats, as well as all-terrain vehicles, horses, and foot patrols. In 2014, CBP had more than 42,000 officers; roughly half of that number serve as Border Patrol agents. Nearly 18,000 agents are assigned to the southwest border of the United States to supervise the entry of goods and people at twenty-four land ports of

---

31. CPB maintains forty-five major land ports of entry, twenty-one along the northern border with Canada and twenty-four along the southwest border with Mexico.

entry. Confronting drug trafficking and illegal immigration at the established entry ports presents the CBP's major challenge.

A primary task of the Border Patrol is to detect and halt illegal immigration, human trafficking, drug smuggling, and unlawful cargo while also providing efficient entry of people and goods at ports of entry. Given the nationwide entry of nearly 25 million containers and more than 170 million nonimmigrant admissions every year, providing efficient entry of people and cargo is a daunting task, to say the least. To improve the efficient processing of cargo, CBP has developed a number of inspection procedures that facilitate container processing. CBP has also created several electronic identification systems that provide permits to preapproved, low-risk travelers.[32] From an operational perspective, however, the fundamental aim is not efficiency but effectiveness—namely, ensuring that only legitimate goods and authorized aliens enter the United States.

For our purposes, the chief responsibility of the Border Patrol is to ensure that immigrants enter the United States lawfully and to reduce, as much as possible, unauthorized entry. At the beginning of the new millennium, the Border Patrol pursued this goal chiefly by apprehending unlawful aliens along the border. The practice at the time was to catch illegal aliens and then allow them to return voluntarily to their homelands. However, this catch-and-release practice did not reduce illegality, because those who were released simply reentered the United States at a later date. In 2005, DHS changed its border strategy by ending voluntary return and requiring the processing of all apprehended aliens. Under the revised system, DHS personnel were allowed to deport unauthorized aliens without a removal order from an immigration judge. Under the so-called reinstatement of removal process, DHS officers can deport unauthorized aliens who have been previously removed. The second process—"expedited removal"—is used to deport aliens who have not been previously charged with an immigration offense but who have entered the United States unlawfully, are within a hundred miles of the border,

---

32. Three of these electronic programs include: (1) the Global Entry Program, which allows preapproved persons to avoid immigration delays at airports by proceeding to a kiosk, where their passport is scanned and their identity is confirmed with fingertip verification; (2) the Secure Electronic Network for Traveler's Rapid Inspection (SENTRI), which distributes electronic identity cards to approved, low-risk travelers based on a background check and an interview—the cards can be used to enter the United States by car in designated lanes at land ports of entry; and (3) NEXUS, which allows prescreened travelers expedited processing when entering the United States from Canada (and also those entering Canada from the United States) at northern ports of entry.

and who have been in the country for two weeks or less. Because of the DHS's shift in strategy, apprehensions have subsequently declined while the number of removals has increased. For example, the Border Patrol apprehended about 1.67 million aliens in 2000 and 1.26 million aliens in 2001. Ten years later (2010), total apprehensions were fewer than 500,000 per year.[33] At the same time, annual deportations have risen significantly, especially during the Obama presidency.

Immigration and Customs Enforcement (ICE)

The third major DHS immigration agency is ICE, the agency chiefly responsible for enforcing immigration laws within the country itself. Whereas the Border Patrol apprehends unlawful aliens at the border and up to one hundred miles inland, ICE is primarily responsible for identifying and removing unauthorized aliens throughout the country as a whole. With 20,000 employees and an annual budget of more than $6 billion, ICE's major law enforcement responsibilities are to identify, apprehend, and deport unlawful aliens, especially those who pose a threat to the country's security and well-being. ICE's work is carried out by two major agencies: Homeland Security Investigations (HSI) and Enforcement and Removal Operations (ERO). The former is chiefly an intelligence agency that investigates the unlawful movement of people and goods across the US border; ERO, by contrast, is the law-enforcement arm that apprehends and deports unauthorized aliens, especially those who have been convicted of a serious crime or who pose a threat to national security. Given the large number of unauthorized aliens in this country, DHS uses "prosecutorial discretion" in enforcing the law by setting detention and removal priorities. As of 2014, the aliens most likely to be detained and deported were those engaged in suspected terrorism or espionage, aliens involved in organized criminal gangs, unauthorized aliens apprehended at the border, and aliens convicted of a felony or aggravated felony.[34]

33. U. S. Border Patrol, "Nationwide Illegal Alien Apprehensions Fiscal Years 1925-2015." Available at: https://www.cbp.gov/sites/default/files/documents/BP%20 Total%20Apps%20FY1925-FY2015.pdf.

34. In November 2014, Jeh Johnson, the head of DHS, issued a directive with law-enforcement priorities. He declared that DHS's highest law enforcement priorities would continue to be national security, public safety, and border security. Available at: http://www.dhs.gov/sites/default/files/publications/14_1120_memo_prosecutorial _discretion.pdf.

Ever since the US government toughened the nation's immigration enforcement system with the passage of the Illegal Immigration Reform and Responsibility Act of 1996, the number of noncitizens who are temporarily detained and subsequently deported has increased significantly. Currently, ICE is required by Congress to maintain detention facilities for 34,000 persons—a so-called bed mandate. Most of the 250 detention facilities located throughout the United States are county jails and for-profit detention centers. As of 2012, ICE was detaining about 400,000 persons per year at a cost of about $1.9 billion. Most unauthorized aliens are detained for under two months, and many are released on bond to await a future hearing at one of many immigration courts.

Department of Justice's (DOJ) Executive Office for Immigration Review (EOIR)

The Department of Justice is responsible for the application and interpretation of immigration law to specific cases, a task administered by the EOIR, which oversees the adjudication of federal immigration law through the work of three agencies: the Office of Chief Immigration Judge, which supervises fifty-nine immigration courts located throughout the United States; the Board of Immigration Appeals, which reviews decisions of immigration judges; and the Office of the Chief Administrative Hearing Officer, which oversees employment cases. As of 2014, there were 243 immigration judges.

Cases are assigned to the DOJ's immigration courts by the Department of Homeland Security. When ICE determines that an alien has violated an immigration law, it charges the person and orders him or her to appear before an immigration judge by issuing a Notice to Appear. Typically, a lawyer from ICE's Office of the Principal Legal Advisor represents the interests of the US government. Since the US government does not provide legal assistance to aliens charged with violating immigration laws, whether or not they receive legal aid will be determined by whether they secure assistance from pro bono human-rights attorneys or have the financial means to secure a personal lawyer.

The most important and voluminous work performed by immigration courts is determining which aliens should be removed. In 2014, the EOIR received 225,896 new cases, of which 95 percent concerned removal.[35] In dealing with new cases, the judge must first decide whether the charges against an alien are valid. If the charges are not sustained, the judge terminates the case. If the charges are sustained, the judge decides whether to order the deportation of the alien or to grant relief. In the decisions made on new cases in 2014, immigration judges terminated 12.4 percent of the cases, granted relief in 14.7 percent, and ordered removal in 72 percent of the cases.[36]

US Department of State

The Department of State is responsible for two important immigration-related tasks. First, the department's Bureau of Consular Affairs (BCA) is responsible for issuing passports (which allow US citizens to travel overseas) and granting visas (the official permits to enter the United States). The BCA issues two types of visas: immigrant visas for those who desire to live and work permanently in this country, and nonimmigrant visas for those who come for tourism, to work temporarily, to study at accredited academic institutions, or to facilitate business enterprises. Though other departments are involved in assessing the legitimacy and suitability of visa applicants, US consular officers in embassies are the first persons who interview visa applicants in order to assess their requests. In 2014, the Department of State issued 9.9 million nonimmigrant visas and 467,000 immigrant visas. Since the Department of State is responsible for the diversity visa program, it hosts an annual lottery that allows some 50,000 aliens to be granted permanent admission into the United States.

The Department of State's second important immigrant-related responsibility is to help identify and select refugees eligible for resettlement in the United States. Although refugee admissions involve cooperation among several US government departments, the Department of State's Population, Refugees, and Migration (PRM) bureau has the lead role in proposing total and regional admissions ceilings as well as the criteria for selection. As noted earlier, the US government maintains the multidepartment Refugee Admissions Program to facilitate coordination among US government agencies and with international governmental and nongovernmental organizations working with refugee affairs. In

35. Executive Office for Immigration Review, *FY 2014 Statistics Yearbook*, Office of Planning, Analysis, and Technology, March 2015, B1.

36. *FY 2014 Statistics Yearbook*, C2.

carrying out its responsibilities, the PRM bureau shares with DHS's Citizenship and Immigration Services the responsibility of identifying those groups and individuals who should be considered for resettlement in the United States. To be eligible to apply for refugee status, the alien must be registered as a refugee with the UNHCR, complete the refugee application, and be interviewed by a US asylum officer. If approved, the refugee—working with the Department of State's PRM personnel—works out travel and arrival arrangements. Once the refugee arrives in the United States, the resettlement process is carried out through domestic agencies, such as Lutheran Immigration and Refugee Services, International Rescue Committee, World Relief, and the Catholic Church's Migration and Refugee Services. Once resettlement is underway, the government's responsibility of oversight is taken over by the Department of Health and Human Services' Office of Refugee Resettlement. After a year in residence, the refugee is allowed to apply for adjustment of status to legal permanent resident.

In 2015, there were between 14 and 16 million refugees worldwide. From an ethical perspective, these refugees have moral priority over immigrants because of the danger and persecution they face in their own countries. Given the enormous humanitarian needs in our contemporary global system, developed industrial states (including the United States) face a daunting challenge in determining the number and criteria for admitting refugees and for granting them asylum. Currently, the United States resettles about 70,000 refugees annually and grants asylum to another 20,000 to 30,000 aliens. But the number of refugees is far greater than the willingness of the United States and other developed nations to accept them for resettlement. As a result, the primary way of caring for their needs is through direct assistance in refugee camps and through multilateral funding of UNHCR and other humanitarian NGOs.

Other departments

The Department of Health and Human Services (HHS) plays an important role in caring for refugees and unaccompanied minors through its Office of Refugee Resettlement (ORR). After refugees arrive in the United States, HHS assumes responsibility for their placement and their ongoing care while they adjust to their new environment. The ORR carries out much of its work via nongovernmental organizations that receive grants and program guidance in dispensing social, medical, and health services.

Similarly, after unaccompanied minors are detained and processed by the Border Patrol, they are transferred within seventy-two hours to HHS personnel. They, in turn, seek to find a safe, appropriate, and less restrictive environment—preferably with a family member—that can provide care for the juveniles while their request for asylum is processed.

The Department of Labor plays an important role in processing employment applications for temporary skilled and unskilled workers as well as permanent foreign employees. Before an employer can apply for an H-2 visa with CIS, a job request must be filed and processed by the Department of Labor. The aim of the department's administrative role is twofold: first, to ensure that there are not enough American workers who are willing and qualified to do the needed work, and second, to ensure that the employment of foreign workers will not adversely affect the wages and working conditions of similarly employed US workers. Once the foreign worker receives an H-2A or H-2B visa, the worker is required to work solely for the particular business that sponsored the visa. Ironically, unauthorized workers have far more flexibility in moving from job to job.

Finally, the Drug Enforcement Administration (DEA), the federal agency responsible for curbing illicit drug trafficking and prosecuting persons involved in it, works closely with CBP and ICE, especially along the United States' southwest border, in order to halt the cross-border transfer of illegal drugs. Because many criminal gangs involved in drug trafficking are also involved in the smuggling of aliens, the Border Patrol and DEA cooperate to identify, detain, and prosecute aliens involved in smuggling people and controlled substances. Given the significant profits provided by smuggling, halting illegal migration and illicit drugs remains an elusive goal.

The Challenge of Legal Enforcement

Illegal immigration did not arise in recent decades. Rather, the intermittent transnational migration of Mexicans finds its roots in the lax controls over the southwest US-Mexico border and increased opportunities for low-wage agricultural work in the United States. A significant number of migrants began crossing the southwestern border in the 1930s to provide temporary agricultural labor to American farmers in southwestern states. Although the *bracero* program sought to regulate the number of peasants working in the United States, the demand for low-wage workers far exceeded the supply, resulting in many unskilled workers entering the United States without border inspection. By the mid-1950s, there were more unauthorized migrant workers than guest workers. To confront the crisis of illegality, US authorities deported some 1.5 million migrants in the mid-1950s. But even after that crackdown on illegal migrants, opposition to guest workers persisted. In the early 1960s the widespread opposition from labor unions succeeded in terminating the *bracero* program. Because of the ongoing demand for low-wage workers, the *bracero* program was soon replaced by a more informal guest-worker initiative centered on direct ties between farmers and migrants. Under this system, the demand for unskilled workers continued to increase as migrants took up work in unskilled areas beyond farms. In addition, a growing number of unauthorized workers brought their families with them and, rather than returning after the temporary work had been completed, began settling permanently in the United States.

The US government has undertaken a number of initiatives to reduce illegal migration. The two most significant measures include the Immigration Reform and Control Act (IRCA) of 1986 and the Illegal Immigration Reform and Immigrant Responsibility Act (IIRIRA) of 1996. However, these and other laws have been unsuccessful in curbing unauthorized immigration, largely because the economic demand for low-wage workers far exceeds the supply of native workers who are able and willing to do the work. Since the US government caps the number of temporary visas for unskilled workers, the availability of low-wage work opportunities encourages many workers to seek to enter the country unlawfully. But in addition to workers and family members who wish to enter the United States, there are millions of other aliens without work or family connections who desire to move to the United States from their homeland. The high demand for entry into the United States is evident from the more than 11 million persons who register to participate in the annual lottery sponsored by the Department of State for 50,000 diversity visas. In short, because of the imbalance between the demand and supply of visas that the US government is willing to authorize, many migrants decide to enter the United States unlawfully—either by overstaying their visas or by avoiding legal inspection when entering the country.

For many years the government's approach to illegal migration has been to identify and repatriate aliens without formal processing. Since most unauthorized aliens were caught at or near the border, the federal authorities would detain and return that alien—a process called "catch and release." But this policy failed to work because the returned aliens would simply attempt later crossings until they succeeded in entering the country. To reduce illegal crossings, US immigration authorities began prosecuting aliens caught entering the country unlawfully. As a result of increased border control and more effective processing, the number of apprehensions declined significantly after about 2005. As a result, the number of prosecutions for illegal border crossings rose dramatically; by mid-2013, they accounted for nearly half of all federal criminal prosecutions.[37]

According to the Pew Research Center, there were 11.2 million unauthorized immigrants in 2012; that number had peaked in 2007 at 12.2 million.[38] Besides the forces of supply and demand for workers, the "wink-and-nod" approach to immigration law enforcement has also contributed to the growth in the number of irregular immigrants. Being in the United States unlawfully is not a felony; rather, it is a misdemeanor that is punishable by detention and removal. But given competing economic and social forces, coupled with the US government's commitment to both human rights and the rule of law, the large number of unlawful migrants presents a daunting challenge to government institutions. To effectively confront unlawful presence, government officials must identify, detain, process, and remove irregular migrants, and it must be done in a way that is consistent with the nation's democratic values and humanitarian sensibilities. Given the complexity of this task, administrations have relied extensively on prosecutorial discretion, focusing the government's resources in those areas they consider most important. But reliance on executive discretion has impaired consistent policy implementation, which, in turn, has undermined the credibility of the rule of law.

The American people remain staunchly opposed to illegal immigration, believing it is detrimental to the country. A CBS News poll in 2014, for example, found that 84 percent of the respondents believed that illegal immigration was a "very serious" or "somewhat serious" issue.[39] Both the Select Commission on Immigration and Refugee Policy, chaired by Rev. Theodore Hesburgh, and the US Commission on Immigration Reform, chaired by former Congresswoman Barbara Jordan, emphasized the harmful impact of unauthorized immigration and offered

37. Hiroshi Motomura, *Immigration Outside the Law* (New York: Oxford University Press, 2014), 50.

38. "Five Facts about Illegal Immigration in the US," Pew Research Center, November 18, 2014.

39. CBS News Poll, July 29–August 4, 2014. Available at: http://www.pollingreport.com/immigration.htm.

numerous recommendations to strengthen border control and improve legal compliance. The Hesburgh Commission, which called for closing the "back door" of immigration in order to open the "front door" further, influenced public opinion and helped to structure congressional action that resulted in the passage of the Immigration Reform and Control Act (IRCA) of 1986. IRCA is important because it has sought to reduce illegal immigration by requiring employers to verify the legal status of their employees.

The Jordan Commission, which was established by the Immigration Act of 1990, issued two interim reports in 1995—one on illegal immigration and the other on legal immigration.[40] The first report, titled "US Immigration Policy: Restoring Credibility," called for greater efforts to reduce unlawful immigration by strengthening border control and providing for more efficient deportation of unauthorized aliens.[41] It also emphasized the need to establish an effective system of verifying employment eligibility. The interim report declared, "The credibility of immigration policy can be measured by a simple yardstick: people who should get in, do get in; and people who should not get in are kept out; and people who are judged deportable are required to leave." Some of the commission's concerns and recommendations about illegal migration were incorporated into the IIRIRA of 1996.

Historically, the US government has maintained an ambivalent attitude toward illegal immigration.[42] On the one hand, business groups

---

40. US Commission on Immigration Reform, "Legal Immigration: Setting Priorities." Available at: https://www.utexas.edu/lbj/uscir/exesum95.pdf. The legal report called for modest reductions in the number of total immigrant admissions to foster deeper assimilation of American values and traditions. It also called for the scaling back of family-based migration in order to contain chain migration, expanding immigration of skilled workers, and eliminating the diversity visa program. The proposed reduction in family-based migration was to be accomplished by limiting preferences to three categories: first preference, spouses and minor children of US citizens; second preference, parents of US citizens; and third preference, spouses and minor and adult dependent children of LPRs.

41. US Commission on Immigration Reform, "US Immigration Policy: Restoring Credibility." Available at: https://www.utexas.edu/lbj/uscir/exesum94.pdf.

42. According to legal scholar Hiroshi Motomura, this ambivalence toward unauthorized aliens living in the United States has resulted in an "inconclusive" approach toward unlawful presence. He argues that the policy of "acquiescence or tolerance" is not a failure to implement laws but rather a direct result of the design of policy. He writes, "A highly restrictive admissions system predictably produces a large unauthorized population, to which the response is selective enforcement, which various government actors administer with broad discretion that can be unpredictable, inconsistent, and sometimes discriminatory" (Motomura, *Immigration Outside the Law*, 52).

and farmers have desired a large pool of low-wage migrant workers to support their enterprises in a predictable and efficient manner. And when businesses have been unable to meet their own employment needs with domestic and legal foreign workers, they have not hesitated to use unauthorized migrants, that is, alien workers who have entered the United States without formal inspection. On the other hand, citizens also want laws enacted that are just and are enforced with uniformity and consistency. The rule of law is not an ancillary attribute of representative government; rather, it is the moral foundation of legitimate governmental rule based on consent. To be sure, legal compliance is never completely fulfilled. But when a significant portion of a people disregards a law, this failure not only undermines a specific statute but can also call into question the credibility of the government's ability to ensure legal compliance with any law.

The presence of a large number of unlawful aliens in the country is significant because it potentially calls into question the competence of government and the rule of law. Furthermore, when aliens who circumvented admission procedures are allowed to legalize their status, this can undermine the perceived legitimacy of existing laws. The tension between the perceived legitimacy of legal and illegal immigration was illustrated by an Indian alien, Manmeet Singh, who was following the slow and cumbersome process of securing legal status. In his "Lament of a Legal Alien," he writes that he has lived in the United States for seven years and is married to a US citizen. Although Singh has completed his medical training, he is still waiting for a green card. He notes that if he had entered the United States illegally and married his wife, he would have received legal status by now. Mr. Singh is troubled by the fact that legal immigrant applications are being delayed because priority is being given to processing deportation deferrals. He writes, "What is really surprising is that, in a nation that prides itself on being a nation of laws, the enforcers of the law are told to deliberately look away when it comes to illegal immigration. . . . As the debate in Washington and the media centers on the plight of willful wrongdoers, America's reputation as a nation of laws and as a nation of immigrants is at stake here."[43]

43. Manmeet Singh, "Lament of a Legal Alien," *The Wall Street Journal*, August 12, 2014.

Border protection

To address the growth of unlawful migration, Congress has greatly increased the number of personnel working in border protection and immigration enforcement. The Border Patrol, for example, had 2,268 agents in 1980, but its size had increased to nearly 21,000 agents by 2014. In addition, the government has built a border wall to deter illegal entry, covering close to 800 miles of the 2,000-mile border with Mexico. As result of these and other measures, the number of border apprehensions has fallen dramatically, from a peak of 1.7 million in 1986 to roughly 400,000 in 2013.[44] Ironically, however, the rise in border control has had the unfortunate effect of impeding aliens who are returning to their homeland.

In addition to strengthening of the CBP, the US Congress has also bolstered the enforcement of immigration laws. This has been realized by greatly expanding the number of ICE personnel and by strengthening statutes and policies to ensure compliance with the most important immigration rules. The most significant legal development was, without a doubt, the passage of the IIRIRA (1996), which increased the ability of the government to remove unauthorized aliens by reducing the avenues available for relief from deportation and by establishing an expedited nonjudicial removal process.

According to the IIRIRA law, aliens who have been unlawfully present in the United States and desire to legalize their status must now depart the country and remain outside the United States for a specified period of time before being allowed to apply for a visa. While the aim of the 1996 law was to deter illegal immigration, the effect of the law was to trap unauthorized aliens in the United States, making it especially difficult to legalize their status. Since the only way for an alien to enter the United States is to first secure a visa, this means that those who have been in the United States unlawfully must leave and secure a visa at a US consular office abroad. But if they depart the country, the three- and ten-year bars will prohibit them from returning immediately. Indeed, they will be unable to secure a visa because they will be regarded as inadmissible for having violated immigration law by previously entering the United States unlawfully—that is, without inspection. The unlawful presence bars are a humanitarian challenge for unauthorized aliens who are married and have children and seek to legalize their status.

44. William A. Kandel, "US Immigration Policy: Chart Book of Key Trends," Congressional Research Service, December 17, 2014, 16.

ICS has established two relief programs to waive the three- and ten-year bars for aliens who have lived in the United States without legal authorization and who have qualifying relatives (parents or spouse) in the United States. The *traditional waiver* works as follows: when the unauthorized alien leaves the United States to apply for an immigrant visa (green card) at a US consulate, he or she triggers the three- and ten-year bar. After the alien is refused the visa, a qualifying relative in the United States can apply for a waiver—a process that takes a minimum of six months, and up to a year. If the waiver is granted, the alien applies and typically receives a visa that permits the unification with family members. The *provisional waiver*, which was established in 2013 to expedite the time for processing waivers, allows unauthorized aliens to request relief while still remaining in the United States. To be eligible to apply for this waiver, the alien must have an immediate relative who is a US citizen, must be physically present in the United States, must have a crime-free background, and must prove that the denial of the waiver would cause his or her US relatives "extreme hardship." After being approved by an ICS officer, the alien leaves the country to be interviewed by a consular officer. Assuming no grounds of inadmissibility are found, the alien is allowed to return to the United States with the knowledge that the Border Patrol will permit entry. Although the provisional waiver helps keep families together while the alien seeks relief, the waiver is difficult to obtain because the applicant must show that the denial of an immigrant visa would cause significant hardship to his or her US relatives.

Deportation

The basis for deportation is set forth in the INA. According to the INA § 237(a), an alien can be deported if she or he: (1) is inadmissible at the time of entry or violates his or her immigration status; (2) commits certain crimes; (3) fails to register or commits document fraud; (4) is a security risk; (5) becomes a public charge within five years of entry; or (6) votes unlawfully. The standard process for removal is carried out in an immigration court in which an attorney for the US government presents the case for why the alien should be removed, and the alien's attorney presents the case for his or her client. The immigration judge then determines whether the alien should be removed. An alien might also short-circuit the legal process by agreeing with the charge and accepting removal (known as stipulated removal). In addition, aliens may ask for relief or even apply for asylum if they have a credible fear of persecution upon returning to their homeland.

From a legal perspective, unauthorized immigration is not considered a crime; rather, it is a civil offense (a misdemeanor). As a result, the detention of immigrants is not viewed as punishment but as a necessary way by which the government can carry out its immigration responsibilities. This means that detained aliens are not entitled to constitutional protections that are afforded criminals. Whereas persons charged with crimes have legal rights, such as the right to counsel at government expense, detained aliens are not entitled to appointed counsel and have fewer due-process protections.[45]

The 1996 IIRIRA statute is important because it has streamlined the process of removing aliens. It has done so by simplifying removal procedures and increasing the speed with which an alien can be removed. This new process—known as expedited removal—allows DHS personnel to remove aliens who lack documentation or have committed fraud or willful misrepresentation in gaining admission without resorting to the judicial process of immigration courts. Typically, such removals are applied at the border or within one hundred miles of the border (within a two-week period of entry). Aliens who are in the expedited removal process must remain in detention until they are removed. If they have a credible fear of persecution and harm, however, they can request asylum. The alien must complete an asylum application, which is processed immediately by an asylum officer. If the officer concludes that the alien has a legitimate claim, the case goes to an immigration court, where a judge makes a final decision. If the asylum officer or the immigration judge denies the request, the alien must depart the country. Once aliens are deported under this process, they are barred from reentering the United States for at least five years.[46]

Given the large number of unauthorized aliens in the United States, the strategy of the US government is to use its limited law enforcement resources by focusing on those issues of greatest concern to American society. To this end, the Department of Homeland Security maintains enforcement priorities when apprehending, detaining, and removing undocumented immigrants. The most recent of these,

45. Jennifer M. Chacón, "Immigration Detention: No Turning Back?," *The South Atlantic Quarterly* 113 (Summer 2014): 621-23.

46. For an informative overview of current alien deportation policy, see Alison Siskin, "Alien Removals and Returns: Overview and Trends," Congressional Research Service, February 3, 2015.

announced in November 2014, set forth the following immigration enforcement priorities: priority 1 involves a threat to national security, border security, and public safety; priority 2 involves misdemeanors and new immigration violators; and priority 3 sets forth other immigration violations.[47] Examples of aliens in the highest priority are those who pose a threat to US security, who are apprehended at the border while trying to enter the country unlawfully, who have been convicted of an offense as a gang member, who have been convicted of a felony, or who have committed an "aggravated felony." In carrying out their enforcement responsibilities, DHS personnel will necessarily be required to use "prosecutorial discretion." In addition to following the three priorities above, enforcement officials are also encouraged to take into account other factors, such as extenuating circumstances involved in the criminal conviction; length of time since the conviction; length of time in the United States; military service; family ties in the United States; and humanitarian considerations such as poor health, age, or serious illness of a relative.

From 1996 to 2012 the United States deported more than 4.5 million aliens. Beginning in 2010, the United States significantly increased annual removals, averaging more than 360,000 from 2012 through 2014. Of those removed in fiscal year 2014, 56 percent (177,960) had previously been convicted of a crime, while 67 percent (213,719) were removed while attempting to unlawfully enter the United States. Of the aliens who were removed from the interior of the United States, 85 percent (102,224) had been previously convicted of a crime.[48] It is interesting to note that 94 percent of all those removed in 2014 came from four countries—Mexico, El Salvador, Guatemala, and Honduras—with Mexico alone accounting for more than half of that total.[49]

In mid-2014, immigration authorities were confronted by a border crisis precipitated by the illegal crossing of more than 56,000 unaccompanied minors, most of them from El Salvador, Guatemala, and Honduras, along the southwestern border, principally in the Rio Grande Valley in Texas. That crisis was not the result solely of violence and deprivation

47. Jeh Charles Johnson, "Policies for the Apprehension, Detention and Removal of Undocumented Immigrants," DHS memorandum, November 20, 2014. Available at: http://www.dhs.gov/sites/default/files/publications/14_1120_memo_prosecutorial_discretion.pdf.

48. US Immigration and Customs Enforcement, "ICE Enforcement and Removal Operations Report, Fiscal Year 2014," DHS, December 19, 2014, 7.

49. "ICE Enforcement and Removal Operations Report, 2014," 9.

but also a deliberate campaign to guide children across the US border unlawfully. The ostensible promise was that smugglers would enable children to cross the Rio Grande in the hope that they would be given asylum. According to the Pew Research Center, the percentage increase in children apprehended at the border between 2009 and 2014 was 707 percent for El Salvador, 930 percent for Guatemala, and 1,271 percent for Honduras.[50] As of 2015, the number of unaccompanied children crossing the US border had receded significantly, in large part due to greater efforts by authorities in Mexico to police its southern border with Guatemala.

Unlike adults, who can be immediately deported after they are apprehended and processed, the law requires that juveniles (under the age of eighteen) be placed in removal proceedings before an immigration judge.[51] Furthermore, US law, based on the so-called Flores Settlement Agreement, requires that children be granted a "general policy favoring release" and that custody be transferred to relatives or foster parents.[52] Thus, once unaccompanied children are detained and processed, they are transferred to the Department of Health and Human Services, which in turn is responsible for finding an environment conducive to the child's well-being, such as with relatives or a guardian family. The guardians have a duty to care for the child's welfare and to ensure that they appear in court on the appropriate dates.

The 2014 border crisis was also aggravated by the illegal entry of some 61,000 "family units"—essentially, mothers and children. The challenge facing immigration authorities was how to treat families. Since the gov-

---

50. Jens Manuel Krogstad and Ana Gonzalez-Barrera, "Number of Latino Children Caught Trying to Enter US Nearly Doubles in Less Than a Year," June 10, 2014. Available at: http://www.pewresearch.org/fact-tank/2014/06/10/number-of-latino-children -caught-trying-to-enter-u-s-nearly-doubles-in-less-than-a-year/.

51. This feature applies, ironically, to unaccompanied children from Central American states but not to neighboring Mexico or Canada. The requirement to give children added protection derives from the 2008 William Wilberforce Trafficking Victims Protection Reauthorization Act. That act, which was designed to curb human trafficking, sought to give protection to women and children forcibly transported across international borders into a world of sexual slavery and coerced labor.

52. In *Flores v. Meese*, the Supreme Court remanded the case to the district court. Before the court could make a determination on the dispute, the parties reached an accord called the Flores Settlement Agreement, which the court approved. According to the accord, a detained juvenile without a criminal background must be held in the least restrictive setting and must be released without delay to a relative, legal guardian, or other appropriate adult.

ernment seeks to keep family members together, the government had to decide whether the family units should be treated as adults and deported, or as unaccompanied children, subject to the Flores stipulations. In 2005, the George W. Bush administration decided to deny Flores protections to family units. In 2009, President Obama reversed this policy, closing all but one small family detention center. But when the border crisis emerged in 2014, the government again changed course, denying Flores protections to parents and children. The change in policy was to a significant degree a consequence of responding to a humanitarian crisis with limited available resources. Since the US government had only one small family detention center with a capacity for ninety-five persons in the fall of 2013, the sudden influx of family units forced the authorities to create several temporary centers.[53] Because the aim of the centers was to facilitate deportation, not to process asylum requests, the centers were viewed as short-term holding establishments. In testimony before the US Senate in July 2014, Jeh Johnson, secretary of the Department of Homeland Security, declared, "Then there are adults who brought their children with them. Again, our message to this group is simple: We will send you back."[54] As of mid-2015, ICE had three detention centers, with about three thousand beds, in order to confront further family crossings along the Rio Grande.

The challenges arising from the dramatic rise in unlawful entry by children in 2014 and 2015 suggest that immigration policy must be sufficiently flexible to respond to unexpected crises like the unlawful entry of the unaccompanied children. Because children are legally entitled to greater human-rights protections than adults, US government agencies made their status and well-being a priority. But in addressing children's needs, the government was forced to shift its attention and resources from other, longer-term immigration concerns to the pressing issue of how to care for children. Thus, though the federal government needs to establish clear, enforceable immigration policies, it must also be prepared to respond with flexibility to address unexpected problems.

In conclusion, the United States maintains a complex immigration system. As domestic political demands and international pressures have

53. The first center, in Artesia, New Mexico, was closed in December 2014, while two other larger facilities were established in Dilley, Texas, and Karnes, Texas. The Dilley center has a capacity of 2,400 beds, while the Karnes center has a capacity for five hundred persons.

54. Wil S. Hylton, "The Shame of America's Family Detention Camps," *The New York Times Magazine*, February 4, 2015.

shifted over time, the US government has continued to amend its basic immigration law (the INA). Despite efforts to address the continuing shifting domestic political demands, the US immigration system suffers from many shortcomings. Because of the large number of unauthorized migrants living in the United States—plus the belief that the government does not issue sufficient visas for skilled and unskilled workers—there is a broad consensus that the US system needs reform. In the next chapter, therefore, I will assess the effectiveness of the immigration system by highlighting some of its major strengths and limitations.

« 3 »

The Immigration System in Practice

How well does the US immigration system work? Does the system admit a sufficient number of skilled and unskilled workers to encourage economic growth? Does the government provide sufficient assistance to people in need? Should the United States welcome more refugees who are fleeing their homelands because of violence and fear of persecution? Do the principles governing US immigration provide a fair balance between the wants and needs of citizens and those of foreign nationals? Are the rules just?

Conventional wisdom holds that the US system is "broken." One does not have to look far to see evidence of this. One manifestation of the system's "brokenness" is the inability of the government to resolve the status of children who are transported unlawfully to the United States. Congress sought to address this issue by proposing the Development, Relief, and Education for Alien Minors (DREAM) Act, but the bill failed to pass. As a result, President Obama, using executive authority, decided to address this issue. In June 2012, he announced a temporary immigration initiative known as Deferred Action for Childhood Arrivals (DACA). The President's executive order provided that US authorities would defer the deportation of young people.[1] The order gave undocumented youth the right to work and not be deported for two years, subject to renewal for an

---

1. To be eligible, young people had to meet the following criteria: (1) they had arrived before their sixteenth birthday; (2) they were under the age of thirty-one and had no valid immigration status; (3) they had lived continuously in the United States during the previous five years (since 2007); (4) they were currently in school or had graduated from high school or obtained a GED or were honorably discharged from the armed forces; and (5) they had not been convicted of a serious crime.

additional two years.[2] According to the CIS, the department responsible for implementing DACA, more than half a million persons applied for this program in the first year.[3] In November 2014, President Obama announced two additional initiatives—one for young people and the other for adults. A federal district judge temporarily barred implementation of the two programs. A court of appeals subsequently affirmed the original legal order. In June 2016, the Supreme Court, in a split 4–4 decision, remanded the case back to the court of appeals, thereby upholding its earlier judgment.

A further manifestation of the immigration system's "brokenness" is the lack of coherence between local, state, and federal authorities. While immigration policy is fundamentally a federal issue, the effects of the system's shortcomings are felt in local communities. An example of the incoherence of immigration policies is the January 2013 California Supreme Court ruling that an undocumented alien who had completed law school could be licensed to practice law. The immigrant, who had been brought to the United States as a child by his Mexican parents, had been living without federal authorization. The California Court's chief justice declared that "the fact than an undocumented immigrant's presence in this country violates federal statutes is not itself a sufficient or persuasive basis for denying undocumented immigrants, as a class, admission to the State Bar."[4] In light of the court's ruling, the unauthorized alien could practice law in the *state* of California, but because he was not a lawful permanent resident from a *federal* perspective, he was not authorized to work in the United States.

The failure of federal authorities to limit illegal immigration has led some cities to enact local ordinances to discriminate against unauthorized aliens (by prohibiting property rentals and employment). Other localities have decided not to cooperate with the federal authorities in enforcing immigration laws. In 2008, the US government initiated the Secure Communities program, which permitted the federal government to check on the immigration status of persons arrested by local police. Though the program called on local authorities to inform federal agen-

2. To a significant extent, this initiative was undertaken because of the failure of Congress to adopt the DREAM act in 2010. That act would have granted lawful status to qualified immigrants who were brought unlawfully to the United States as children.

3. Jose Palazzolo, "Can Illegal Immigrants Practice Law?," *The Wall Street Journal*, September 3, 2013.

4. Catherine Shoichet and Tom Watkins, "No Green Card? No Problem—Undocumented Immigrant Can Practice Law, Court Says," CNN, January 3, 2014.

cies of the identity of arrested persons, some localities refused to participate in the program. Some cities, such as San Francisco, even went so far as to declare themselves "sanctuary cities." This lack of cooperation between local and federal agencies was highlighted in mid-2015 when an unauthorized alien from Mexico with a lengthy criminal record shot and killed an American woman on a pier in San Francisco. The man, who had been deported five times, was prosecuted in 2009 for a felony of illegal entry and then served four years in a federal prison. Upon completion of his sentence, he was sent to a San Francisco prison based on a warrant for a twenty-year-old felony marijuana charge. Since a San Francisco ordinance restricted local police from cooperating with immigration officials, the city failed to notify ICE of his whereabouts, even though ICE was set to deport him again. Instead, a local judge dismissed the marijuana charge, and prison authorities released the alien soon thereafter, unaware that he was slated for deportation.[5]

The inability to manage immigration has also led some states to seek to adopt initiatives that restrict benefits and social services to unauthorized aliens. The most important of these was California Proposition 187, which was adopted in 1994 with 60 percent of the vote. The measure, however, was never implemented because the US Supreme Court ruled it unconstitutional. Other, more moderate initiatives seeking to restrict the behavior of unauthorized aliens have been adopted by other states, including Alabama, Arizona, Indiana, Georgia, Nevada, South Carolina, and Utah. Of these measures the most important is Arizona's Support Our Law Enforcement and Safe Neighborhoods Act (SB 1070), adopted in 2010. The measure aimed to curb illegal immigration. According to the law, state and local law enforcement could make an effort to determine the immigration status of a person during routine stops, detentions, or arrests if there was a "reasonable suspicion" that the person was an alien who "was unlawfully present in the United States."[6] Although the US Supreme Court declared some elements of the statute unconstitutional in 2012, it affirmed the right of law enforcement agencies to investigate the legal status of detained persons.

Cases such as these suggest broad dissatisfaction with the existing US immigration system. Some critics believe that the government does

5. Julia Preston, "Murder Case Exposes Lapses in Immigration Enforcement," *The New York Times*, July 8, 2015.

6. Alberto R. Gonzales and David N. Strange, *A Conservative and Compassionate Approach to Immigration Reform: Perspectives from a Former US Attorney General* (Lubbock: Texas Tech University Press, 2014), 39-45.

not provide enough visas for skilled and unskilled workers; others argue that more visas should be available to expedite family reunification; still others support a reduction in family-based visas as a way of encouraging more employment-based immigration; and some are more concerned with America's inability to control its borders. Arguably, the most widespread concern is how to respond to the millions of unauthorized aliens living in the United States. The problem in addressing this issue is the division between those who support a liberal, expansive immigration policy and those who advocate for significant reductions in the total number of immigrants.

As I noted in the preceding chapter, the US immigration system involves complex practices and institutions that have been established through a slow, incremental process of policy-making by the US Congress. Given the multidimensional and multi-institutional nature of immigration, any effort to improve immigration should be undertaken with caution and care, lest the reform initiative fail to resolve the major problems or even create additional, unintended shortcomings. In this chapter I assess the effectiveness of the US immigration system, first identifying some of its key strengths and then examining some of its major perceived limitations. Second, since illegal immigration remains one of the most contentious and intractable challenges in the immigration debate, I analyze some of the factors that help to sustain unauthorized migration. Finally, I examine some of the political conditions that impair the development and implementation of effective immigration policies.

Strengths of the Current System

The US immigration system represents a formidable political achievement. It reconciles conflicting interests of different social, ethnic, political, and economic groups in American society. While immigration critics may not like the existing immigration policies, the current system is the result of long negotiations between leaders of political parties, pro-immigrant groups, and anti-immigrant groups to balance competing interests. The current policy attempts to find a satisfactory middle ground that gives appropriate significance to both business interests and family preferences. It is noteworthy that despite divergent and variable group interests on core immigration issues, the US government has succeeded in both establishing overall ceilings for annual immigrant admissions and setting forth criteria by which aliens are to be selected for admission.

Despite some obvious limitations, the US immigration system does have a number of important strengths, including a generous admissions policy for immigrants and refugees, a priority for family reunification, an emphasis on global inclusiveness, a strong commitment to due-process protections, and a special commitment to people who have suffered human rights abuses or who face oppression and persecution in their homelands.

A generous system

The United States maintains one of the most open immigration policies in the world, admitting more than a million new legal permanent residents (LPRs) every year. From 2004 to 2013, the United States granted LPR status to more than 10.5 million persons.[7] With the close of the Cold War, the United States admitted a record 1.5 million and 1.8 million LPRs in 1990 and 1991, respectively. As of 2014, the United States had more than 46 million foreign-born residents—more than any other country in the world. Typically, the US government allows about 70,000 refugees the right to resettle in the United States each year. According to the DHS's Office of Immigration Statistics, from 1980 to 2013, the United States accepted more than 2.7 million refugees—or roughly an average of 81,000 per year.[8] Based on the level of immigrant and refugee admissions, Stephen Bouman and Ralston Deffenbaugh write that the United States "is the most generous country in the world in admitting refugees for resettlement, taking in more than half of all refugees resettled worldwide."[9]

The US government provides a relatively efficient system for foreigners to come to this country temporarily to study, visit, or work. In 2013, there were 173 million temporary (nonimmigrant) admissions to the United States, most of them involving multiple border crossings for work.[10] Most international migration is for short periods of time for tour-

7. Office of Immigration Statistics, "Persons Obtaining Lawful Permanent Resident Status: Fiscal Years 2004-2013," *Yearbook of Immigration Statistics: 2013*, August 2014.

8. Office of Immigration Statistics, "Refugee Arrivals: 1980 to 2013," *Yearbook of Immigration Statistics: 2013*, August 2014.

9. Stephen Bouman and Ralston Deffenbaugh, *They Are Us: Lutherans and Immigration* (Minneapolis: Augsburg Fortress, 2009), 63.

10. Mexican nationals who legally work temporarily in the United States can be issued a border-crossing card, a machine-readable card to expedite border entry.

ism, work, or family visits. Ninety percent of the 61 million nonimmigrant admissions in 2013 were for pleasure or business.[11]

The priority of family ties

A further strength of the immigration system is the priority it gives to family relationships. As I observed above, roughly 70 percent of immigrant visas are allocated to relatives of US citizens and legal permanent residents. Moreover, an unauthorized alien who has a spouse who is either a US citizen or an LPR—or who has children who are US citizens (by virtue of their birth in the United States)—are potentially eligible to apply for relief from deportation. Unauthorized aliens with a crime-free background who are facing deportation are potentially able to secure some relief if they have immediate family members who are US citizens or LPRs. The family-friendly policy also manifests itself in the treatment of spouses and minor children. For example, when aliens are granted an H–2 visa for temporary work, the applicants can also apply to bring their spouses and children for the duration of their temporary employment. Similarly, students who have secured an educational visa to carry out graduate study at an accredited institution can also apply to bring their spouses and children with them.

The priority of keeping family members together is evident in the detainment and processing of unaccompanied minors who have entered the United States unlawfully (generally by crossing the Rio Grande in Texas).[12] Once minors are apprehended, they are transferred to the Department of Health and Human Services (HHS) to undergo separate processing from adults. By law, immigration authorities must process the children expeditiously so that children can be placed in a safe and relatively unrestrictive environment as soon as possible, preferably within seventy-two hours. HHS's Office of Refugee Resettlement (ORR), responsible for the welfare of children while their cases are pending, works

11. Katie Foreman and Randall Monger, "Nonimmigrant Admissions to the United States: 2013," Office of Immigration Statistics, Annual Flow Report, July 2014.

12. The challenge of unaccompanied minors became a significant issue in mid-2014 when the number of children coming from El Salvador, Guatemala, and Honduras increased dramatically. Where fewer than 10,000 minors had crossed the southwest US border illegally in previous years, in 2014 the number rose to more than 65,000, precipitating a logistical challenge for authorities as they sought to process and care for all of these children.

through nongovernmental humanitarian organizations to provide minors with educational, social, medical, and health services. If family members are in the United States, ORR seeks to transfer responsibility to them while the children await a court hearing.

The priority of families is also evident in how detained mothers and children are processed. When the number of unauthorized mothers and children surged in 2014, federal authorities decided to keep families together in newly constructed detention centers while their requests for relief from deportation were being processed. Thus, unlike unaccompanied minors who are released expeditiously to family members or relief organizations, the DHS holds families indefinitely while the courts process their requests to defer further unlawful border crossings. Many criticize these detention facilities without realizing that the facilities were constructed with the good intention of keeping mothers and children together. Still, the detention facilities are just that: jails that restrict movement. In July 2015, a federal court ruled that the existing family detention practices were illegal because they did not meet the minimum required protections for children as established in an important legal settlement in 1997, known as the Flores Accord.[13]

Inclusiveness

In the early part of the twentieth century, US immigration policy favored migration from Europe. After 1965, the amended INA eliminated the national-origins criteria that had previously governed immigration and replaced it with criteria that sought to make immigration more global. The 1965 Hart-Celler Act distinguished family-based immigration from employment-based immigration and established ceilings for both the Eastern and Western Hemispheres. In addition, the law placed an annual per-country ceiling of 20,000.[14] In 1990, the INA increased total annual family-based and employment-based immigration and created a special category of "diversity" visas for underrepresented countries. The goal of the diversity program was to strengthen global inclusiveness. In addition, the INA capped annual immigration per country at 7 percent of

13. Julia Preston, "Judge Orders Immigrant Children and Mothers Released from Detention," *The New York Times*, July 26, 2015, 14.

14. Originally, the Hart-Celler Act placed country ceilings only on the Eastern Hemisphere; subsequently, the annual caps were extended to the Western Hemisphere as well.

the annual total, which roughly amounts to an annual ceiling of 25,600 visas per country.

It is important to emphasize that the aim of US statutes has been to make immigration globally inclusive. Despite the INA's global goals, the policy outcomes have been far less inclusive. For example, of the roughly one million persons granted LPR status in 2013, 135,000 (13.6 percent) were from Mexico, while China, India, and the Philippines accounted for 71,000 (7.2 percent), 68,500 (6.9 percent) and 54,500 (5.5 percent), respectively.[15] According to the Department of Homeland Security, in 2013 there were 13.1 million LPRs ("green card" holders), of which 3.3 million (25 percent) were from Mexico. The three other countries with most LPRs were China, the Philippines, and India, which accounted for 5 percent, 4.4 percent, and 4.1 percent, respectively.[16]

Due-process protections

As I have noted above, unauthorized aliens are not entitled to the constitutional protections accorded to citizens and legal residents. They are not, for example, entitled to legal counsel at government expense or to plead their case in immigration court for a repeat unlawful border-crossing. In the latter case, ICE can process and deport the alien without a removal order from an immigration judge. Nevertheless, the US immigration authorities seek to ensure that all persons who are in custody are treated with respect and are given the opportunity to plead their case before an immigration judge when the circumstances justify it.[17] After an unauthorized alien has exhausted all legal ways to prevent deportation, an immigration judge will inquire if the defendant has reasons to fear persecution upon returning to his or her home country. If so, the judge will point out the opportunity to apply for asylum.[18]

15. Randall Monger and James Yankay, "US Lawful Permanent Residents: 2013," DHS: Office of Immigration Statistics, May 2014, 4. Available at: http://www.dhs.gov/sites/default/files/publications/ois_lpr_fr_2013.pdf.

16. Bryan Baker and Nancy Rytina, "Estimates of Legal Permanent Resident Population in the United States: January 2013," DHS: Office of Immigration Statistics, September 2014. Available at: http://www.dhs.gov/sites/default/files/publications/ois_lpr_pe_2013.pdf.

17. The author witnessed the priority of due process protections on numerous occasions while visiting federal immigration courts in Chicago.

18. To apply for asylum, the defendant must complete a detailed application (Form

The effort to protect aliens' basic rights is further illustrated by how government officials responded to the 2014 border crisis precipitated by the illegal arrival of unaccompanied children. After minors are processed (separately from adults) and transferred to the care of the Department of Health and Human Services, they are placed by the HHS with family members or with foster-care programs. The care for children remains the responsibility of HHS, which ensures that minors receive proper care while they await a court hearing before an immigration judge.[19] Due-process protections are also evident in how the US immigration authorities have addressed the challenge posed by children and mothers entering the country illegally. When "family units" are detained, agencies make every effort to keep mothers and children together—even at greater expense to the government.[20] These family detention centers, however, have been ruled illegal because children are not being accorded swift release. Again, these various actions suggest that unauthorized aliens are being granted significant legal protections.

It was evident to me, after observing numerous immigration court proceedings, that immigration judges made every effort to treat detained aliens in a dignified, humane way, providing them with ample opportunities afforded under the law to seek relief from deportation. Such opportunities include providing a translator to explain court proceedings,

---

I-590) and be interviewed by an asylum officer. If a plausible case is made for asylum, the case returns to an immigration judge, who makes the final determination. The case for asylum must be based on a well-founded fear of persecution on account of one of five factors: race, religion, nationality, membership in a particular social group, or political opinion. Fear and insecurity because of political instability or widespread criminal activity are not sufficient bases for the judge to grant asylum.

19. The special treatment accorded minors stems from the William Wilberforce Trafficking Victims Protection Reauthorization Act of 2008, a law that was designed to offer protection to children and adults facing human trafficking. Unlike the earlier Trafficking Victims Protection Act of 2000, the 2008 law granted unauthorized minors entering the United States alone substantial protection from being returned quickly to their home country. The aim of the law, which exempted minors from Canada and the United States, was not to prevent deportation of minors but rather to protect minors who were victims of sexual slavery. See Carl Hulse, "Immigrant Surge Rooted in Law to Curb Child Trafficking," *The New York Times*, July 7, 2014.

20. Religious groups and human rights advocates have argued that the family detention centers are not well equipped to provide care for children. The problem, of course, is not so much the inadequacy of the family detention centers but the long and indefinite nature of some of the detentions. But this problem arises from the backlog of cases in immigration courts that is further compounded by the spike in arrivals of unaccompanied children as well as "family units."

delaying proceedings to give additional time to secure legal counsel, reminding aliens of their rights of due process, and explaining possible avenues to find relief, such as applying for asylum.

Special concern for victims of persecution and abuse

Finally, US immigration authorities provide special treatment to aliens who face abuse and oppression in their homelands, as seen by the effort to resettle between 60,000 and 80,000 refugees annually. In addition, the United States grants asylum to some 20,000 to 30,000 persons who are already in the United States and seek to remain here because of substantial fears of persecution and systemic violence if they were to return to their home country.

The US government also grants protection to aliens who are likely to face significant human-rights abuses if they were to return to their country. Special programs are available for two types of nonimmigrants: victims of human trafficking and victims of crimes resulting in substantial mental or physical abuse. The first, the T visa, is reserved for people in the United States or at a port of entry who have been subjected to human trafficking. Applicants for the T nonimmigrant visa must be in the United States or at a port of entry; they must be willing to assist federal authorities in the investigation and prosecution of human trafficking crimes; and they must demonstrate that they would suffer severe harm if they were removed from the United States. The second humanitarian visa applies to aliens who have suffered significant mental or physical abuse in the United States. To be eligible for the U visa, the alien must be a victim of a qualifying crime and be willing to provide information that will assist in the prosecution of the offenders. This type of visa, which was created with the Victims of Trafficking and Violence Protection Act of 2000, is designed to protect victims from domestic violence and sexual assault. Although unauthorized aliens are ineligible for federal benefits, the 1996 welfare reform law created an exception by allowing battered women and children to receive public benefits.

Shortcomings of the Current System

Notwithstanding these and other advantages, the current immigration system is beset by many limitations. Some are rooted in the laws and policies themselves, while others stem from ineffective implementation. Some of the major shortcomings include insufficient visas to meet the business demands for skilled and unskilled workers (both temporary and permanent); long delays in securing family-based visas; weak enforcement of employment verification; inadequate tracking of people who arrive and depart the country; weak border security; excessive discretion in enforcing immigration laws; long delays in immigration judicial proceedings; and chain migration. While each of these concerns is important, the source complicating each of these problems and the fundamental issue driving the contemporary immigration reform debate is the question of what to do with the more than 11 million unauthorized aliens. Should they be allowed to remain unlawfully in the United States, or should authorities make an effort to give them legal status? If they pursue legalization, what preconditions should be established? What should be done about the unauthorized aliens who do not participate in an amnesty or legalization program? In what follows I briefly describe each of these problems and explain why resolving them presents daunting challenges.

Inadequate work visas

US law allows businesses to sponsor up to 140,000 permanent professionals per year. In addition, businesses can request a limited number of temporary workers through the H-1 and H-2 visa program. The H-1 program allows employers to petition skilled workers for a maximum of six years. The annual numerical cap for this type of visa is 65,000. The H-2 program is for temporary unskilled workers in agricultural (H-2A) and nonagricultural work (H-2B). Both of these visa categories are limited to about 66,000 per year and are good for one year. Although such visas can be renewed, a worker is limited to three years, after which he or she must leave the country for at least three months. Business leaders claim the current ceiling for permanent and temporary foreign workers is inadequate. Union leaders, by contrast, oppose additional increases in temporary unskilled workers, lest such an expansion in the labor pool result in a decline in the wages of American workers. Some countries, such as Australia and Canada, give precedence to workers, especially skilled workers, rather than to family reunification. To implement this policy, these countries have developed a quantitative system to identify skilled workers who are most likely to meet the needs of their enterprises. Similarly, the 2013 Senate bill 744, developed by a bipartisan group of eight senators (the "Gang of Eight"), recognized the need for more skilled labor and called for a significant rise in the number of employment-based visas.

Chain migration

Chain migration refers to the process by which family-sponsored migration results in expanding migration flows from immigrants who gain LPR status or citizenship and then sponsor other relatives. Because nearly two-thirds of all US immigrant visas are based on family reunification, migrant diasporas grow large rapidly through family-based visas. This process of concentration is evident in the recent distribution of persons gaining LPR status. In 2013, for example, of the nearly one million persons gaining this status in 2013, 13.6 percent were from Mexico, 7.2 percent were from China, and 6.9 percent were from India.[21] Family-based migration is an especially salient political concern when applied to unauthorized immigrants. When the 1986 IRCA law granted amnesty to 3 million unauthorized aliens, those aliens also gained the right to eventually sponsor family members. However, some observers perceived this as unjust and morally problematic. As a result, the Jordan Commission on Immigration Reform recommended in 1995 that amnestied beneficiaries should not have the same rights as immigrants who arrived lawfully. The 1995 Commission report declared this view as follows: "To further reward their earlier illegal entry by giving equal or higher priority to the entry of their relatives sends the wrong message at a time in which the US must obtain greater control over abuse of its immigration laws."[22]

Even though unauthorized aliens and recently amnestied aliens are unable to sponsor family members, they can potentially take advantage of family reunification priorities by marrying a US citizen or by being parents of children born in the United States.[23] Although minors are unable to sponsor parents, once they become adults (i.e., twenty-one years of age), they are eligible to sponsor parents and other relatives. President Obama's 2014 Deferred Action for Parents Act (DAPA) initiative dramat-

21. Randall Monger and James Yankay, "US Lawful Permanent Residents: 2013," Annual Flow Report, Office of Immigration Statistics, May 2014, 4.

22. Quoted in Robert Suro, *Watching America's Door: The Immigration Backlash and the New Policy Debate* (New York: Twentieth Century Fund, 1996), 64.

23. The Fourteenth Amendment to the US Constitution specifies that persons born in the United States are automatically US citizens.

ically illustrates the importance of children in immigration issues. This executive program, which was ruled unconstitutional in mid-2016, would have given temporary relief to some 3-4 million undocumented aliens.[24]

Delays in family reunification

This problem arises from citizens' and LPRs' high demand to sponsor additional family members. Since immediate family members (spouses, children, and parents) are not subject to immigration quotas, ordinarily there is little delay in their being granted immigration visas. The backlog arises for family members in the other lower-level family preferences, because the INA not only maintains quotas for each category but for countries as well.[25] Since the number of foreign nationals petitioning for immigrant visas greatly exceeds the number of immigrants that can be admitted under current law, a visa queue, or waiting list, has formed: in 2014 the waiting list was estimated to be at 4.2 million persons.[26] The delays are greatest for nationals from countries with a large number of visa applicants, such as China, India, Mexico, and the Philippines. According to the Department of State's Bureau of Consular Affairs November 2014 bulletin, 1.3 million nationals from Mexico and 428,000 nationals from the Philippines were waiting for a family-sponsored immigrant visa.[27]

Of course, the delays in granting immigrant visas to family members are a direct byproduct of the generosity of the American immigration system, which facilitates family reunification for citizens and LPRs. Because family-sponsored visa petitions are processed separately from the granting of the visas, the large delays generate not only frustration

24. In a split 4-4 decision, the Supreme Court sent the case back to the court of appeals, which had earlier ruled that DAPA exceeded the president's constitutional authority.

25. As I noted in the preceding chapter, the INA provides for four family-preference categories to cover family members beyond the immediate family.

26. William A. Kandel, "US Family-Based Immigration Policy," Congressional Research Service (November 19, 2014), 2.

27. US Department of State, Bureau of Consular Affairs, "Immigrant Number for November 2014," *Visa Bulletin*, vol. 9, no. 74, 2. For example, the delays mean that Mexican unmarried sons and daughters of US citizens (first preference) who had been waiting since July 1994 were now eligible to apply for a visa—a delay of close to twenty years; similarly, Filipino brothers and sisters of US citizens (fourth preference) who had initiated their request in May 1991 were now eligible for a visa—a delay of roughly twenty-three years.

and impatience but may contribute to immigrants overstaying their temporary nonimmigrant visas or seeking to enter the country unlawfully. In view of delays in the existing immigration system, some observers have advocated curtailing family-based immigrant visas and increasing employment-based visas. Others, including the Jordan Commission on Immigration Reform, have simply called for limiting family unification to the nuclear family—that is, spouses, minor children, and parents.[28]

Inadequate employment verification

The 1986 Immigration Reform and Control Act was based on a compromise between those advocating amnesty for unauthorized aliens, stronger border security, and compliance with worker verification. The law demanded that employers verify the status of employees by having each employee complete the Employment Eligibility Verification Form (I-9) and provide supporting documentation to the employer in order to verify the worker's legal status. However, rather than contributing to a reliable verification system, the requirement spawned a counterfeit industry in identity and Social Security documentation. To rectify the problem of illicit documentation, the government initiated an electronic verification system known as E-Verify. The internet-based system allows CIS officials to compare the information in the required I-9 Form with immigration and identity data maintained by the US government. If a discrepancy in the data exists, eligibility issues must be resolved before the employee can continue to work. Although E-Verify is not mandatory, close to half a million businesses use this service.

Inadequate tracking of nonimmigrants

A fourth weakness of the American immigration system is the lax accountability in the enforcement of the terms of temporary visas. Tracking of temporary visitors and workers is important because, by one estimate, close to 40 percent of all unauthorized aliens living in the United States are visa overstayers. In the aftermath of the 9/11 terrorist attacks, the US government developed a program (called US-VISIT) that sought to monitor the entry and exit of visitors more rigorously. By 2013 the DHS,

28. Kandel, "US Family-Based Immigration Policy," 12.

in cooperation with the Department of State, had established a mandatory biometric screening of all passengers arriving by air and sea and had instituted biometric screening at selected exit sites. As of 2015, DHS was still exploring how to implement an efficient and cost-effective biometric exit system.[29] In the meantime, significant electronic measures have been devised to identify visitors who fail to depart in accord with the terms of admission.

Weak border security

Ensuring the territorial security of the United States presents major challenges, especially the 2,000-mile US-Mexico border. For many decades there was limited control of the southwest border with Mexico. Migrants found few impediments to crossing the border on either side. Beginning in 1990, the United States began strengthening the border, first by constructing a fence and subsequently by establishing sophisticated monitoring devices to patrol the border. In addition, the US government expanded the size of the Border Patrol, increasing the number of government agents to nearly 20,000. As of 2015, the Border Patrol was the largest and most expensive federal law enforcement agency. As a result of improved border security enforcement, the number of annual apprehensions declined significantly, while the number of deportations increased.[30] Although the border is undoubtedly more secure than it was previously, migrants still find it possible to enter the United States unlawfully with the aid of professional smugglers ("coyotes").

Excessive prosecutorial discretion

Because of the complexity and multifaceted nature of immigration, coupled with the limited resources available to implement established pol-

29. Edward Alden, a senior fellow at the Council on Foreign Relations, argues that the benefits from exit tracking are limited. To be sure, they help to bring integrity to US immigration laws and to discourage illegal immigration, but they contribute little to national security (Alden, "Visa Overstay Tracking: Progress, Prospect and Pitfalls," Council on Foreign Relations, March 25, 2010).

30. During the first six years of the Obama administration, deportations were around 400,000 per year, while the number of border apprehensions declined from more than 1.6 million per year in the mid-1990s to 420,000 in 2013.

icies and procedures, government administrators establish priorities in allocating scarce resources and in enforcing the law. During his tenure as president, for example, George W. Bush sought to strengthen legal compliance with the employment rules by authorizing raids against industries thought to be using illegal workers. By contrast, President Obama has placed far greater emphasis on border security and the deportation of unauthorized aliens, especially those involved in criminal behavior.[31] While reliance on executive discretion may be an inevitable element of governing, lack of consistent policy interpretation and enforcement undermines policies themselves and calls into question the rule of law itself. Thus, when President Obama announced DAPA in 2014, which was designed to temporarily prevent legal action against unauthorized parents of children who are US citizens, the result was the immediate raising of expectations for millions of irregular aliens.[32] But a year later the initiative was being contested in federal courts. In the meantime, the absence of clear, stable rules contributes to uncertainty and inconsistency in perceptions of US policy.

Inefficient judicial proceedings

Another shortcoming of the American immigration system is the lengthy period required to process legal claims within US immigration courts. The Department of Justice's Executive Office for Immigration Review (EOIR) typically receives about 300,000 new cases per year. These cases generally involve such issues as fraud, moral turpitude, aggravated felony, misinformation or the withholding of information on official documents, requests for asylum, removal proceedings, and requests for relief from deportation. Because of the continuing growth in EOIR's workload, immigration courts have been unable to keep pace with the number of cases assigned to them. As a result, the courts had reached a record-high

---

31. In 2013, DHS removed (through a court order) 438,000 unauthorized aliens. In addition, Border Patrol returned some 178,000 unauthorized aliens to their home countries through processes that did not require a formal removal order. See John F. Simanski, "Immigration Enforcement Actions: 2013," Annual Report, Office of Immigration Statistics, September 2014.

32. The DAPA initiative was also supplemented with an expanded version of a program for children that began in June 2012. That program, called Deferred Action for Childhood Arrivals (DACA), provided that legal action would be deferred for two years for young people who came as children and met other eligibility criteria.

backlog of 445,607 cases in 2014. This backlog, aggravated by the sudden increase in unaccompanied children, contributed to long delays in hearing cases. The average wait just to hear a case in 2015 was 612 days; once cases are initiated, it can take three to five years to resolve them.[33] Such delays complicate removal hearings since those being charged have an opportunity to further embed themselves within their communities, thereby creating "virtual amnesty."[34] Of the cases waiting to be heard in 2014, nearly 70 percent involved aliens from four Latin American countries—Mexico, El Salvador, Guatemala, and Honduras.

State-federal inconsistencies

The US Constitution's Tenth Amendment declares, "The powers not delegated to the United States by the Constitution, nor prohibited by it to the States, are reserved to the States respectively, or to the people." Even though the amendment places limits on the role of Congress, the division of responsibility between the federal government and the states has remained an ongoing struggle. Since immigration regulates goods and people across national boundaries, it has historically been regarded as a national (federal) governmental responsibility.[35] However, while federal agencies are solely responsible for maintaining border security, the implementation of federal immigration laws requires cooperation from state and local authorities in identifying and prosecuting unauthorized aliens who have settled in towns throughout the country.

Since the number of undocumented aliens exceeds ten million, the US federal authorities use prosecutorial discretion to focus on those aliens who have committed crimes. To help identify, prosecute, and deport criminal aliens, the George W. Bush administration established

33. Syracuse University, "Immigration Court Backlog Tool," TRAC Immigration, May 2015. Available at: http://trac.syr.edu/phptools/immigration/court_backlog/.

34. Bob Price, "Immigration Courts' Backlog Creates Virtual Amnesty," Breitbart, August 29, 2014. Available at: http://www.breitbart.com/texas/2014/08/29/immigration-court-backlog-creates-virtual-amnesty/.

35. In its decision of June 25, 2012, the Supreme Court ruled in *Arizona v. United States* that several sections of Arizona's Support Our Law Enforcement and Safe Neighborhoods Act (SB 1070) were unconstitutional because they encroached on the federal government's primary responsibility over the regulation of immigration. The Arizona state legislature passed SB 1070 because it was attempting to address problems resulting from the federal government's failure to regulate immigration.

Secure Communities (SC), a program of state and local cooperation with federal immigration authorities. According to the SC program, local and state authorities were required to pass along to ICE the fingerprints of prisoners. If ICE deemed the person a threat, it could issue a detainer, which required local and state law enforcement authorities to hold the alien for up to forty-eight hours. Since many of the detained prisoners were not a high priority for deportation, and because the detainers were issued by government officials rather than by a judge, a number of state and local authorities refused to cooperate with SC. Because of SC's short-comings, President Obama replaced this program in 2015 with a modified initiative known as Priority Enforcement Program (PEP). Like SC, PEP requires local and state law-enforcement authorities to pass along bio-metric data of prisoners to ICE so it can determine whether the individual is a priority for removal. Unlike SC, however, PEP does not automatically issue detainers. Instead, a voluntary request is sent to the appropriate local or state agency once ICE has determined that the criminal alien is a priority.

Although controlling immigration may be a federal task, the effects of immigration have significant impact on the communities where migrants live and work. As a result, immigration remains an ongoing matter of tension between states and the federal government. The most recent illustration of this ongoing federal/state tension is the dispute arising from President Obama's November 2014 executive action to give work permits and defer deportation to some four million unauthorized aliens. After twenty-six states filed suit in federal court challenging the president's authority, a federal judge issued a preliminary ruling in February 2015 that halted the implementation of the initiatives. This ruling was subsequently affirmed by a court of appeals.

Because most health, social, and educational services are provided by state and local governments, the presence of a large number of refugees or unauthorized aliens can present a variety of economic and humanitarian challenges to state and local authorities.[36] And while most aliens are not entitled to federal economic and health assistance, they do receive many state public services. Since illegal immigration can pose significant budgetary challenges to state and local governments, a number of states and cities have sought to adopt measures to restrict public benefits to unauthorized aliens. In 1994, for example, California sought

36. In 1982, the Supreme Court ruled in *Plyler v. Doe* that states had to provide all students, regardless of their legal status, with publicly funded K-12 education.

to restrict state-funded benefits, including public education, to legal residents. In a state referendum, 60 percent of California residents approved Proposition 187, which prohibited virtually all state welfare and public education to unauthorized aliens. Subsequently, however, a federal court invalidated the law. Two other areas where states must decide how to respond to illegal immigration are in-state tuition benefits for students and access to driver's licenses. As of 2015, twenty states permit unauthorized immigrants to receive tuition benefits, while eleven states allow them to get a driver's license.[37]

Illegal immigration

A major shortcoming of the current immigration policy of the United States is the large number of unauthorized aliens living and working in this country: according to the DHS, in 2012 there were 11.4 million unauthorized aliens (6.7 million from Mexico, and 1.7 million from the three neighboring Central American countries of El Salvador, Guatemala, and Honduras) living in the shadows of society, which is a serious social, political, and legal concern.[38]

Unlawful migration has a number of harmful effects. First, the existence of a large number of persons living "in the shadows" creates a division in society between those living openly and those seeking to remain hidden from legal authorities. In a 1998 report of the Committee on Migration of the US National Conference of Catholic Bishops titled "One Family under God," the bishops declare, "It is against the common good and unacceptable to have a double society, one visible with rights and one invisible without rights—a voiceless underground of undocumented persons."[39]

Second, the presence of a large number of low-wage unauthorized workers creates the temptation for employers to exploit them and even abuse their basic rights. Since unlawful aliens do not have the legal right to work in the United States, they seek cash-based employment in small-

37. Julia Preston, "States Are Divided by the Lines They Draw on Immigration," *The New York Times*, March 29, 2015.

38. Bryan Baker and Nancy Rytina, "Estimates of the Unauthorized Immigrant Population Residing in the United States: January 2012," Population Estimates, Office of Immigration Statistics, March 2013, 5.

39. Committee on Migration, US Catholic Conference, "One Family under God" (Washington, DC: US Catholic Conference, 1998), 8.

scale enterprises, such as restaurants, small construction contractors, and roofing contractors, where they are less likely to be noticed by federal agencies.

Third, unskilled illegal workers tend to depress the wages of unskilled citizens. Economic theory would tell us that in the absence of a commensurate rise in demand, the increased supply of workers will tend to depress wages. Although this conclusion is contested among scholars, what is generally acknowledged is that the economic benefits of unlawful migration accrue disproportionately to wealthier citizens, who are able to secure basic services at lower cost.

Fourth, unlawful migration tends to increase domestic economic inequality. This conclusion is reinforced by Philip Cafaro's claim that since legal immigration creates "winners and losers," an inevitable outcome of rising immigration levels is increased economic inequality among the citizenry.[40] Economist Paul Collier similarly argues that while most indigenous workers benefit from immigration, the poorest workers end up losing. He writes, "There seems to be reasonable evidence that at the bottom of the income spectrum indigenous workers face slightly lower wages, reduced mobility, and larger losses on social housing, but most workers gain."[41] Thus, if lawful immigration contributes to domestic economic inequality, unlawful migration is even more likely to reinforce this trend. To be sure, the migrants themselves benefit economically from being able to work in a developed economy. The impact on citizens, however, will disproportionately favor the wealthy (and those who employ migrant labor) and harm unskilled citizens.

Fifth, unlawful migration contributes to broken families. Although some married migrants enter the United States unlawfully as a family, most enter as individuals. Once they settle in a community, they seek to bring their spouses and children into the country. In other cases, unauthorized aliens who are single may get married and have children after they arrive in the United States. Whether they marry a US citizen or another alien, they create what scholars call "mixed-status families," where only some members of the family are unlawful.[42] Family separa-

40. See Philip Cafaro, *How Many Is Too Many? The Progressive Argument for Reducing Immigration into the United States* (Chicago: University of Chicago Press, 2015), esp. chap. 4.

41. Paul Collier, *Exodus: How Migration Is Changing Our World* (New York: Oxford University Press, 2013), 123.

42. For a discussion of "mixed status families," see April Schueths and Jodie Lawston, eds., *Living Together, Living Apart* (Seattle: University of Washington Press, 2015).

tion arises when a parent commits an offense that leads to incarceration and eventually to deportation. Family separation became more frequent after the passage of the 1996 Illegal Immigration Reform and Immigrant Responsibility Act, which increased the number of deportable offenses. Regardless of the factors precipitating deportation, the separation of families involves serious social, economic, and moral issues.

Finally, unlawful migration nurtures further illegality. Since ongoing participation in society requires documentation, unauthorized aliens rely on fraudulent documents to live and work in society. Most significantly, the toleration of a large segment of the population living in the shadows means that society becomes accustomed to unlawful behavior, thereby undermining the rule of law. The US Select Commission on Immigration and Refugee Policy, chaired by Rev. Theodore Hesburgh, declared in its final report (1981) that "the toleration of large-scale undocumented/illegal immigration can have pernicious effects on US society. . . . Most serious is that illegality breeds illegality. The presence of a substantial number of undocumented/illegal aliens in the United States has resulted not only in a disregard for immigration laws but in the breaking of minimum wage and occupational safety laws, and statutes against smuggling as well. As long as undocumented migration flouts US immigration law, its most devastating impact may be the disregard it breeds for other US laws."[43]

Despite numerous initiatives to curb unlawful migration, the US government has not developed a successful policy to address this issue. Since most of the immigration policy shortcomings are caused or exacerbated by aliens living and working secretly in the United States, we next explore some of the causes and ramifications of illegal immigration.

Confronting Illegal Immigration

The passage of IRCA and IIRIRA did not reduce illegality. Indeed, unauthorized migration continued to increase throughout the 1990s and 2000s, peaking at more than 12 million irregular aliens in 2007. Some scholars have argued that given the increasing porosity of borders in an age of globalization, it is virtually impossible to halt unlawful migration. Others attribute the inability to regulate migration to a decline in state

---

43. US Select Commission on Immigration and Refugee Policy, "US Immigration Policy and the National Interest," March 1, 1981, 41–42.

sovereignty—a development also linked to increased globalization and global governance.[44] By contrast, Christian Joppke argues that it is the government's willingness to limit its capacity to act, not a decline in state sovereignty, that is the real cause of unwanted immigration. He calls this perspective "self-limited sovereignty." According to Joppke, unwanted immigration is fueled in democratic systems by "client politics" in which small, well-organized groups pursue their own interests and "constitutional politics." Such groups are especially effective in democratic systems when they emphasize a commitment to human rights for all persons, regardless of political or legal status. Thus, for Joppke, "liberal states are internally, rather than externally, impaired in controlling unwanted immigration."[45]

How should the United States address the issue of unauthorized aliens living and working in the country? In view of the conflicting moral, legal, political, and humanitarian dimensions of this issue, it is not surprising that the American people remain conflicted over this issue. A 2014 *ABC News/Washington Post* poll, for example, illuminated this division. When respondents were asked whether undocumented aliens should have the right to live and work in the United States, nearly the same percentage supported legalization (46 percent) as those who opposed it (50 percent).[46] While Americans find it difficult to determine the appropriate way to reconcile human rights and the rule of law, they nevertheless tend to favor the legalization of unauthorized aliens, including a pathway to citizenship.[47] Unlike the amnesty provided in 1986 through IRCA, current proposals call for conditional legalization—what some euphemistically call "earned citizenship"—based on meeting a number of preconditions, including paying fines for unlawful entry, along with back taxes and a criminal background check.

---

44. See, e.g., Wayne A. Cornelius, Philip L. Martin, and James F. Hollifield, "Introduction: The Ambivalent Quest for Immigration Control," in Wayne A. Cornelius et al., eds., *Controlling Immigration: A Global Perspective* (Palo Alto: Stanford University Press, 1994).

45. Christian Joppke, "Why Liberal States Accept Unwanted Immigration," *World Politics* 50 (January 1998): 271.

46. See ABC News/Washington Post Poll, September 2014. Available at: http://www.pollingreport.com/immigration.htm.

47. A spring 2015 CBS/New York Times poll, for example, found that 57 percent of the survey participants supported giving illegal immigrants a way to eventually gain citizenship. Similarly, a July 2014 poll by the Public Religion Research Institute found that 58 percent of the respondents favored conditional citizenship for unauthorized immigrants. Available at: http://www.pollingreport.com/immigration.htm.

At the same time, a significant portion of Americans believe that giving unauthorized aliens a pathway to citizenship is unjust because it disregards the original offense and treats legal and illegal aliens alike. Political scientist Peter Skerry, for example, argues that the United States should seek to legalize as many unauthorized immigrants as possible but not offer them the option of citizenship. He proposes instead that illegal aliens should be given the option of permanent noncitizenship.[48] This notion is also supported by other scholars and public officials, including former Governor Jeb Bush of Florida and former Attorney General Alberto Gonzales. In a jointly authored book on immigration, Jeb Bush and Clint Bolick argue that illegal immigrants should be allowed to regularize their status after pleading guilty to unauthorized entry and receiving an appropriate punishment. The legalization process could result in the LPR status but would not lead to citizenship. "To do otherwise," they argue, "would signal . . . that people who circumvent the system can still obtain the full benefits of American citizenship."[49] Similarly, Alberto Gonzales and coauthor David Strange argue that unauthorized aliens should not be promised citizenship since "they did not follow the rules before making it available to those who did."[50] Instead, they argue that legalization should involve the grant of US nationality to those who are eligible and who pay a fine for their unlawful entry.[51] While Gonzales and Strange acknowledge that many activists are likely to oppose their recommendation, they defend it by arguing that unauthorized aliens came to the United States not to become citizens but to find work.[52]

Three domestic conditions continue to impair immigration policy and facilitate unlawful migration. First, because the American people hold opposing—even contradictory—opinions about immigration, not

48. Peter Skerry, "Splitting the Difference on Illegal Immigration," *National Affairs* 14 (Winter 2013).

49. Jeb Bush and Clint Bolick, *Immigration Wars: Forging an American Solution* (New York: Threshold Editions, 2013), 43.

50. Gonzales and Strange, *Conservative and Compassionate Approach*, 53.

51. A noncitizen national has many of the same rights as a citizen but is prohibited from participating in the political life of the country, such as voting, holding public office, and serving on a jury.

52. A poll by the Pew Research Center found that Hispanics are more concerned with legalization than with citizenship. In the 2013 survey, 55 percent of the participants indicated that they considered legalization more important than citizenship, while 35 percent gave priority to the latter over the former (Pew Research Center, "Hispanics Prioritize Legalization for Unauthorized Immigrants over Citizenship," January 23, 2014).

only is the development of immigration laws challenging, but implementing the rules consistently is especially difficult. Second, the debates concerning immigration reform are influenced unduly by "client politics." This means that specific interests and values of some groups cannot be reconciled with those of the general public. As a result, the laws and policies that emerge are a result of bargaining among competing groups, but such agreements may not advance either the national interest of American society or the common good. Third is the multiplicity of government agencies involved in the creation and implementation of policy. The first two conditions are political, while the third is institutional in nature. The dysfunctional political dynamics inhibit consensus on immigration policy and help to sustain political fragmentation on core conflicts, including issues such as human rights versus the rule of law, employment-based versus family-based immigration, economic interests in fostering growth versus political concerns in fostering national solidarity, and beneficence toward foreigners (especially refugees) versus the pursuit of national interests. The third factor is rooted in the interaction among different governmental institutions involved in the regulation of immigration.

Fragmented public opinion

Public opinion surveys have repeatedly shown that Americans remain divided about the nature and scope of immigration. They consistently show, for example, that a large majority of Americans are opposed to increased immigration: in a 2013 Gallup poll, only 22 percent of the respondents favored increased immigration, while 41 percent supported decreased immigrant flows.[53] And yet, despite the public's preference for decreased immigration—a perspective that political scientist Peter Schuck calls "restrictionism"—high levels of annual immigration have persisted for years.[54] According to Schuck, several factors explain the continued disconnect between public attitudes and immigration policy:

53. Gallup immigration surveys in 2001, 2005, and 2009 also found that the percentage of respondents favoring a decrease in immigration was roughly twice as large as the percentage favoring increased immigration. See Gallup, "Immigration," 1. Available at: http://www.gallup.com/poll/1660/immigration.aspx.

54. Peter H. Schuck, "The Disconnect Between Public Attitudes and Policy Outcomes in Immigration," in Carol M. Swain, ed., *Debating Immigration* (Cambridge: Cambridge University Press, 2007), 20.

the different distributional costs and benefits of immigration; the important role of ethnic and business lobbies; the ideological belief that the United States is a nation of immigrants; pro-immigration mass media; and the low salience of immigration when compared to economic and security concerns.[55] At the same time, it is important to emphasize that Americans have been reluctant to close the immigration door. Public opinion surveys continue to affirm that the American people believe that immigration is beneficial to the United States. For example, a 2014 Gallup poll had 63 percent of the respondents opining that immigration was good for the country.[56]

The desire for continued migration, however, does not translate into support for open, unregulated immigration. Indeed, when people have been asked whether the US government should focus on border security and enforcement or the legalization of unauthorized aliens, the public has tended to support both alternatives, but with a majority preference for border security.[57] At the same time, most Americans are opposed to mass deportation, viewing it as an unrealistic and harmful policy.[58] And while the American public is divided over the use of deportation as a policy tool, American society tends to support the removal of unauthorized aliens that have committed serious crimes.[59] In short, American people remain, as Yuval Levin has observed, deeply ambivalent about immigration, especially unauthorized immigration. Writing about unauthorized aliens, he notes that the United States has "invited them in even as it has pushed them away."[60]

55. Schuck, "Disconnect," 28–30.

56. See Gallup "Immigration," 6. Available at: http://www.gallup.com/poll/1660/immigration.aspx.

57. A Survey by the Pew Research Center in August 2014 found that 33 percent of the respondents emphasized border security, 23 percent gave a priority to legalization, while 41 percent believed that both alternatives should receive equal support.

58. A spring 2015 CBS/*New York Times* Poll found that only 29 percent of respondents felt that illegal immigrants should be required to leave the United States. Available at: http://www.pollingreport.com/immigration.htm.

59. According to a Pew Research Center poll in February 2014, respondents were evenly divided over the deportation of unauthorized immigrants: 45 percent believed deportation to be beneficial, and 45 percent deemed it undesirable. Available at: http://www.pollingreport.com/immigration.htm.

60. Yuval Levin, "The Immigrant Middle Ground," *National Review Online*, August 14, 2014.

Clientist politics

The second impediment to effective policy-making is seen in the diverse interests and values of competing interests groups. Some groups—such as the business community, churches, human-rights groups, ethnic groups, and liberal political organizations—favor increased immigration and legalization of unauthorized aliens. By contrast, other groups, such as labor unions, unskilled native workers, and conservative political organizations, want greater control over the border and a more restrictive immigration policy.

But the existence of deep differences in attitudes and interests on immigration alone does not explain the intractability of immigration politics. Rather, what further complicates policy-making is "clientist politics," which emerges in the immigration policy debates because the interest groups that are most committed to change are those whose constituents are likely to gain the most. When the benefits are concentrated and the costs are dispersed, group activists are likely to be better organized and devote more resources to their own cause than would the unorganized general public. Social scientists call such an issue a collective action problem. Thus, when group interests are diverse and group concerns diverge from those of the general public, reconciling competing interests and conflicting values can make for a daunting challenge.

Support for an open, flexible immigration system is captured by media outlets such as *The Wall Street Journal* and think tanks like the Cato Institute, a libertarian research organization in Washington, DC. The groups that are most vociferous in calling for increased labor migration are high-tech companies, which seek greater access to skilled and technologically trained professionals, and agricultural and service industries, which call for higher numbers of temporary, low-wage foreign workers. Since the United States is the world's leader in higher education, high-tech companies have encouraged the government to allocate green cards to all foreign students graduating with advanced degrees from American universities, but political leaders have been unsuccessful in raising the quota for skilled immigrants. Because of their inability to secure a sufficient number of skilled domestic workers, some companies, such as Apple Computer and Microsoft, have established plants overseas instead of in the United States.

Similarly, the desire to produce goods and services efficiently has led farmers and service industries to hire low-wage workers, even if they have entered or remained in the country unlawfully. Indeed, the rise of illegal aliens in the United States is a direct byproduct of the unrelenting demand for foreign low-wage labor. Ever since the creation of the *bracero* program in the 1940s, American farms, especially those employing a large number of unskilled workers, have sought to hire low-wage laborers—particularly in seasonal agricultural production. This demand has been so significant that even when the *bracero* program was operational, US farmers came to depend on unauthorized workers to supplement the formal guest-worker program. In time, other industries, including construction, roofing, meat processing, poultry, and hotels and restaurants, began to meet their demand for unskilled workers by hiring unauthorized aliens. In short, unauthorized aliens come and remain in the United States because a significant number of the American people (and American companies) favor the economic benefits from low-wage migrant labor.

In contrast to the pro-immigration groups, some American interest groups favor reduced immigration and are opposed to the legalization of unlawful migrants. To a significant degree, opposition to immigration is rooted in the fear that high levels of migration could harm the economic well-being of native workers, and thus unskilled American workers tend to oppose any expansion in the foreign labor pool.[61] Also labor unions, not surprisingly, tend to favor reduced immigration and oppose guest-worker programs. In 1964, the US government terminated the *bracero* program because of organized labor's continued opposition to it.

In addition to economic concerns, anti-immigrant groups argue that high levels of immigration can threaten a nation's culture and shared political values and thereby undermine national solidarity. Paul Collier argues that high levels of immigration can weaken a society's social capital, or what he terms "mutual regard." Mutual regard is important, argues Collier, because it facilitates trust and cooperation in society and thereby contributes to the empathy among people that makes redistribution feasible.[62] A study by political scientist Robert Putnam found that high levels of immigration are associated with lower levels of mutual trust between immigrants and natives. Even more significant, however,

---

61. Recognizing the potential harm to native wages, the Department of Labor mandated that a US business that seeks an employment-based visa must demonstrate in its filing that there are no domestic workers that can meet the needs of the company and that it will pay the prevailing wages to its new employees.

62. Collier, *Exodus*, 63–73.

the study found that the higher the level of immigration in a community, the lower the trust was among the immigrants themselves.[63]

Institutional complexity

A third factor contributing to a variable and inconsistent immigration policy is the diverse and complex set of institutions involved in US immigration. Three different types of institutions contribute to the inherent conflicts within the US government: first, the competition among the three branches of the federal government; second, the competing interests and concerns of multiple government agencies and bureaucratic offices; and third, the ongoing tensions between national and state governments.

Perhaps the most important tensions in the US immigration policy arise from the conflicts between the President, Congress, and the Supreme Court. The tension between Congress and the President was evident in the public and congressional response to President Obama's November 2014 executive action initiating deferred action for unauthorized parents of US citizens (DAPA) and expanding the scope and benefits of minors who had been brought unlawfully to the United States (DACA). The president justified his initiatives on the inherent prosecutorial discretion of the executive and indicated that he had taken these executive actions because of Congress's failure to reform immigration policy. These two initiatives, while strongly supported by the Hispanic community, elicited strong opposition from Congress and from numerous interest groups. Since the two programs could potentially provide temporary relief and work permits to as many as four million unauthorized aliens, some critics argued that because DAPA and DACA involved fundamental modifications in immigration policy, they necessitated congressional approval. Furthermore, public opinion polls found that more than 50 percent of respondents opposed these initiatives.[64]

Another major federal tension is between the Congress and/or the President and the federal courts. The courts have repeatedly intervened on immigration concerns to defend human rights and to ensure basic

---

63. Collier, *Exodus*, 74.

64. CNN/ORC Poll, November 21-23, 2014. N=1,045; margin of sampling error is plus or minus 3%. http://i2.cdn.turner.com/cnn/2014/images/11/26/cnnorc -immigration-poll112614.pdf

constitutional protections. When Texas sought to deny public education to the children of illegal aliens, the Supreme Court ruled in 1982 in a landmark case *(Plyler v. Doe)* that all children regardless of legal status were entitled to free schooling (K–12). More recently, when California sought to deny basic educational and social services to unauthorized aliens in 1994, a federal judge ruled that the citizen-supported measure was unconstitutional.

The second type of institutional complexity arises from the competition and conflicts among different government agencies involved in immigration affairs. Since government agencies typically develop their own procedures and perspectives, coordination and consistent implementation of immigration rules are difficult because personnel in different agencies and subagencies approach immigration with different organizational interests and perspectives.[65] The Department of Homeland Security, for example, is chiefly concerned with ensuring that the goods and people entering the United States are lawful and do not pose a threat to the security and well-being of the nation. In contrast, the Department of Justice is concerned chiefly with the application and interpretation of immigration laws. It particularly seeks to ensure that the human rights of citizens and noncitizens are protected. The Department of Health and Human Services, which is charged with caring for refugees and unaccompanied minors, is primarily concerned with the human welfare of migrants. The issuing of temporary worker visas requires the cooperation of the Department of Labor, DHS's Citizenship and Immigration Services, and the Department of State's Consular Services. Similarly, addressing the unlawful border crossing by unaccompanied children involves the Border Patrol, ICE, and the HHS's Office of Refugee Resettlement. Although each of these agencies has different procedures and interests, the President and cabinet officers make every effort to advance policies in a coherent and consistent fashion. Still, significant intergovernmental tensions arise that result in ambiguous and variable immigration policies and practices.

Inconsistencies in the implementation of rules also arise from shifting priorities of different administrations. When the Eisenhower administration was confronted with a large influx of illegal migrants in 1954, President Eisenhower ordered law-enforcement agents to deport them.

---

65. In his path-breaking study *Essence of Decision: Explaining the Cuban Missile Crisis* (Boston: Little, Brown, 1971), Graham Allison argues that policy-making is not simply a set of unified, coherent government actions but a process that emerges from competing and conflicting interests of different government departments.

The deportation campaign, called "Operation Wetback," was carried out by federal agents with the support of state and local authorities and resulted in the deportation of some 1.3 million Mexican aliens. And when 125,000 Cubans suddenly arrived in Key West, Florida, in the spring of 1980 from the port of Mariel, the Carter administration treated those aliens as refugees.[66] The so-called Mariel boatlift was halted almost immediately by means of an accord between the United States and Cuba after US immigration officials discovered that the Castro regime had released prisoners and mental health patients as part of the exodus. And when 70,000 unaccompanied children were able to enter the United States unlawfully in 2014, the Obama administration had to shift resources away from the regular immigration policies to address the sudden border crisis precipitated by minors. In short, the enforcement of rules is not consistent and is, at times, discretionary. ICE, for example, is charged with enforcing immigration laws; but clearly, if the laws were enforced consistently, it would be unlikely that eleven million aliens would be living in the United States. For example, the statutory requirement (established by IRCA in 1986) that businesses hire only legal workers has not been enforced consistently. Few aliens have been deported, and even fewer firms have been penalized. Law professor Hiroshi Motomura argues that the unlawful presence of millions of aliens in the United States is a direct byproduct of the selective and discretionary application of existing statutes. In his view, immigration laws are regarded as "malleable."[67]

Finally, immigration practices suffer because of the different ways that federal, state, and local authorities respond to immigration issues. In particular, the tensions between federal and state authorities greatly complicate the work of enforcing immigration rules and meeting the needs of immigrants. Immigration policy is fundamentally a federal responsibility. But since health, social, and educational services are typically distributed at the state and local levels, state and local governmental institutions are inevitably confronted by the challenge of how to meet the needs of new immigrants. This is especially true of illegal immigration,

66. The Mariel exodus arose in response to the sudden downturn in the Cuban economy that encouraged Cubans to flee and to seek diplomatic asylum. When some 10,000 Cubans were able to enter the Peruvian embassy compound and request asylum, Castro responded to the crisis by declaring that Cubans could leave the country through the port at Mariel. This precipitated the Mariel boatlift.

67. Hiroshi Motomura, *Immigration outside the Law* (New York: Oxford University Press, 2014), 191.

which can involve significant health and education costs to communities. Budgetary imbalances arise from the fact that payroll and federal income taxes are paid to the federal government, while most social, medical, and school expenditures are covered by state and local taxes.

In view of escalating costs of the state benefits for unauthorized aliens, in November 1994, voters in California adopted Proposition 187, an initiative designed to prohibit social and educational services to undocumented aliens. Immediately after the law was enacted, a federal district judge issued a permanent injunction against the measure and did not issue the court's ruling until three years later. Judge Mariana Pfaelzer declared that Proposition 187 was unconstitutional because it infringed on the federal government's exclusive jurisdiction on immigration concerns. She declared, "California is powerless to enact its own legislative scheme to regulate immigration. It is likewise powerless to enact its own legislative scheme to regulate alien access to public benefits."

In conclusion, the American immigration system is a complex set of rules and practices that has emerged from the competing and conflicting political and economic interests of the American people. Although the system has many laudable features, it also suffers from major limitations in both design and implementation. These shortcomings, especially the inadequate number of visas for temporary and permanent workers, along with the large number of unauthorized aliens living in the United States, have led civic leaders to demand comprehensive immigration reform. But devising a more just immigration system is a difficult task. Not only are Americans divided about desired policy changes, but they also approach immigration with different conceptions of the international community. Because these alternative global perspectives play a critical role in how migration concerns are conceived, we turn next to an analysis of alternative international-relations paradigms.

« 4 »

Theories of International Migration

International-relations scholars have developed a variety of approaches to the field of global politics. These approaches, or paradigms, are important because they help to structure the analysis of global affairs. In effect, they not only help us see and understand important dynamics in international relations but prescribe solutions to the predicaments of global politics in general and to specific challenges like the problems posed by international migration. Because of the important role that paradigms play in structuring the analysis of international affairs, I devote this chapter to an analysis of how paradigms influence conceptions of international justice and membership in nation-states. Although scholars have developed numerous approaches to global affairs, three paradigms have dominated contemporary international-relations scholarship: realism, communitarianism, and cosmopolitanism.[1]

The first perspective, *realism*, views the world as composed of distinct political communities. Each of these communities is independent and sovereign, and each one pursues its short- and long-term interests in the international system based on its wealth and power. Morality and law are not important in how states relate to each other; the obligations of states are chiefly to their own people. The second perspective, *communitarianism*, is similar to realism, but it assumes, in addition, that there

---

1. In an important study on world order, Hedley Bull, an Australian scholar, anticipated the development of these approaches by arguing that the international community could be conceived either as a system of states, as a society of states, or as a world community. Although he used different terms to describe each paradigm, the three perspectives align closely with realism, communitarianism, and cosmopolitanism (Hedley Bull, *The Anarchical Society: A Study of Order in World Politics* [New York: Columbia University Press, 2002]).

are transnational interests and transcendent moral values that constrain states. States are the major actors in global society, but morality and law also influence government decisions. According to the communitarian perspective, the international community is a society of states because interstate relations are structured not only by power but also by morality and law. The third perspective, *cosmopolitanism*, represents the ideal of a just world community where individuals are the primary focus of political action. According to this approach, universal reason provides the basis for pursuing the individual and collective well-being of all humans. Although states exist in the world community, the cosmopolitan approach gives moral primacy to global welfare and regards state sovereignty as unimportant. Because this book is about how moral values should constrain and guide immigration policy, and because morality is largely absent from the realist worldview, the following analysis focuses only on the communitarian and cosmopolitan perspectives.

I divide this chapter into five parts: in the first section I contrast the two dominant international-relations theories—communitarianism and cosmopolitanism. In the second section I explore how these alternative paradigms structure migration issues. In the third section I explore how Christian perspectives align with the two alternative paradigms and suggest, in section four, the need for a global communitarian ethic that combines insights from both cosmopolitanism and communitarianism. In the fifth section, I examine the challenge posed by refugees, persons who have fled their homeland because of war and persecution. Since refugees are persons without a homeland, their protection and well-being depends ultimately on the willingness of states to provide temporary or permanent asylum through resettlement.

Alternative Paradigms of the International Community

The norms of international law stipulate that people have a right to emigrate from their homeland but not a right to immigrate to a particular country. The right of entry can be granted only by the country of destination. Since the cosmopolitan and communitarian perspectives play an important role in how citizenship and migration are conceived, I will next examine the key features of each of these paradigms.

Communitarianism (the real world)

Communitarianism accepts the existing community of states as normative, believing that the quest for human dignity is best secured within and through each of the distinct political societies of the international system. Although states can impede justice, they also serve as the primary political organizations to advance human rights domestically and peace internationally. However, the communitarian approach recognizes that because domestic order is not sufficient to ensure human dignity, pursuing peace and justice among states is also necessary. Thus, a central concern of the communitarian perspective is to define the moral and legal obligations that can contribute to a just world.

Foreign policy practitioners approach foreign policy either through realism or communitarianism. Most scholarship and journalism about foreign affairs is about how government leaders and diplomats work with officials from others states to advance shared interests. Such efforts are undertaken through bilateral or multilateral channels, as well as through international governmental organizations and influential nongovernmental organizations. While numerous scholars have set forth analyses of the communitarian perspective, John Rawls's writings are especially significant because they provide a compelling moral defense of this framework.

Rawls is arguably the most influential American political theorist of the latter part of the twentieth century. His classic work *A Theory of Justice* sets forth a moral framework for pursuing social and political justice in domestic societies. The theory, however, neglects international relations altogether. Rawls addresses this omission in his book *The Law of Peoples*.[2] In this book Rawls seeks to uncover the principles that can advance a just international order based on "the political world as we see it," using what he terms a perspective of "realistic utopia" (83). His theory builds on the following premises: First, peoples, not states, are the key actors. Unlike conventional international-relations theories focused on the rights, duties, and interests of states, Rawls focuses on the institutions and moral character of societies. He does so in order to identify those political communities that are most effective in securing human rights. Second, a just international order is possible only among well-ordered societies. Such societies comprise two types of regimes: "liberal peoples," constitutional,

2. John Rawls, *The Law of Peoples* (Cambridge, MA: Harvard University Press, 1999). Hereafter, page references to this work appear in parentheses within the text.

democratic regimes that protect human rights domestically and fulfill international responsibilities; and "decent hierarchical peoples," nondemocratic regimes that respect human rights and are nonaggressive in global society. Third, the international community is also composed of societies that are not well-ordered and are therefore incapable of contributing to international peace and justice.[3]

Since liberal societies are thought to be reasonable and rational, Rawls claims they will tend to work with other liberal societies in establishing "fair terms of political and social cooperation" (35). Such cooperative action is important because it illuminates the core moral principles that govern the international community and thereby sets forth the structure of international justice. According to Rawls, liberal societies are characterized by such practices as respecting the freedom and independence of other societies; honoring human rights; observing treaties; acknowledging the equality of societies; and providing aid to poor people (37).

Rawls's theory illuminates the quest for justice among distinct nations. Admittedly, he focuses on peoples, not states, but he does so only to highlight the fact that international peace and justice are dependent on the nature of the societies themselves. For Rawls, international justice can be secured only if two conditions are fulfilled: first, states are well ordered and protect human rights, and second, states respect the autonomy of other states and cooperate to ensure a peaceful, stable, and prosperous international community.

In sum, Rawls's communitarian perspective assumes that a peaceful and just world is best advanced through the right actions of member states. Political ethicist Michael Ignatieff has argued powerfully for the importance of sovereign states in promoting human rights and prosperity. He writes, "If we want individuals to face less oppression, violence, and fear in this world, we should wish for stronger sovereigns, not weaker ones. By stronger I mean more capable, more responsible, and more legitimate. If we want human rights to be anchored in the world, we cannot want their enforcement to depend on international institutions and NGOs. We want them anchored in the actual practice of sovereign

3. These nonliberal societies are of three types: "outlaw states"—societies that do not respect human rights; "burdened societies"—those that are incapable of protecting human rights because they lack the institutions, cultural values, resources, and human capital necessary for maintaining a decent, well-ordered society; and "benevolent absolutisms"—societies that protect many human rights but do not allow their people to participate in political decision-making.

states."[4] Thus, if the goal is to advance human rights and prosperity in the world, one needs to nourish nation-states that are strong and benevolent, effective and democratic. Providing economic resources to failed states is unlikely to foster humane regimes. And simply allowing people from poor, failing states to migrate to prosperous countries is also unlikely to promote the well-being of such societies, because the people most willing and able to migrate are not the ones who are most impoverished.

Cosmopolitanism (the ideal world)

The cosmopolitan paradigm focuses on human well-being and assumes that global or cosmopolitan bonds should have precedence over state boundaries. The origins of cosmopolitanism date from the fourth century BCE, when Cynics coined the term "cosmopolitan" (meaning "citizen of the world"). Stoics subsequently developed the idea by emphasizing the fundamental equality of persons by virtue of human reason. For many cosmopolitans, the suffering and injustice in the world is a direct product of self-interest and greed among states. War, famine, and human-rights abuses are a direct byproduct of the existing decentralized global order that facilitates and fosters competition and conflict among member states. Although some cosmopolitan thinkers view local, national, and regional affinities as legitimate, they claim that the primary bonds of humans are to global society. Indeed, when conflict arises between a commitment to a state and to the world, the latter allegiance must take precedence. Moreover, since state sovereignty is not morally significant in the cosmopolitan paradigm, international morality requires the subordination of state boundaries to human dignity. Thus, whereas communitarianism accepts the legitimacy of the existing international order, the cosmopolitan approach denies the moral significance of the existing neo-Westphalian order. (The Peace of Westphalia, which ended the Thirty Years' War in 1648 and heralded the beginnings of the modern nation-state, gave political leaders supreme sovereignty over the affairs within their territorial boundaries, thus affirming that sovereign leaders had the right to decide their state's official religion.)

Because of its idealistic nature, the cosmopolitan perspective is defended and promoted primarily by political theorists, moral utopians,

4. Michael Ignatieff, "The Return of Sovereignty," *The New Republic*, February 16, 2012, 28.

and religious leaders. One leading scholar who has championed this perspective is ethicist Peter Singer. He argues, in *One World*, that globalization has been having the effect of a more interdependent global society—a world with one atmosphere, one economy, one law, and one community. Since globalization makes state boundaries more porous and undermines state sovereignty, he suggests that the time is ripe for a new political morality that gives precedence to universal obligations over nationalistic interests. In his view, the rise of the "global village" demands a "new ethic" that can serve the interests of all persons. As a leading utilitarian philosopher, he wants to advance the greatest good for the greatest number of persons in the world. Thus he emphasizes global responsibilities over the specific duties to fellow citizens. "Our newly interdependent global society, with its remarkable possibilities for linking people around the planet," Singer says, "gives us the material basis for a new ethic."[5]

The foundation of this new political morality is that people matter; state sovereignty is an outmoded concept that unnecessarily confines people's interests and obligations. Building on the foundational premise that human beings are the "basic unit of concern for our ethical thinking," Singer calls for an ethic of impartiality where political and national identities cease to be morally important. Whereas Rawls pursues justice through the existing global order of states, Singer seeks to promote an alternative global system in which sovereignty is no longer ethically significant. He writes, "A global ethic should not stop at, or give great significance to, national boundaries. National sovereignty has no intrinsic moral weight. What weight national sovereignty does have comes from the role that an international principle requiring respect for national sovereignty plays, in normal circumstances, in promoting peaceful relationships between states."[6]

Singer's cosmopolitan project does not seek to eliminate all cultural and political differences. Rather, it highlights the universal bonds among all persons, regardless of where they live. However, if legitimate social and cultural differences are to be respected and protected, pluralism must become a widely and deeply accepted worldview. But until the world becomes one culture and one society, political institutions will be required to secure human rights in global society. Devising a

5. Peter Singer, *One World: The Ethics of Globalization*, 2nd ed. (New Haven, CT: Yale University Press, 2002), 12.

6. Singer, *One World*, 148.

new ethic will not be sufficient to ensure a just and peaceful world. Global institutions will also be necessary to balance the demands of universalism and particularism. Singer argues that the world needs to strengthen global institutions in order to meet growing challenges and demands (199).

In his book *The Life You Can Save*, Singer applies his cosmopolitan perspective, or what he terms a "planetary focus," to the issue of global poverty. He begins the book with a hypothetical case of a child who is in danger of drowning in a shallow pond. All that is required to save the child is to wade into the pond and rescue him or her. In his view, most people would walk into the pond and rescue the child, even if they ended up wet and dirty or damaged their clothes and shoes. From this hypothetical account, Singer explores how rich people should respond to those suffering from extreme poverty. He claims that, based on UNICEF statistics, close to ten million children under the age of five years die each year from poverty-related causes. In his view, if we are willing to save a drowning child, we should be willing to do far more for the millions who are perishing from hunger. Rich people, he argues, should help alleviate global poverty. Such giving would not only help reduce child mortality and improve the lot of many but also mark "the first step toward restoring the ethical importance of giving as an essential component of a well-lived life."[7]

Justice and International Migration

Communitarianism and cosmopolitanism give rise to two distinct conceptions of political justice. For the communitarian, states are the primary actors in global society and thus are presumptively legitimate and entitled to sovereignty. Because communitarianism is concerned mainly with the promotion of a just peace among states, global political ethics is approached as a quest for *international justice*, involving equity and peace among member states. Communitarians recognize that the quest for interstate justice will not ensure justice within states. Indeed, some regimes might deliberately pursue policies that inflict great harm on their people. Because communitarians believe that the protection of existing rules of global society is foundational to domestic and international order, they are reluctant to override the sovereignty norm in the name of human

7. Peter Singer, *The Life You Can Save* (New York: Random House, 2010), 152.

rights. Thus, when gross human-rights abuses occur within a state, or the government is unable to establish a humane order on which economic development can be undertaken, it is the people of that community who must seek to redress the offenses and restore a humane order. Military intervention by foreign powers should be undertaken only as a last resort.

Cosmopolitanism, by contrast, is concerned mainly with the well-being of persons. Cosmopolitan thinkers argue that states have a moral obligation to defend and protect basic rights; when they fail to do so, they lose their moral standing within international society. Because cosmopolitans view nation-states as legitimate political actors only to the extent that they protect and secure human rights, state boundaries are not morally significant.[8] While affirming the legal principle of nonintervention, *world justice* assumes that the existing structures and rules of international society should not be used to protect injustice within states. Therefore, when gross human rights abuses occur and domestic institutions are unable or unwilling to halt the injustice, foreign intervention by the United Nations may be necessary. States that fail to uphold human rights and maintain a humane public order are illegitimate, according to cosmopolitanism. They have no moral standing in the international community.

These two competing worldviews give rise to different perspectives on international migration. In the following, I explore how each of these paradigms addresses immigration.

The communitarian view of migration

According to communitarians, people have an inherent right to membership in a political community. Because human beings are only fully human in association with others, the longing to belong to a community is fundamental to personal identity.[9] Article 15 of Universal Declaration of Human Rights expresses this basic truth by declaring that "everyone has the right to a nationality." But people also have a right to freedom and, in particular, to freedom of movement. As a result, individuals have

---

8. For a full exposition of this position, see Charles Beitz, *Political Theory and International Relations* (Princeton, NJ: Princeton University Press, 1979), which applies John Rawls's theory of justice to international affairs.

9. In South Africa, the sense of belonging is captured by the word *ubuntu,* which is generally translated as "humaneness" and expresses itself in the phrase "people are people through other people."

a right to leave their own homeland. The right of emigration, like the right to be a part of a nation, has become a central claim of contemporary international human-rights law. This claim is stated in Article 13 of the Universal Declaration of Human Rights as follows: "Everyone has the right to leave any country, including his own." The moral basis of the right of emigration is rooted in the voluntary character of democratic societies. Alan Dowty explains the priority of the right to emigrate this way:

> The right to leave thus gets at the very essence of government by consent—a concept that has achieved near universal acceptance in principle, even amongst states that rarely abide by it. Since government by consent holds that citizenship is a voluntary act, the right to leave a country implicitly serves to ratify the contract between an individual and society. If a person who has the right to leave chooses to stay, he has signaled his voluntary acceptance of the social contract. From this follows his obligation to society. But if he does not have the option of leaving, then society's hold on him is based only on coercion.[10]

Dowty argues that the character of a regime is revealed by the respect it accords to personal self-determination and, in particular, to the right of emigration. In his view, the degree of personal autonomy is a measure of a country's "overall social health."

Although individuals have the right to emigrate, they do not necessarily have the right to immigrate to a particular state. This is because governments, not international organizations or migrants themselves, determine admission into sovereign countries.[11] Although people have a right to a nationality and to change their national affiliation, this claim does not entitle a person to reside in a country of his or her choice. As Brian Barry has noted, "It is a general characteristic of associations that people are free to leave them but not free to join them."[12] Thus, emigra-

---

10. Alan Dowty, *Closed Borders: The Contemporary Assault on Freedom of Movement* (New Haven, CT: Yale University Press, 1987), 15.

11. The right of return is a delimited claim for admission. The right of return applies mainly to peoples seeking to return to their nation's homeland on the basis of historic ties of prior membership. For a discussion of how this right applies to Palestinian and Jewish people within Israel, see W. Gunther Plaut, *Asylum: A Moral Dilemma* (Westport, CT: Praeger, 1995), 82-88.

12. Brian Barry, "The Quest for Consistency: A Skeptical View," in Brian Barry and Robert E. Goodin, eds., *Free Movement: Ethical Issues in the Transnational Migration of People and of Money* (University Park: Pennsylvania State University Press, 1992), 284.

tion and immigration are morally and legally asymmetrical. The moral asymmetry between exit and entry, departure and arrival, is illustrated in everyday social and economic life. For example, workers have a right to leave their place of employment, but they are not entitled to another job of their own choosing. Employers, not prospective employees, determine employment. Similarly, students may withdraw from colleges and universities at any time, but their desire to continue their studies at another academic institution depends wholly on their admittance to that institution.

Michael Walzer, a leading communitarian, has set forth a powerful argument about the ethics of border regulation. He claims that regulating membership through admission and exclusion is essential in preserving "communities of character"—that is, "historically stable, ongoing associations of men and women with some special commitment to one another and some special sense of their common life."[13] Walzer explains the necessity of regulating migration as follows: "The distinctiveness of cultures and groups depends upon closure and cannot be conceived as a stable feature of human life without it. If this distinctiveness is a value . . . then closure must be permitted somewhere. At some level of political organization something like the sovereign state must take shape and claim the authority to make its own admissions policy, to control and sometimes restrain the flow of immigrants."[14]

Walzer illustrates the nature and importance of membership by comparing political communities with neighborhoods, clubs, and families. Just as neighborhood unity is rooted in shared values and customs, national cohesion similarly derives from common cultural and political norms and widely shared communal aspirations. States are also like clubs in that membership is entirely up to the members themselves to decide. Admissions policies, like immigration laws, are a significant feature of communal life because they contribute to the maintenance of cohesion and a sense of shared purpose. Finally, states resemble families in that they can help meet the human needs of nonmembers. Although family commitments are generally directed toward next of kin, families also provide periodically for the well-being of strangers; similarly, states frequently extend refuge to persons in need even when there is no religious, ethnic, or political bond between the refugees and the state's citizens.[15]

13. Michael Walzer, *Spheres of Justice: A Defense of Pluralism and Equality* (New York: Basic Books, 1983), 62.

14. Walzer, *Spheres of Justice,* 9-10.

15. Walzer, *Spheres of Justice,* 35-42.

Walzer's analysis suggests that political communities have the right to protect their distinctive cultural, social, and political features and to seek to perpetuate those distinctive qualities through immigration controls. At the same time, political communities, he suggests, have a moral obligation to strangers, especially those who suffer persecution and destitution. Walzer's arguments provide moral justification for the contemporary immigration regime based on widely shared rules and procedures governing migration flows. Myron Weiner characterizes this emerging consensus as follows: ". . . that no government is obligated to admit migrants, that migration is a matter of individual national policy, that most governments need more effective control over their borders, that more forceful measures are needed to halt illegal migration and the growth of worldwide migrant smuggling, that improved procedures are needed to distinguish genuine asylum seekers and refugees suffering from persecution and violence from individuals who use these procedures to migrate, that 'temporary' guest-worker policies do not work."[16]

Using Walzer's communitarian perspective, political theorist Stephen Macedo argues that political communities are morally important and that regulating borders is essential to the protection and advancement of the well-being of its members, especially those who are disadvantaged socially and economically. Macedo says that self-governing communities are morally important because they give rise to powerful bonds of mutual concern. He writes, "Citizens have powerful obligations of mutual concern and respect, and mutual justification, to one another because they are joined together—as constituent members of a sovereign people—in creating binding political institutions that determine patterns of opportunities and rewards for all."[17] While Macedo claims that better-off people have moral obligations to help the least well-off, he argues that the needs of citizens should have priority over those of nonmembers. He provides two justifications for this claim: first, developed societies like the United States have many citizens who are poor and deserving of aid; and second, the pursuit of social or distributive justice can be undertaken only within a state—a community with authoritative institutions that can allocate scarce resources. According to Macedo, fulfilling the needs of deserving low-income native workers is especially important since their

16. Myron Weiner, "Ethics, National Sovereignty and the Control of Immigration," *International Migration Review* 30 (Spring 1996): 192.

17. Stephen Macedo, "The Moral Dilemma of US Immigration Policy," in Carol M. Swain, ed., *Debating Immigration* (Cambridge: Cambridge University Press, 2007), 74.

own economic well-being has suffered as a result of the rising number of low-wage immigrants.

The preferential treatment of citizens does not mean, however, that people in developed societies should not assist foreigners. Rather, it requires that the US government, for example, when designing immigration policies, should give significant consideration to the needs of unskilled American workers. Macedo declares, "Justice demands that we craft policies . . . from the standpoint of the least well-off among our fellow citizens. . . . An immigration policy cannot be considered morally acceptable in justice unless its distributive impact is defensible from the standpoint of disadvantaged Americans."[18]

Economist Paul Collier similarly argues that sustaining strong political communities is important in meeting human needs. Such communities can be sustained, however, only if migration is regulated in order to maintain social solidarity—or what he terms "mutual regard."[19] Communal solidarity is important because it facilitates two kinds of economic actions that are indispensable to successful societies, namely, financial transfers from rich people to those who are poor and cooperation among community members in devising common policies and providing for public goods. More important, mutual regard enables a society to nurture cooperation and trust, or what political scientist Robert Putnam calls "social capital." Since trust and cooperation do not arise automatically, they must be created and sustained through deliberate policies that contribute to group solidarity. According to Collier, mass immigration can easily undermine such cohesion by impeding "mutual regard." "Moderate migration," he writes, "is liable to confer overall social benefits, whereas sustained rapid migration would risk substantial costs."[20]

Collier cites a study by Robert Putnam that shows that higher levels of immigration in a community are associated with lower levels of social trust. The reduced solidarity was not limited to lower levels of mutual trust between immigrants and natives but also among migrants themselves, a striking outcome that indicates how the dislocations associated with migration can have a destabilizing effect on everyone.[21] The implication of Collier's analysis is that if the well-being and prosperity of a society is to be advanced, community membership must be regulated.

18. Macedo, "Moral Dilemma," 81.

19. Paul Collier, *Exodus: How Migration Is Changing Our World* (New York: Oxford University Press, 2013), 61.

20. Collier, *Exodus*, 63.

21. Collier, *Exodus*, 74–75.

The cosmopolitan view of migration

Although cosmopolitan scholars differ on what institutions are necessary to pursue peace and justice in the international community, there is significant consensus that transnational institutions and intergovernmental organizations must play a more important role than states do. As I observed above, cosmopolitans do not believe that territorial borders are morally significant. For them, justice is about the welfare of people, not the rights of states. As a result, human-rights claims must take precedence over sovereignty.

More than any other scholar, Joseph Carens has devoted a lifetime to exploring the ethics of immigration. Although he himself denies that his scholarship is an expression of cosmopolitanism, his focus on global human rights, advocacy of "open borders," and commitment to justice rooted in equality are fundamental ideals of the cosmopolitan perspective.[22] He declares that states do not have "a fundamental moral right to control immigration" (10; see also chap. 11). Further, he assumes that a world of open borders among distinct but relatively equal states would be a more just world—one in which the problem of unlawful migration would all but disappear (288). Unlike some cosmopolitans, many of whom deprecate the state and celebrate international governmental and nongovernmental organizations, Carens focuses his analysis on human rights. Yet he fails to explain how such rights can be advanced by undermining the state's regulatory responsibilities for borders. Carens's cosmopolitan leanings are revealed in the following statement:

> I think that the way the world is organized today is fundamentally unjust. It's like feudalism in important respects. In a world of relatively closed borders like ours, citizenship is an inherited status and a source of privilege. Being born a citizen of a rich country in North America or Europe is a lot like being born into the nobility in the Middle Ages. It greatly enhances one's life prospects (even if there are lesser and greater nobles). And being born a citizen of a poor country in Asia or Africa is a lot like being born into the peasantry in the Middle Ages. It greatly limits one's life chances (even if there are some rich peasants

22. In setting forth his "theory of social membership," Carens argues that some cosmopolitans regard human rights as solely determinative and denigrate communal bonds. He says that this is not his view and that *belonging* matters. See Joseph H. Carens, *The Ethics of Immigration* (New York: Oxford University Press, 2013), 161. Hereafter, page references to this work appear in parentheses within the text.

and a few gain access to the nobility). These advantages and disadvantages are intimately linked to the restrictions on mobility that are characteristic of the modern state system, although the deepest problem is the vast inequality between states that makes so many people want to move. This is not the natural order of things. It is a set of social arrangements that human beings have constructed and that they maintain.[23]

To illuminate some of the distinctive features of a cosmopolitan view of migration, I will examine some of the principal claims of Carens's *The Ethics of Immigration*.

Carens's book, which represents the culmination of three decades of scholarship on immigration ethics, examines how democratic regimes should address immigration. In the first part of the book he explores how immigrants should be treated; in the second part he analyzes what criteria should be used in the admissions process. He sets forth his own perspective in chapter 11, titled "The Case for Open Borders." Since he is aware that a borderless world is unlikely to be accepted, he seeks to theorize about immigration by beginning his analysis using assumptions rooted in the existing state-centric system. His temporary acceptance of the right of states to regulate immigration—what he terms the "conventional view"—is designed to morally assess current immigration practices so that, in the end, he can persuade readers of the unimportance of border regulation. In carrying out this task, he attempts to work from the ground, basing his arguments on widely accepted democratic principles, including freedom, participation, rule of law, and equality.

Two core democratic assumptions structure Carens's analysis: individual freedom and the equal moral worth of all humans. Because people are entitled to freedom by virtue of their human dignity, they have an inherent right to move and live where they desire. Carens acknowledges that the freedom of movement is accepted domestically but not transnationally. But he argues that if the world is to become more just, it needs to extend the right of movement across borders. Only then can the equal worth of persons be fully realized.

A central element of Carens's analysis is his theory of social membership. The theory suggests that peoples' social interactions over time are the foundation of communal life. What matters, according to the theory, is not legality but social engagement. People develop a sense of be-

23. Gary Cutting and Joseph Carens, "When Immigrants Lose Their Human Rights," *The New York Times*, November 25, 2014.

longing by participating in the social life of communities. Carens writes, "What matters most morally with respect to a person's legal status and legal rights in a democratic political community is not ancestry or birthplace or culture or identity or values or actions or even the choices that individuals and communities make but simply the social membership that comes from residence over time" (160). Even though states may have a right to control admissions, if migrants manage to enter a country unlawfully, remain undetected, and develop communal associations, Carens believes that they should be allowed to stay. Governments can regulate borders, but if people can avoid government controls for a number of years, they should be allowed to remain, even though they entered the country unlawfully. In his view, the right to apprehend and deport unauthorized aliens "erodes with the passage of time" (150). As such migrants become more settled, their social connections become deeper and more extensive and gain moral importance. At the same time, the original offense of entering without permission becomes less important. Thus, for him, time as a law-abiding member of a community overcomes the legal barrier created by the original offense (150).

Building on his theory of social membership, Carens argues that unauthorized aliens (he uses the term "irregular migrants") who have established roots in a foreign land should be allowed to stay. This is especially the case for children who have been brought to a foreign country unlawfully by parents. Since social membership does not rest on legal permission but simply on the fact of participating in communal life, Carens does not regard unlawful border crossing as morally significant. What is important is the extent to which people establish a web of social ties with others. "People who live and work and raise their families in a society," he writes, "become members, whatever their legal status" (150). This is why deportation is morally problematic. Although Carens believes that states need to establish policies to address illegal migration, he is opposed to periodic amnesties or to giving relief to individuals based on humanitarian considerations. Instead, states should legalize aliens after they have resided in a community for a fixed period of time: five to seven years, he believes, should be sufficient to establish the claim of social membership (151).

Although Carens begins his book by accepting the idea that states have a right to regulate borders, his analysis does not reinforce this view. He does not further illuminate how or why states should protect borders, because he does not believe that borders are morally important. What matters is the well-being of people. The protection of all people's human rights is so important that he believes that a "firewall" should exist between the enforcement of immigration laws and the enforcement of other national statutes. Entering the United States without admission is an administrative offense (a misdemeanor), not a crime, and most US deportation occurs when an alien is caught at the border.[24] US immigration authorities typically do not target for deportation unauthorized aliens who manage to live and work and remain crime-free. But when unauthorized aliens commit crimes, such as fleeing the scene of a traffic accident, driving under the influence (DUI), or committing aggravated assault, those offenses often come to the attention of federal authorities and will generally lead to deportation proceedings. The aim of Carens's "firewall" is thus to interfere with the collaboration between local law-enforcement agencies and federal organizations in the enforcement of immigration policies.

The two global paradigms I have examined point to different ways of conceiving of immigration. For the communitarian, states are the primary institutions for protecting human rights. Advancing basic rights, including freedom and equality, is only feasible within a strong state, where the rule of law is institutionalized. This means that laws, including those pertaining to immigration, must be enforced. The cosmopolitan approach, by contrast, regards the nation-state as an impediment to human rights and global justice. The "real world" is unjust because it helps to sustain egregious inequalities among states and impedes people from migrating freely from poor, fragile societies to developed states. Cosmopolitan advocates call for open borders in the belief that a more coherent global society will advance human rights. Cosmopolitans rightly insist that people are morally more important than states, but such a claim is meaningless if institutions are not available to secure and protect those rights.

Although these paradigms present contrasting perspectives of world order, they are not mutually exclusive. Rather than viewing cosmopolitanism and communitarianism as dichotomous perspectives, it is useful to view the paradigms along a continuum ranging from complete political fragmentation anchored in state sovereignty to a unified world society anchored in global governance. The communitarian perspective does not endorse nationalistic appeals that seek to advance national interests with

---

24. However, if the person has been deported and returns, the second unlawful entry is considered a crime (a felony) and is subject to a prison term, followed by deportation.

disregard for the well-being of aliens. Rather, communitarianism calls for the preferential treatment of its members while also seeking to care for foreign peoples who face famine, deprivation, and oppression. To some extent, current US immigration practices reflect elements of both worldviews by seeking to regulate immigration and control borders while simultaneously affirming the inherent dignity of persons, especially those who are fleeing political oppression or are unaccompanied minors who have crossed the US border covertly.

The Christian Faith and Immigration Reform Paradigms

This book is not about international relations but the political ethics of immigration. More specifically, I seek to illuminate elements of a Christian worldview relevant to migration and to describe and assess the role of religious actors on the public debate over US immigration policy. I have examined the different ways communitarians and cosmopolitans approach immigration issues in order to highlight the significant role that such paradigms have in structuring an analysis of immigration. To be sure, churches and religious coalitions engaged in immigration advocacy rarely make explicit the worldviews that influence their policy analysis. Indeed, they may be unaware of the underlying assumptions about global order that guide their thinking. And some Christian groups, especially Evangelicals, may wish to justify advocacy of immigration reforms by turning to the Bible. But whether or not they acknowledge the underlying assumptions about world order, they nonetheless build their immigration analysis and advocacy using presuppositions about the international community.

In chapters 6 through 8 below, I will examine biblical and moral principles that Catholics, Evangelicals, and Mainline Protestants have used in addressing immigration. Here I will highlight the important role that global worldviews have in structuring the moral reasoning on international migration. When churches and advocacy groups assess migration, they rely not only on moral principles and religious teachings but also on a particular conception of the international community. Such a conception typically corresponds with cosmopolitan norms rather than with communitarian precepts.

The contribution of cosmopolitan ideals

A Christian worldview shares with cosmopolitanism three central beliefs: first, the well-being of persons is primary; second, because people are entitled to dignity and equality, the international community is an inclusive moral society; and third, because the international community is a coherent ethical society, people have a right to migrate.

The alignment of a Christian worldview with cosmopolitanism is first based in the priority of persons and their inherent right to dignity. A core claim of the Christian faith is that all persons are made in the image of God and thus have equal and infinite worth. According to George Weigel, "the inalienable dignity and value of every human being . . . is the bedrock personalist principle from which Catholic thinking about public policy begins."[25] Although differences in culture, nationality, language, social and economic status, and education divide and separate people, Christians affirm the inherent equal worth of all persons regardless of such differences. In her book on Christian ethics and immigration, Kristin Heyer argues that a Christian view of persons is bound to foster "relational agency, family flourishing, and solidarity." As a result, the humanity of persons overrides any boundaries that divide people.[26]

Transnational solidarity, the second feature shared with cosmopolitanism, has led some Christians to view the international community as a family and to express such inclusivity with slogans such as "strangers no more," "welcoming the stranger," and "loving our neighbor." Protestant ethicist Dana Wilbanks argues that since "a Christian perspective is not a nationalistic one," believers should favor relatively free transnational migration.[27] The Conference of US Catholic Bishops declared in a 1988 statement on US immigration that "the Church must be the first to insist that love knows no borders."[28] According to Drew Christiansen, since the Roman Catholic Church regards the world as a unified human family, Catholic social teaching approaches international relations from

25. George Weigel, "An Immigration Debate Primer," *The Catholic Difference*, May 19, 2010. Available at: http://eppc.org/publications/an-immigration-debate-primer/.

26. Kristin E. Heyer, *Kinship across Borders: A Christian Ethic of Immigration* (Washington, DC: Georgetown University Press, 2012), 6.

27. Dana W. Wilbanks, *Re-creating America: The Ethics of US Immigration and Refugee Policy in a Christian Perspective* (Nashville: Abingdon, 1996), 95.

28. Quoted in David Simcox, "The Roman Catholic Church's Position on Immigration Is Irresponsible," in Scott Barbour, ed., *Immigration Policy* (San Diego: Greenhaven, 1995), 51.

"a universalist" perspective—one where people are potentially neighbors to every other person.[29] This universalist perspective is manifest in the 2003 US-Mexican Catholic bishops' pastoral letter "Strangers No Longer," which captures the bishops' approach to migration in the following declaration: "We recognize the phenomenon of migration as an authentic sign of the times. . . . To such a sign we must respond in common and creative ways so that we may strengthen the faith, hope, and charity of migrants and all the People of God. Such a sign is a call to transform national and international social, economic, and political structures so that they may provide the conditions required for the development for all, without exclusion and discrimination against any person in any circumstance."[30] While the bishops acknowledge that states have a right to control borders, the overall message of the letter is to facilitate transnational bonds between the people of Mexico and the United States. Indeed, to the extent that the bishops address US border control, they do so, in Peter Meilaender's view, in an "unremittingly critical" fashion.[31]

The third assumption shared with cosmopolitanism is the claim that human beings have a right to migrate. In his encyclical *Pacem in Terris* ("Peace on Earth"), Pope John XXIII articulates this right as follows: "Every human being has the right to the freedom of movement and of residence within the confines of their country; and, when there are just reasons for it, the right to emigrate and take up residence elsewhere." In an address in 1985, Pope John Paul II declared, "Every human being has the right to freedom of movement and of residence within the confines of his own country. When there are just reasons in favor of it, he must be permitted to migrate to other countries and to take up residence there. The fact that he is a citizen of a particular state does not deprive him of membership in the human family, nor of citizenship in the universal society, the common worldwide fellowship of men."[32] And Pope Francis's 2015 address to Congress emphasizes the need to respond compassion-

---

29. Drew Christiansen, SJ, "Movement Asylum, Borders: Christian Perspectives," *International Migration Review* 30, no. 1 (Spring 1996): 10-11.

30. "Strangers No Longer: Together on the Journey of Hope," A Pastoral Letter Concerning Migration from the Catholic Bishops of Mexico and the United States, 2003, para. 102. Available at: http://www.usccb.org/issues-and-action/human-life-and-dignity/immigration/strangers-no-longer-together-on-the-journey-of-hope.cfm.

31. Peter C. Meilaender, "Immigration: Citizens and Strangers," *First Things* (May 2007).

32. Pope John Paul II, "Address to the New World Congress on the Pastoral Care of Immigrants," October 17, 1985.

ately to those who migrate to improve their standard of living: "On this continent, too, thousands of persons are led to travel north in search of a better life for themselves and for their loved ones, in search of greater opportunities. Is this not what we want for our own children?" There can be little doubt that people have a right to freedom of movement. But as I have noted repeatedly above, the right to emigrate is not synonymous with the right to immigrate. People are allowed to leave their own communities, but they do not have an inherent right to join other communities.[33]

Protestants have also emphasized the right of migration. For example, Dana Wilbanks calls into question the moral foundations of the Westphalian system of nation-states, arguing that territorial borders protect "unjust privilege." In his view, the "presumption in Christian ethics would seem to be an open-border policy."[34] Similarly, M. Daniel Carroll R. (Rodas), an evangelical professor of biblical studies, argues in his book *Christians at the Border* that Scripture provides a framework for assessing immigration. For Carroll, the biblical disposition is more concerned with inclusion than exclusion, with hospitality than with law. He writes, "[Immigration] is a topic close to the heart of God and inseparable from the life and mission of God's people. Openness to sojourners is a virtue, and concern for their well-being is manifested tangibly in Old Testament law."[35]

The cosmopolitan ideals of human dignity, global solidarity, and freedom of movement are important because they are essential in defining and pursuing justice. But moral norms alone are insufficient to advance human rights, promote just immigration policies, and contribute to international peace and global prosperity. If Christians are to contribute to a more effective and more just immigration policy, the analysis and advocacy of immigration reform must also incorporate communitarian precepts that acknowledge the fragmented nature of global society and the essential role of states in advancing human rights. To be sure, not

33. It is noteworthy that the educational resources distributed by the US Conference of Catholic Bishops, such as the program "Justice for Immigrants," repeatedly affirm the right of the state to control immigration. But, whereas the documents make human well-being primary, there is little analysis of how border regulation can be strengthened or how to respond to those migrants who seek to bypass border controls altogether. In effect, the church pays lip service to border control but justifies people's right to migrate.

34. Wilbanks, *Re-creating America*, 180.

35. M. Daniel Carroll R., *Christians at the Border: Immigration, the Church, and the Bible* (Grand Rapids: Baker Academic, 2008), 112.

all states may wish to promote human rights or to advance global order. Moreover, some states may inhibit migration altogether. But given the existing decentralized nature of the international community, the promotion of human rights, including the right of migration, presupposes constitutional sovereign states—that is, strong states that are also good. So long as the United Nations global order persists, governments of nation-states—not global governance—will have the final responsibility for securing human rights, whether they do so individually within their own borders or multilaterally in foreign countries.

Since the ideals of caring for neighbors and welcoming strangers are insufficient in themselves to guide policy-making, the promotion of just migration will necessarily entail communitarian principles building on the existing institutions that structure contemporary international affairs. Consequently, the cosmopolitan ideals that undergird much of the analysis and political advocacy of Christian groups on US immigration should be supplemented with precepts from a communitarian perspective.

The contribution of communitarian perspectives

The communitarian paradigm offers principles and perspectives that can strengthen a Christian approach to migration in several ways. First, a communitarian approach contributes to communal solidarity. Unlike cosmopolitanism, which emphasizes universal bonds among all persons, communitarianism focuses on the special bonds that people have with their local communities and nations. Since a person's humanity is expressed through communal life, and since proximity contributes to stronger social ties, membership in limited communities is especially important to human well-being. Nation-states are arbitrary political creations that include many different ethnic, religious, and social groups. Still, the solidarity of the nation-state, sometimes expressed overtly through nationalism, can foster legitimate social and political ties that enhance human dignity.

A second contribution of communitarianism is its recognition of the inevitability of human competition and conflict. To Christians, such conflict is rooted in a realistic conception of human nature: one that acknowledges both the human capacity for love and generosity and also the capacity for evil and injustice. And though Christians celebrate human dignity, the Christian faith also teaches that humans are sinful and in need of divine redemption. According to Christian teaching, sin is *total* and *universal:* total because all of a person's being (will, reason, and emotions) is subject to human will; universal because it afflicts all persons regardless of nationality, ethnicity, or social class. The late Rev. John Stott, an influential British evangelical pastor, once observed that a Christian view of human nature is paradoxical, involving beneficial dispositions that contribute to love of neighbor, creativity, and prosperity but also harmful dispositions that contribute to greed, oppression, and destruction. He called the first dimension "the glory of humanness" and the second "the shame of humanness."[36] According to Stott, the Christian view of the person provides a "radical realism of the Bible," avoiding the easy optimism of the humanist and the dark pessimism of the cynic. Given the dual nature of persons, ethicist Reinhold Niebuhr similarly argues that a sound approach to politics needs to avoid the extremes of idealism and pessimism. The "children of light" were those who were overconfident that intractable problems could be resolved through reason, while the "children of darkness" were persons who thought that problems arising from greed and self-interest could only be addressed through power.[37] Of course, not all human conflict arises from selfishness and greed, since competition is a natural byproduct of people's freedom in pursuing individual and shared interests. Nevertheless, communitarianism's acknowledgment of the inherent nature of the conflict in social and political life provides important perspectives that can help foster and sustain communal solidarity and avoid the limitations of utopian cosmopolitanism.

Communitarianism's third contribution to a Christian approach to migration is its acceptance of the existing decentralized global order. The Westphalian system of state sovereignty that emerged in the mid-seventeenth century is not a divinely mandated political order. Other systems have existed in the past, and other forms of global order could arise in the future. But for the present, the current system is rooted in the legitimacy of sovereign nation-states. Although such a decentralized system permits competition and war among member states, it also allows for cooperation in promoting the common good and in confronting evil and injustice via the individual and the collective. From a moral perspective, the decentralized global system allows states to challenge each other through the balance of power. Just as checks and balances and federal-

---

36. Reverend John Stott discussed the Christian view of human nature in a chapel address on January 25, 1994, at Wheaton College, Wheaton, Illinois.

37. Reinhold Niebuhr, *The Children of Light and the Children of Darkness* (New York: Charles Scribner's Sons, 1944).

ism contribute to the pursuit of the common good in the United States, so does the balance-of-power system allow states to confront injustice internationally.

A fourth (and related) strength of communitarianism is its acknowledgment of the important role of the state in advancing human rights. Unlike the cosmopolitan perspective, which celebrates global solidarity and deprecates the state, the communitarian approach recognizes that government institutions are essential in making and enforcing laws that protect human dignity. Acknowledging the important role of government is especially important for Christians, because they are aware of how greed, selfishness, and avarice can undermine the common good. In public affairs, sin is manifested in the decisions and actions of individuals and collectives as they pursue their own interests in disregard of—and at the expense of—the well-being of others. If sin were not part of the human condition, the pursuit of a just world order and equitable migration practices would not present intractable obstacles. But because greed and selfishness predominate in communal life, sovereign governments must seek to rectify offenses and advance proximate justice through the maintenance of order and the rule of law. Governments are divinely instituted in part to undertake the responsibility of caring for the needs and interests of their own citizens, but to the extent that it is possible, they can also pursue these moral goals in foreign lands through multilateral initiatives.

Finally, the communitarian perspective contributes to a Christian approach to migration by highlighting the dual responsibilities of citizens and foreigners. Whereas the cosmopolitan perspective treats all persons as members of a coherent global community, the communitarian worldview distinguishes between obligations to citizens and responsibilities to foreigners, giving the interests of their citizens precedence over those of strangers. This does not mean that human beings are morally unequal or that states can disregard the wants and needs of noncitizens. Rather, a moral approach to migration must advance the interests of citizens while taking into account the wants and needs of others. Since communal life can only be sustained if membership is regulated, the challenge in making immigration policy is controlling migration in order to protect the inherent values, traditions, and aspirations of a community while also responding to the needs and wants of migrants. There is no simple solution to the balancing of these dual obligations; rather, government officials must seek to devise policies based on multiple claims through prudence.

The Contribution of Global Realism

Both the communitarian and cosmopolitan perspectives provide important insights that can contribute to a peaceful and humane international community. By emphasizing transnational bonds, the cosmopolitan perspective nurtures the equality of persons and the universality of human dignity. According to political theorist Martha Nussbaum, cosmopolitanism is important because it shifts people's allegiance from the nation to the international community, thereby nurturing the ideal of a global moral community made up by "the humanity of all human beings."[38] At the same time, the communitarian worldview reminds us that human beings achieve their full humanity through social interaction in specific communities—by fostering a sense of belonging within families, neighborhoods, and nations. Political theorist Benjamin Barber says that the challenge is not to eliminate patriotism and nationalism but "how to render them safe." "Cosmopolitanism as an attitude may help us in that effort," he says, "but cosmopolitanism as a political destination is more likely to rob us of our concreteness and our immediacy and ultimately can only benefit the less wholesome aspects of the yearning for community and identity."[39] Social theorist Gertrude Himmelfarb similarly questions the cosmopolitan worldview because she believes that it impairs essential human attributes—the "givens of life" such as family, religion, heritage, history, culture, tradition, and nationality.[40]

Given the contributions of both universalist and communal perspectives, a Christian approach to migration should be rooted in both the idealism of cosmopolitanism and the realism of communitarianism. How these two worldviews are integrated in addressing migration will, of course, vary in accordance with the specific challenges facing states. For example, for the United States, faced with the challenge of enforcing immigration laws, the communitarian model provides a helpful framework. Such a model can remind political leaders and policy advocates of the important role of sovereign states in securing human rights through the rule of law while fulfilling the wishes of a reasonable number of visa applicants. For the European countries, by contrast, the current challenge in meeting the security and welfare needs of refugees calls for a cosmo-

38. Martha C. Nussbaum, "Patriotism and Cosmopolitanism," in Joshua Cohen, ed., *For Love of Country: Debating the Limits of Patriotism* (Boston: Beacon, 1996), 7.

39. Benjamin R. Barber, "Constitutional Faith," in Cohen, *For Love of Country*, 36.

40. Gertrude Himmelfarb, "The Illusions of Cosmopolitanism," in Cohen, *For Love of Country*, 77.

politan perspective, one that gives priority to persons fleeing violence over the legal prerogatives of states. But even in responding to mass migration, states play an indispensable role in processing refugee claims, formally admitting those with legitimate claims, and providing aid in their resettlement.

A review of major declarations and documents issued on US immigration policy by Catholics, Mainline Protestants, and Evangelicals suggests that the dominant paradigm structuring the assessment of migration is a cosmopolitan worldview. While lip service is paid to the governmental responsibility to regulate borders, the fundamental message of church pronouncements is that all people are made in God's image and that they are a part of an inclusive moral community. As a result, church groups and religious advocacy groups favor comprehensive immigration reform that involves increased legal immigration, more rapid family reunification, and the legalization of irregular aliens. But such an approach overemphasizes social inclusion—"welcoming the stranger"— and de-emphasizes obedience to lawful authority, that is, rendering to Caesar the things that are Caesar's. Inclusion is a hallmark of the church, but the international community is a society of states, each with its own laws, customs, and social practices. Because the kingdom of Christ is a universal community, the church can exist without boundaries. The state, however, is responsible to control the affairs within its territorial boundaries. Without sovereign control, there is no state, and without government, no law enforcement is possible.

A major limitation of the ecclesiastical analyses of US immigration is the disregard of the state. Terms such as nation, state, government, rule of law, citizenship, passport, and legal justice are often minimized or even absent, while the moral language of inclusion, hospitality to strangers, and compassion dominates the analysis. The clerical approach to immigration reform might be characterized as heavy on ethics and light on political science. "Strangers No Longer," the joint pastoral letter by the Catholic bishops from the United States and Mexico, for example, celebrates the rights of persons and the universal solidarity of the international community but is reticent to acknowledge the important role of the nation-state in protecting human rights and advancing economic prosperity.[41] In discussing the needs of migrants, the bishops treat American society and its institutions as a market, a place where strangers work

41. "Strangers No Longer: Together on the Journey of Hope," A Pastoral Letter Concerning Migration from the Catholic Bishops of Mexico and the United States, 2003.

and pursue their economic interest, not a society where people share common bonds and shared responsibilities. Similarly, the 2009 resolution of the National Association of Evangelicals (NAE) on immigration minimizes the role of civil authorities in regulating migration. Rather than illuminating the tensions of loving both citizens and foreigners and between the rule of law and the acceptance of unauthorized aliens, the resolution offers recommendations that seek to advance a more inclusive, flexible, and expansive immigration policy.[42]

Stephen Macedo argues that political communities are essential in protecting and advancing the well-being of its members, especially those who are disadvantaged socially and economically. While Macedo claims that the rich have moral obligations to help the poor, he argues that the needs of citizens should have priority over those of nonmembers. In his view, the needs of deserving low-income workers is especially important since their own economic well-being has suffered as a result of the rising number of low-wage immigrants. The preferential treatment of citizens does not mean, however, that people in developed societies should not assist foreigners. Rather, it requires that government, when designing immigration policies, give significant consideration to the needs of unskilled American workers.

Collier similarly argues that sustaining strong political communities is important in meeting human needs. Such communities can be sustained, however, only if migration is regulated in order to maintain group solidarity—or what he calls "mutual regard."[43] Communal solidarity is important because it facilitates two kinds of economic actions that are indispensable to successful societies, namely, financial transfers from rich people to those who are poor and cooperation among community members in devising common policies that provide public goods. More importantly, mutual regard enables a society to nurture cooperation and trust, or what social scientists call "social capital." Since trust and cooperation do not arise automatically, they must be created and sustained through deliberate policies that contribute to group solidarity. And because mass immigration can impair communal trust, Collier argues that managing international migration is an important government responsibility.

While nation-states have been crucial to the promotion of human

---

42. National Association of Evangelicals, "Immigration 2009." Available at: http://nae.net/immigration-2009/.

43. Paul Collier, *Exodus: How Migration Is Changing Our World* (New York: Oxford University Press, 2013), 61.

rights, not all states serve the common good. Some states are unjust, and others are simply incapable of making and enforcing laws. To advance a just peace, the world needs strong states (i.e., states with strong institutions that can rule) that are also good (i.e., states with constitutionally democratic institutions that protect human rights through the rule of law). Because of ongoing civil wars and ethnic and religious conflicts, a growing number of countries have been unable to constitute and maintain a sovereign government, one with the authority to make and enforce rules. The result of failing regimes, such as those in the Democratic Republic of Congo, Libya, Somalia, South Sudan, and Syria, is rampant killing, gross human rights abuses, and economic devastation. In light of the suffering arising from weak and failing states, it would be wrong to conclude that the time had arrived to jettison the sovereign state.

As I have suggested earlier, a Christian perspective on immigration should be rooted in both the universal ambitions of cosmopolitanism and the concern with communal solidarity found in communitarianism. Such a combined approach could be called realistic idealism or global realism. Since Christian groups addressing US immigration reform have been influenced overwhelmingly by cosmopolitan sentiments, Christians seeking to devise a more balanced advocacy strategy should also consider the claims and insights of the communitarian paradigm. Such insights include the belief that constitutionally democratic governments are essential in protecting and advancing human rights and that human flourishing is maximized within communities that enjoy high levels of trust and voluntary cooperation. Social solidarity is not an automatic byproduct of interactions among people. Rather, communal solidarity is a human creation—a byproduct of shared customs and traditions, common moral values and aspirations, and the work of political institutions. In particular, advancing human rights within and among nation-states will necessarily require working through governmental institutions that emphasize the rule of law, citizenship, and the regulation of membership. Thus, while emphasizing the universal bonds of the human family is important, a Christian perspective on immigration must acknowledge the important contribution of the state in regulating membership.

The Moral Claims of Refugees

The most challenging problem in migration politics is undoubtedly the question of the responsibility for the protection and care of refugees.

Fundamentally, refugees are persons who have fled their homeland because of war, ethnic strife, religious persecution, political oppression, or other significant threats to personal security and human dignity.[44] When people flee their communities because of security threats but remain within their own country, they are classified as "internally displaced persons." Over the past two decades the persistence of political, religious, and ethnic conflicts has resulted in many bitter wars. Since these disputes have brought about discrimination, ethnic cleansing, political oppression, and even the collapse of state authority, they have resulted in enormous human suffering and systematic abuse of human rights. As of 2015, domestic wars, ethnic persecution, and religious conflicts had resulted in close to twenty million refugees who had fled their homelands and close to forty million internally displaced persons. According to the United Nations High Commissioner for Refugees (UNHCR), the year 2014 recorded the largest increase in internally displaced persons in a single year since that organization was established in 1952.[45]

It is generally acknowledged that in addressing the needs of refugees, the most desirable long-term solution for refugees—for communal reasons—is repatriation back to the home country. Although the Universal Declaration of Human Rights enshrines the right of return (repatriation), the ability and willingness of people to avail themselves of this right depends largely on local political conditions. Repatriation can be more difficult, even untenable, when the political instability, oppression, and enmity that originally forced people to flee continue. As a result, refugee protection sometimes involves long-term humanitarian assistance by the UNHCR or even requests by refugees for permanent resettlement. Third-country resettlement, however, is generally regarded as the least desirable solution, partly because of the great cultural, social, and economic challenges that refugees must overcome in becoming fully integrated into a new society.

Several factors make the plight of refugees legally and morally challenging. Because refugees fall, as Louis Henkin has noted, "in the interstices of state boundaries," they suffer from a lack of protection from

---

44. According to the 1951 UN Convention on the Status of Refugees, a refugee is a person "who owing to well-founded fear of being persecuted for reasons of race, religion, nationality, membership of a particular social group or political opinion, is outside the country of his nationality and is unable, or owing to such fear, is unwilling to avail himself of the protection of that country."

45. UNHCR, "Global Trends Report: World at War" (2014).

authoritative institutions.[46] While international humanitarian organizations, such as the UNHCR, play a major role in caring for refugees, it is actually nation-states that serve as the principal caregivers. When civil wars erupt and intensify, people typically flee to neighboring states, where temporary camps are set up with the assistance of local authorities and the UNHCR. For example, the Syrian civil war, which emerged in the aftermath of the Arab Spring in 2011 and continues in 2017, has forced more than four million to flee to neighboring Turkey, Lebanon, Jordan, and Iraq, but it has also encouraged more than a half million persons to seek refuge in Europe, fleeing by land through Turkey or by boat to either Greece or Italy. At the same time, tens of thousands of refugees have applied for protection in distant countries. As a result, US government officials announced that the United States would seek to admit 10,000 Syrian refugees for resettlement in 2016.

While there is broad international consensus on the criteria for refugees, determining which persons are entitled to refugee protection is difficult, especially since officials must ascertain the credibility of refugee claims, often with limited data. This task is also made more challenging because the mass movement of migrants frequently includes not only those who are fleeing war but also those who are seeking a better standard of living. Following international law, US law (INA, 101) defines refugees as those individuals who have a "well-founded fear of persecution on account of race, religion, nationality, membership in a particular social group, or political opinion." To be considered for admission, refugees (i.e., persons living in a foreign country, outside their homeland) must complete a detailed application (Form I-590) and be interviewed by an asylum officer. The process also applies to asylees, that is, persons who apply for asylum after arriving in the United States.

Finally, because of the large number of persons requesting asylum, the US government establishes annual ceilings and criteria for the resettling of refugees. The US government annually sets an overall cap as well as ceilings for different geographical regions. In the fiscal year 2015, for example, the overall ceiling was set at 70,000 refugees, and in 2016 the cap was set at 85,000.

Although scholars and public officials generally concur that resource-rich states should care for refugees, there is little agreement on how international organizations or states should respond to the plight of refugees.

46. Louis Henkin, *The Age of Rights* (New York: Columbia University Press, 1990), 48.

Cosmopolitans, for example, argue not only that refugee resettlement should be greatly increased but that international institutions should be strengthened so that they can assume greater responsibility for caring and resettling refugees.[47] For cosmopolitans, giving aid to refugees is a moral obligation, whereas communitarians assume that states have a moral responsibility to provide humanitarian assistance but not necessarily an obligation to accept refugees. Myron Weiner expresses the communitarian view as follows: "If someone is in urgent need and the risks and cost of giving aid are low, we ought to help the injured stranger—not on the basis of justice but on the basis of charity."[48]

In summary, the communitarian and cosmopolitan perspectives of global society provide important ideals in addressing immigration concerns. From a Christian perspective, it is clear that a cosmopolitan paradigm provides important insights in its emphasis on the universality of human dignity and the equality of persons. While the world can be regarded as a coherent moral community, it is not a unified political society but a fragmented community of sovereign nation-states. As a result, while cosmopolitanism offers important moral ideals, it is incapable of providing a sufficient basis for devising immigration policy. A Christian approach to immigration must necessarily incorporate communitarian insights by acknowledging the indispensable role of political community in advancing human well-being. Communal solidarity is not a natural byproduct of social life. Rather, governments must establish laws and practices that protect and nurture solidarity, trust, and cooperation. Since social capital is a human creation, political communities must establish rules to regulate not only life within their boundaries but also ties with other political communities. States regulate immigration because it is a means by which they seek to balance the needs and wants of their own people with those of people desiring to join the community. Therefore, the challenge in immigration policy is to affirm the universality of human dignity but to also nurture communal solidarity so that people can flourish as they develop and use their God-given gifts and abilities to the maximum.

47. For example, Peter and Renata Singer, following the principle of "equal consideration of interests," argue for greatly increasing the number of refugees resettled in rich countries. See Peter and Renata Singer, "The Ethics of Refugee Policy," in Mark Gibney, ed., *Open Borders? Closed Societies? The Ethical and Political Issues* (New York: Greenwood, 1988), 122-28.

48. Myron Weiner, "Ethics, National Sovereignty and the Control of Immigration," *International Migration Review* 30 (Spring 1996): 175.

Christian Ethics, the Bible, and Immigration

The study of Christian political ethics concerns the moral principles that emerge from the teachings of Christianity about social, economic, and political life. Since the Christian faith is a religion, not an ideology, it is primarily concerned with foundational issues regarding the meaning and purpose of life, not with social and political issues. Therefore, Christianity does not offer ready-made prescriptions for temporal issues and problems. This does not mean that membership in the "city of God" does not have implications for citizenship in the "city of man." Rather, Christians seeking to discern and fulfill their social and political obligations require sound biblical and theological knowledge, an understanding of domestic and international affairs, and prudential competence in public affairs. While the Bible is not a manual on political and economic life, it nevertheless provides general principles and broad perspectives that can help guide thought and action on public-policy issues, such as immigration. John C. Bennett, a mid-twentieth-century Protestant theologian, argued in *Foreign Policy in Christian Perspective* that although the Christian faith could not provide specific answers to the problems of international affairs, it could help structure moral reasoning by offering "ultimate perspectives, broad criteria, motives, inspirations, sensitivities, warnings, moral limits rather than directives for policies and decisions."[1]

In this chapter I describe some of the pillars of Christian political ethics, and this will serve as an introduction to some of the major features of Catholic, Mainline Protestant, and Evangelical political theology that address the immigration issues that I will then examine in the next three chapters.

---

1. John C. Bennett, *Foreign Policy in Christian Perspective* (New York: Charles Scribner's Sons, 1966), 36.

Catholic Social Thought

In carrying out its spiritual mission, the Roman Catholic Church relies on a three-legged stool of revelation, reason, and tradition. The basis of Catholic teaching is God's revelation in Scripture, which is not, however, to be interpreted by believers alone; rather, it is to be interpreted under the direction of bishops and priests, who provide formal biblical teachings and serve the sacraments. Unlike Protestants, who hold that every believer can understand and apply biblical truth individually, the Catholic Church assigns a far more important role to the clergy for its teaching and discipleship. The second element in the Catholic Church's ministry is human reason, which the Church regards as an indispensable resource in understanding nature, using the material world to advance human well-being, and interpreting God's special and general revelation in Scripture and nature. Since God created a rational world, humans apprehend, enjoy, and participate in the ongoing work of divine creation through reason. Furthermore, because of its belief in the reliability of reason, the Catholic Church relies on natural law to justify its teachings and moral claims.[2] In summary, the Roman Catholic Church bases its teaching authority on Scripture supplemented by the traditions of the church and reason.

Catholic social thought (CST) is a body of church doctrine on social, political, and economic justice. The teachings, which set forth principles for advancing the common good of communities, are based on Scripture, church teachings, and natural law and are derived from the teachings of the Catholic Church and, more specifically, papal encyclicals, Vatican documents, and bishops' pastoral letters. The body of doctrine is not a fixed group of norms but rather a dynamic set of teachings developed in response to changing circumstances and social and political challenges.[3] The principles comprising CST do not provide ready-made answers to contemporary social challenges; instead, they offer a structure that can guide moral reasoning on issues and problems in social, economic, and political life.

In 2007, the American bishops issued an important document that was designed to assist Catholics in fulfilling their responsibilities as

2. The natural-law tradition assumes that immutable moral laws exist and can be apprehended through reason.

3. Michael P. Hornsby-Smith, *An Introduction to Catholic Social Thought* (Cambridge: Cambridge University Press, 2006), 85.

citizens. The document, titled "Forming Consciences for Faithful Citizenship," declares that the Christian faith demands the church's participation in shaping the moral character of society. Its task is not to tell political rulers what to do. Rather, its mission is to provide the moral structure for addressing social, political, and economic issues. The report states, "The obligation to teach about moral values that should shape our lives, including our public lives, is central to the mission given to the Church by Jesus Christ."[4] The report goes on to illuminate the Catholic Church's vital teaching responsibility as follows: "We [the Church] are to teach fundamental moral principles that help Catholics form their consciences correctly, to provide guidance on the moral dimensions of public decisions, and to encourage the faithful to carry out their responsibilities in political life."[5] Finally, the report highlights the need for prudence in addressing complex policy issues. While a well-formed conscience is necessary for advancing justice, prudence—the capacity to use reason in selecting an action from among moral alternatives—is also essential.

The roots of CST go back to biblical times, but some scholars argue that Pope Leo XIII laid its formal origins in his 1891 encyclical *Rerum Novarum* ("On the Condition of Labor"). Additional papal encyclicals and conciliar documents subsequently reinforced this initiative. Some of the most significant include:

- Pope Pius XI, *Quadragesimo Anno* ("After Forty Years"), 1931
- Pope John XXIII, *Mater et Magistra* ("Christianity and Social Progress"), 1961; *Pacem in Terris* ("Peace on Earth"), 1963
- Vatican Council II, *Gaudium et Spes* ("Joy and Hope"), Pastoral Constitution on the Church in the Modern World, 1965; *Dignitatis Humanae* ("Declaration on Religious Freedom"), 1965
- Pope Paul VI, *Populorum Progressio* ("On the Development of Peoples"), 1967
- Pope John Paul II, *Laborem Exercens* ("On Human Work"), 1981; *Centesimus Annus* ("The Hundredth Year"), 1991

Examining the individual content of each of these significant documents is beyond the scope of this book. But what is noteworthy about

4. USCCB, "Forming Consciences for Faithful Citizenship: A Call to Political Responsibility from the Catholic Bishops of the United States" (Washington, DC: USCCB, 2007), 3.

5. "Forming Consciences," 5.

these and other church encyclicals is the priority given by popes and bishops to the biblical and moral dimensions of the social, economic, and political life. The Catholic Church does not view social justice as an ancillary or subsidiary concern. Rather, it regards social justice as an important part of the church's mission. Indeed, the Vatican's "Compendium of the Social Doctrine of the Church" (issued by the Vatican's Pontifical Council for Justice and Peace in 2006) declares that the church's social doctrine "is an integral part of her evangelizing ministry."[6] Since caring for humans is a dimension of the gospel of Christ, Roman Catholics regard CST as a body of doctrine that can help advance the work of Christ. It does so not by providing preplanned or ready-made answers but by offering principles that can guide ethical reflection on the social, political, and economic changes facing societies.

Theologians and scholars are divided about the most important themes or elements of CST. The US Bishops' Conference, for example, highlights the following seven themes: (1) life and dignity of the human person; (2) call to family, community, and participation; (3) rights and responsibilities; (4) the priority of the poor and vulnerable; (5) the dignity of work and the rights of workers; (6) solidarity; and (7) care for God's creation.[7] In his introductory text on CST, Michael Hornsby-Smith lists six principles that he considers central to the Catholic Church's social teachings: human dignity; common good; subsidiarity; preferential option for the poor; solidarity; and preferential option for nonviolence.[8] The Vatican's "Compendium of the Social Doctrine of the Church" undoubtedly provides the most authoritative overview of the Catholic Church's social doctrine. The document's first three chapters address "God's Plan of Love for Humanity," "The Church's Mission and Social Doctrine," and "The Human Person and Human Rights." Only after addressing theological and anthropological issues does the document take up "Principles of the Church's Social Doctrine" in the fourth chapter. And the document's second section explores additional Catholic Church teachings, focusing on the family, work, economic life, domestic political society, the inter-

---

6. Pontifical Council for Justice and Peace, "Compendium of the Social Doctrine of the Church" (The Vatican, 2006). Available at: http://www.vatican.va/roman_curia/pontifical_councils/justpeace/documents/rc_pc_justpeace_doc_20060526_compendio-dott-soc_en.html.

7. USCCB, "Themes of Catholic Social Teaching." Available at: http://www.usccb.org/beliefs-and-teachings/what-we-believe/catholic-social-teaching/seven-themes-of-catholic-social-teaching.cfm.

8. Hornsby-Smith, *Catholic Social Thought*, 104-7.

national community, environmental protection, and the promotion of peace.

The Catholic Church gives priority to four principles of CST: the common good, subsidiarity, participation, and solidarity. The *common good* is conceived of as the shared well-being of persons in community. Because people can fulfill their true humanity only in association with others, justice in communities can be advanced only when the shared (or "common") interests of all are advanced.[9] *Subsidiarity* is the belief that decision-making should be decentralized in order to empower responsible human action. Since human beings are entitled to freedom, *participation* is the right and responsibility of people to be involved in their personal and collective affairs: participation permits people to be responsible human agents. Finally, *solidarity* is the commitment to care for the dignity and well-being of all people. Since human beings seek their own interests, often at the expense of others, solidarity is the call to care for neighbors near and far. Since human beings are equal and entitled to respect, solidarity is the means of manifesting concern for all persons, whether at the familial, local, national, or international level.

In the next chapter I examine Catholic teachings on migration. Though there is no church document that provides an authoritative listing of CST principles relevant to the challenges of transnational migration, it is possible to discern some of the major elements of the Catholic Church's approach to these issues from papal encyclicals, Vatican documents, and pastoral letters and declarations by the US Conference of Catholic Bishops (USCCB).

Protestant Political Ethics

In the early sixteenth century, a number of religious leaders, led by Martin Luther in Germany and Huldrych Zwingli in Switzerland, rebelled against some of the established teachings and practices of the Roman

9. In covering the common good, the document addresses two subsidiary themes: private property and the preferential option for the poor. The Catholic Church acknowledges that human freedom and personal responsibility are inextricably associated with ownership of material goods. The aim of individual ownership is not simply to enhance the quality of life but to empower human agency. The preferential option, a norm that emerged in the late 1960s from the teachings of Latin American bishops, emphasizes the social priority of people who are poor and vulnerable. Just as Christ gave priority to those who were sick, weak, and oppressed, the church must give preferential care to the poor.

Catholic Church. That renewal movement, known as the Reformation, proclaimed that Christian belief and practice are based solely on the Bible (*sola Scriptura*); it also emphasized that each person can read and understand God's Word as revealed in Scripture, and everyone can receive salvation in Christ without the assistance of clergy. In addition, the Reformers emphasized that salvation in Christ (the gospel) is a gift, which is to be received by faith alone. Salvation is not mediated by priests, nor is it dependent on a person's works. Because of God's unlimited love for humans, redemption from sin is solely a divine gift.

The Reformation was a revolutionary challenge to the power and influence of the Roman Catholic Church. The teachings gave birth to church groups that rapidly spread throughout Europe, with the most important new church groups being the Lutheran churches in Germany and Scandinavia and the Reformed churches in Switzerland, the Netherlands, and Great Britain. In time, the Protestant faith spawned many other church groups, including Puritan, Presbyterian, Anglican, Methodist, Mennonite, and Brethren churches. Although each of the major church groups held distinct doctrinal beliefs and was structured according to a variety of different governmental designs, Protestant churches continued to uphold the central tenets of classical faith: the authority of Scripture, personal salvation through faith in Christ, and the priesthood of believers. Beginning in the late nineteenth century, however, some American Protestant churches began to challenge elements of the traditional faith. Where classical Protestant churches had been rooted in traditional, orthodox beliefs, the emergence of progressive Christianity in the early twentieth century began to undermine those beliefs. That liberal American faith movement of major Protestant denominations increased its influence up through the Cold War era, but then it began to decline in membership. By the late twentieth century the so-called Mainline Protestant churches had lost much of their influence. To a significant degree, their influence was replaced in the post–Cold War era by the rise of Evangelicalism.

The reemergence of orthodox Protestantism (Evangelicalism) during World War II was a byproduct of the rise of liberal, progressive Protestantism at the end of the nineteenth century: the growth of the latter increased tensions between them and believers committed to the classical evangelical faith. As this conflict intensified in the early twentieth century, the traditionalists called for a return to the fundamentals of Christianity and for separation from Mainline churches. As a result, traditionalist Protestants established the Fundamentalist movement, which emphasized not only biblical religion but also a separatist, exclusionary faith. With Fundamentalism's exclusionary nature in view, some traditional Protestant leaders sought to restore a more balanced biblical faith in the early 1940s. Since they were guided by the biblical faith that had characterized the traditional orthodox Protestant faith, the new movement was termed "neo-Evangelicalism" to distinguish it from the eighteenth- and nineteenth-century expressions of the Evangelical religion. While both Evangelicals and Fundamentalists were committed to biblical religion, they differed on the degree of social engagement that Christians should have. For Evangelicals, authentic faith required not only holy living and the sharing of the good news of the gospel; it also called on believers to care for the temporal needs of fellow humans.[10]

Although Protestantism is expressed in many different forms in the United States, my analysis here is limited to Evangelical and the Mainline denominations. In what follows I examine some of the major elements of Protestant political theology.

God's sovereignty

Since God is sovereign, his authority extends to all peoples and all nations throughout time. All creation lives under the providence and judgment of God. This means all human actions are always subject to God's sovereign will. The prophet Isaiah captures the greatness of God and the frailty of nations when he says, "Behold the nations are like a drop from the bucket, and are accounted as the dust on the scales" (Isa. 40:15). And again: "He sits enthroned above the circle of the earth, and its people are like grasshoppers. He stretches out the heavens like a canopy, and spreads them out like a tent to live in. He brings princes to naught, and reduces the rulers of this world to nothing" (Isa. 40:22–23). Though God is sovereign, he uses humans to accomplish his purposes in the world. Thus Christians, as God's children, must obediently promote righteousness and justice within the international community. Finally, individuals and collectives are accountable to God and will be subject to his judgment.

Abraham Kuyper, a late-nineteenth-century Dutch pastor, academician, politician (prime minister of the Netherlands), and influential

---

10. For a discussion of the nature and rise of modern Evangelicalism, see Mark Amstutz, *Evangelicals and American Foreign Policy* (New York: Oxford University Press, 2014), chap. 2.

Christian thinker, argued that God implemented his sovereign will through the lives, work, and service of Christian believers. In his inaugural convocation at Amsterdam's Free University he declared, "There is not a square inch in the whole domain of our human existence over which Christ, who is sovereign over all, does not cry 'Mine!'"[11] While some Protestants emphasize individual, personal spirituality, Kuyper argues that when God saves people, he incorporates them into a community of faith that is called to serve the whole world. Christians worship a sovereign God who, in the words of Richard Mouw, "commands us to be active witnesses in our daily lives to God's sovereign rule over all things."[12]

Theologian John Bennett writes that since God is love, his love transcends all nations "in such a way that he keeps all their ideals and achievements and ideologies under judgment."[13] The truth about God's sovereignty and all-encompassing love is important because it means that human initiatives are always an incomplete and partial fulfillment of divine will. Indeed, human initiatives will always be tainted because, as St. Paul declares, they "fall short of the glory of God" (Rom. 3:23). However, recognizing God's sovereignty and transcendence over nations can free humans from national idolatry—from believing that they have a unique role in resolving the problems of global politics. The divine answer to human frailty is the acknowledgment of sin through repentance, both individual and collective.

The legitimacy of the state

States—political communities ruled by government—are morally legitimate because they are a part of God's created order. In his letter to the Romans, Paul writes that persons should be "subject to the governing authorities. For there is no authority except from God" (Rom. 13:1). And the writer of 1 Peter declares, "Be subject for the Lord's sake to every human institution, whether it be to the emperor as supreme, or to governors as sent by him to punish those who do wrong and to praise those who do right" (1 Pet. 2:13–14). Based on a careful analysis of Scripture, philosopher Nicholas Wolterstorff concludes that govern-

---

11. Quoted in Richard J. Mouw, *Abraham Kuyper: A Short and Personal Introduction* (Grand Rapids: Eerdmans, 2011), 4.

12. Mouw, *Abraham Kuyper*, 5.

13. Bennett, *Foreign Policy*, 37.

ment is divinely instituted "as part of God's providential care for his human creatures."[14]

Christians are called to fulfill their temporal responsibilities in the state and their spiritual responsibilities to the kingdom of God. When government rulers issue commands contrary to Scripture, believers must follow their moral conscience and disregard temporal commands. From a biblical perspective, governmental power must always be subservient to God's authority. Although the Bible encourages obedience to legitimate government authority, Scripture is also clear that believers should disobey rulers when their demands contradict divine commands. When Peter and other apostles were brought before the Jewish Council (Sanhedrin) to answer for their teaching of allegedly false doctrines, they declared that their first responsibility was to God, not the state. Peter boldly declared, "We ought to obey God rather than men" (Acts 5:29). Jesus himself says that his disciples should first pursue the "kingdom of God" and then fulfill other desires and obligations (Matt. 6:33).

While Scripture affirms the legitimacy of governmental authority, it does not specify the best kinds of institutions to advance justice and human dignity. As a result, Christians have historically been a part of a wide range of political regimes.[15] As I note in the next chapter, the Catholic Church has historically regarded the world as a global society, and it came to terms with the notion of state sovereignty only reluctantly in the nineteenth century. By contrast, Protestant churches coming out of the Reformation have been supportive of state sovereignty, a fragmented global order, and divided government authority within states. As a result, while both Protestants and Catholics affirm the legitimacy of government, they hold different conceptions of the importance of state sovereignty and the need for protecting territorial borders. But since the well-being of people is a primary concern for all Christians, responding to the needs of refugees is considered a moral imperative. This explains

14. Nicholas Wolterstorff, "Theological Foundations for an Evangelical Political Philosophy," in Ronald J. Sider and Diane Knippers, eds., *Toward an Evangelical Public Policy* (Grand Rapids: Baker Books, 2005), 160.

15. Historically, political communities have been organized in a variety of ways, ranging from highly centralized governments (like tyrannies), absolute monarchies, and totalitarian dictatorships to participatory systems that seek to constrain government power, such as populist regimes, revolutionary governments, and constitutional democracies. Regimes have also varied according to their institutional character, ranging from centralized global empires to less centralized systems, like confederations, nation-states, and city-states.

both Catholics' and Protestants' propensity to justify the transnational movement of persons and to question the legitimacy of the Westphalian global order. Even evangelical statements and resolutions that call for a more liberalized immigration system all tend to repeat the claim that states have a right to protect borders and to regulate immigration.

The priority of love

Jesus expressed the centrality of love when he declared that the first commandment was to love God "with all your heart, and with all your soul, and with all your mind, and with all your strength" and that the second commandment was to "love your neighbor as yourself" (Mark 12:30-31). Love involves unqualified giving, expressing human dignity through an all-encompassing, unselfish concern for others. Its purest expression is sacrificial love, while its most common manifestation in human communities is mutual love. Love, in short, provides the basis for building and sustaining human communities.

Since God's love is total and universal, Christians are called to follow his example by caring for others, whether they live in crowded cities or remote villages. This responsibility is challenging because it means that believers must reconcile the demands of love among different human communities, including family, friends, neighbors, professional colleagues, citizens, and persons from other nations. The real impediment to expressing love is not the challenge posed by the natural inclination to be partial toward family and friends but the failure to overcome self-love. Religious moralists, Reinhold Niebuhr believed, were not very helpful in politics because they proclaimed the ideal of love as if it were self-enforcing. "The law of love" was not only an inadequate and incomplete political strategy; it was also a false religion. The gospel, he says, is not simply that we ought to love one another. Rather, it is the truth that people violate the law of love and need God's mercy and forgiveness.[16]

Since human beings cannot fulfill the demands of love fully or consistently, the ethic of love—expressed as mutual love—cannot be a reliable foundation for political society. While love is necessary for brotherhood, it is insufficient to sustain communal life. To be sure, love can contribute to

16. Reinhold Niebuhr, "Why the Christian Church Is Not Pacifist," in Robert McAfee Brown, ed., *The Essential Reinhold Niebuhr: Selected Essays and Addresses* (New Haven, CT: Yale University Press, 1986), 111.

harmonious cooperation and voluntary communal compliance, but only government has the capacity and legitimacy to ensure compliance from recalcitrant members. Thus, while love provides the moral foundation for communal solidarity, government provides the indispensable institutions to sustain communal order and foster social and political justice.

The dignity and equality of persons

Because human beings are created in God's image *(imago dei)*, they have infinite worth and are entitled to dignity and respect. Although human beings may differ in their social, economic, political, and intellectual capabilities, as bearers of God's image they are fundamentally equal. And because God's love is unconditional and all-inclusive, human dignity is universal, extending to every person, regardless of age, social status, race, gender, or nationality. Glen Tinder argues that the most fundamental premise of Western social and political theory is the notion of human dignity, which he defines as "the idea of the exalted individual."[17] The idea of exalted individuals is important because it provides the basis for claims of human rationality, sociability, creativity, and moral autonomy. More particularly, the notion of the uniqueness of persons is the foundation for the claim of inalienable human rights, including freedom. Liberty is essential to authentic personhood because moral agency—that is, the assumption of responsible action—is only possible when people are responsible for their own thoughts and actions. Indeed, without freedom there can be no responsible action: no authentic expressions of love, no pursuit of the common good, no creative labor, and no justice.

The universality and totality of sin

Because the Bible teaches that all persons "have sinned and fallen short of the glory of God" (Rom. 3:23), Evangelicals emphasize the universality and comprehensive reach of sin. Tinder, after acknowledging that people are "exalted," argues that a Christian worldview assumes that individuals are "fallen." The Christian perspective of human nature is therefore

17. Glenn Tinder, "Can We Be Good without God?," *The Atlantic Monthly*, December 1989, 71-72.

paradoxical: human beings "are sacred and none are good." According to Tinder, the human inclination toward evil "is primarily an inclination to exalt ourselves rather than allowing ourselves to be exalted by God."[18] Similarly, Reinhold Niebuhr argues that sin involves excessive self-love and pride, resulting in the effort to replace God's authority with the self. In his view, sin reveals the fundamental moral limitation of people: "Sin is occasioned precisely by the fact that man refuses to admit his 'creatureliness' and acknowledge himself as merely a member of a total unity of life. He pretends to be more than he is."[19]

For Protestants, sin is universal and comprehensive, affecting all persons and every aspect of human life. No person is exempt from sin, and no human action can successfully overcome the grip of excessive self-love. Since reason itself is tainted by sin, reliance on natural law, moral principles, and other rational constructs can provide only a proximate guide to ethical action; it cannot serve as a reliable moral map in overcoming individual and collective injustice. Even if reason could devise just actions, the implementation of any reasonable act could be compromised by self-righteousness. Since sin compromises all individual and collective actions that seek to advance the common good, Christians should pursue political action with humility and guard against self-righteousness.

The dual nature of Christian citizenship

Protestant political ethics also emphasizes the dual nature of citizenship. Like the Israelites who lived as aliens in Egypt, Christians live as aliens in this world. Just as Abraham was a stranger in a foreign land (Heb. 11:9), so Christians are sojourners in this world as they journey to their celestial home. But while they reside on earth, they are citizens of a temporal city and fulfill obligations to that city, which means that Christians are citizens of two kingdoms—the earthy city and the heavenly kingdom. One of the most perceptive descriptions of how believers fulfill their dual obligations to the temporal and heavenly cities was set forth in the third century, when Roman authorities were persecuting Christians. The anonymous *Letter to Diognetus* says in part,

18. Tinder, "Can We Be Good Without God?," 77.
19. Reinhold Niebuhr, *The Nature and Destiny of Man*, vol. 1, *On Human Nature* (New York: Charles Scribner's Sons, 1964), 16.

Christians are indistinguishable from other men either by nationality, language or customs. They do not inhabit separate cities of their own, or speak a strange dialect, or follow some outlandish way of life. . . . With regard to dress, food and manner of life in general, they follow the customs of whatever city they happen to be living in, whether it is Greek or foreign. And yet there is something extraordinary about their lives. They live in their own countries as though they were only passing through. They play their full role as citizens, but labor under all the disabilities of aliens. Any country can be their homeland, but for them their homeland, wherever it may be, is a foreign country. Like others, they marry and have children, but they do not expose them. They share their meals, but not their wives. They live in the flesh, but they are not governed by the desires of the flesh. They pass their days upon earth, but they are citizens of heaven.

The classic statement on dual citizenship was set forth by Saint Augustine in the fifth century in his masterpiece *The City of God*. According to Augustine, two worldviews (or ways of life) resulted in the establishment of two distinct societies, or "cities." The earthly realm, or "City of Man," is guided by love of self and relies on power and authority to maintain order, whereas God's love guides the spiritual realm, or the "City of God." In the earthly city, governmental power restrains sin and human greed. By contrast, in the heavenly city, made up of the voluntary community of Christian believers, coercive authority is unnecessary because justice and peace reign as natural byproducts of divinely inspired love.

Ever since the Pharisees asked Jesus whether it was lawful to pay taxes to Caesar, Christians have struggled to define the appropriate boundaries between the altar and the throne, between faith and politics. Jesus's answer—that we should "render to Caesar the things that are Caesar's and to God the things that are God's" (Matt. 22:21)—did not provide a conclusive answer because he did not specify precise boundaries of the temporal realm. As a result, Christians continue to struggle to ascertain how to divide their obligations between the church and the state.[20] According to James Hoffmeier, there is no inherent contradiction between the two obligations.[21] The challenging task, of course, is to define the

20. M. Daniel Carroll R. (Rodas), *Christians at the Border: Immigration, the Church, and the Bible* (Grand Rapids: Baker Academic, 2008), 67.

21. James K. Hoffmeier, *The Immigration Crisis: Immigrants, Aliens, and the Bible* (Wheaton: Crossway, 2009), 140-41.

duties owed to the state and the ones owed to the kingdom of God. From a biblical perspective, governmental power must always be subservient to God's authority. Although the Bible encourages obedience to legitimate government authority, Scripture also clearly states that believers should disobey rulers when their demands contradict divine commands. Living in the "City of Man" while fulfilling the spiritual admonitions and moral obligations of the "City of God" presents a never-ending challenge.

One way to resolve the tension between temporal commitments to the state and the responsibilities toward spiritual authority is either to spiritualize temporal affairs or to pursue a strategy of detachment and withdrawal. The first strategy overspiritualizes issues and concerns, viewing temporal affairs through the prism of the kingdom of God. The second strategy pursues holiness and faithfulness by avoiding social and political engagement altogether. Historically, Fundamentalists and some Evangelicals have been tempted by pietistic disengagement from temporal concerns. But Jesus commands his followers to be in the world but not of it (John 17:15, 16). Believers are to work and serve Christ in the temporal city while maintaining their ultimate allegiance to God.

The demand of justice

A seventh element of a Protestant worldview is justice, one of the most difficult concepts in public affairs. The biblical idea of justice is associated with, among other things, the fair and impartial administration of the law, the proper treatment of the poor, protection of the weak and the oppressed, and support and care for strangers and aliens. It is often associated with righteousness (Ps. 33:5; 112:4; Prov. 29:7). From an Old Testament perspective, the pursuit of justice is rooted in law, which provides standards by which to judge the behavior of individuals and collectives. For Nicholas Wolterstorff, the Old Testament conception of justice is best captured in the vision of *shalom*, or right relationships, an ideal only realized when people are at peace "with God, with self, with fellows, with nature."[22]

The New Testament devotes little space to law and justice. Instead, it emphasizes the fulfillment of justice and righteousness through love. Love, of course, is not justice, since the former involves unqualified giv-

---

22. Nicholas Wolterstorff, *Until Justice and Peace Embrace* (Grand Rapids: Eerdmans, 1983), 70.

ing, while the latter involves calculation and judgment.[23] Divine love, as expressed in the redemptive work of Christ, provides the foundation for justice. Divine love is the only way to partially overcome human sinfulness and finiteness. Rightly understood, the love of God provides a more authentic and complete foundation for pursuing temporal justice in domestic and global affairs. But the most that humans can achieve is a partial or relative justice based on the weighing and balancing of conflicting and competing interests. The communal harmony that is achieved through government and legal institutions is at best an approximation of brotherhood, or mutual love, because humans are never free from the power of egoism. Emil Brunner captures the interrelationship of love and justice as follows: "Justice is nothing but the form of love which has currency in the world of institutions."[24]

The Bible and Immigration

The Bible is not a manual on politics; rather, it is God's revelation on how human beings can find purpose and meaning in life. Fundamentally, Scripture provides guidance on how people can rightly relate to God and to fellow human beings. While biblical knowledge can nurture the spiritual life of individuals, Scripture can also provide general principles and broad perspectives to address social and political concerns. Indeed, the emergence of Christian social and political ethics is a byproduct of the quest to identify Christian precepts relevant to collective life.

For Christians, the Bible can serve two functions in addressing temporal affairs. First, it can provide a worldview, or perspective, on public life. Second, it can provide specific precepts that help guide decision-making. Both elements are important in applying a Christian perspective to immigration. The first provides a moral perspective, or approach, while the second offers specific principles that can help structure analysis and action.

---

23. Emil Brunner once observed that love was always just but that justice was not necessarily love. See Brunner, *Justice and the Social Order* (New York: Harper and Brothers, 1945), 261.

24. Brunner, *Justice and the Social Order*, 261.

Biblical interpretation

Christians have historically been divided on the extent to which the Bible should guide collective decision-making and on how it should be interpreted. For example, the Roman Catholic Church places less emphasis on biblical revelation in addressing public policy concerns and more emphasis on the moral teachings of the church. Thus, when the bishops from the United States and Mexico issued a joint pastoral letter on immigration in 2003, only six paragraphs were devoted to biblical teachings, whereas twelve paragraphs were devoted to the social teachings of the Church.[25] On the other hand, when evangelical denominations have addressed immigration, the bulk of the analyses are derived from biblical teachings. For example, the 2008 immigration report of the Wesleyan Church is almost exclusively devoted to describing "Kingdom values regarding Christians and immigration"—that is, principles based on Scripture that should guide Christian thought and action on migration.[26] Some of these biblical norms include creation, sovereignty, submission, hospitality, and grace. Similarly, the Christian Reformed Church (CRC) issued a detailed commission report on migration in 2010.[27] The report, adopted by the CRC's synod, provides a detailed examination of Scripture and migration, with more than two-thirds devoted to biblical and theological analysis. Finally, the Free Methodist Church issued a statement on the church's position on immigration in 2013.[28] That declaration, developed by a study commission on doctrine, describes biblical principles relevant to immigration. They include the treatment of foreigners, the leveling aspect of the gospel, the instructions to be hospitable, the principle of consequences, and the admonition to work. Each of these norms is justified by scriptural references and brief theological analysis.

The interpretation of Scripture also divides Christians, especially

25. "Strangers No Longer: Together on the Journey of Hope," A Pastoral Letter Concerning Migration from the Catholic Bishops of Mexico and the United States. Available at: http://www.usccb.org/issues-and-action/human-life-and-dignity/immigration/strangers-no-longer-together-on-the-journey-of-hope.cfm.

26. "A Wesleyan View of Immigration, 2008." Available at: https://www.wesleyan.org/237/a-wesleyan-view-of-immigration.

27. CRC, "Committee to Study the Migration of Workers." Available at: www.crcna.org/sites/default/files/Migration.pdf.

28. "The Free Methodist Position on Immigration," Study Commission on Doctrine, 2013. Available at: http://fmcusa.org/files/2014/03/The-Free-Methodist-Church-on-Immigration.pdf.

Evangelicals. Given its centralized teaching authority (through the *magisterium*), the Catholic Church has a far greater hermeneutical consensus than Protestant theologians do. Evangelicals, who place the greatest emphasis on the authority of Scripture, are especially divided over the interpretation and application of Scripture. Old Testament scholar James Hoffmeier has identified four hermeneutical approaches that Evangelicals have applied to Old Testament teachings.[29] The first approach uses a literal correlation between biblical law and modern issues. The second approach focuses on the quest for contemporary justice using the prophetic teachings of the Old Testament. The third approach examines the Torah's legal precepts and seeks to extract ethical principles from those laws in order to use those moral maxims in addressing contemporary affairs. Finally, theologians may engage in interpretation using a comprehensive approach that focuses on theological, social, and economic issues in order to develop a biblical perspective that can be used in evaluating contemporary issues. Hoffmeier argues that this last approach is especially useful because it permits the application of biblical principles to contemporary concerns. The literalistic approach, he thinks, should be avoided because it is simplistic and results in selective application. He further argues that the justice approach is inadequate because it unnecessarily limits Scripture to justice concerns. Although the third approach provides important biblical precepts rooted in Old Testament law, it limits biblical application to the issues covered in the Bible. But since many of our contemporary concerns were not addressed in the ancient world, a more comprehensive hermeneutical model is likely to be most useful in addressing issues such as abortion, international debt, immigration, and nuclear nonproliferation. This is the approach Hoffmeier uses in addressing the Bible and immigration policy.

Biblical principles

Besides using different hermeneutical approaches, Christians also use Scripture in different ways to address temporal social and political concerns. Whereas Roman Catholics and mainline Protestants approach immigration concerns through reason and moral reflection and use Scripture sparingly, evangelicals justify their analyses and advocacy of immigration reform with specific references to the Bible. To be sure, most

29. Hoffmeier, *Immigration Crisis*, 24-27.

Christians regard the Bible as God's revelation to humankind. But while Catholics and Mainline Protestants are reluctant to use biblical justification for specific public policies, Evangelicals are at ease using Scripture to bolster their claims. Indeed, many Evangelicals argue that the moral basis for important public policies, such as immigration, should be the Bible.

While Evangelicals acknowledge that the Bible is not a manual on public affairs, they nevertheless use Scripture to provide, in the words of the National Association of Evangelicals' 2009 resolution on immigration, "a moral compass."[30] Blogger Mark Roberts writes that if Christians desire to address the question of illegal immigration, they should do so by discovering "the mind and activity of God with respect to illegal immigration." This is best done, he believes, by turning to Scripture. He suggests that Evangelicals should begin their analysis from two starting points: first, God's design for the world, as expressed in Genesis 1; and second, the teachings and actions of Jesus, as recorded in the New Testament.[31] Kelly Monroe Kullberg, who founded Evangelicals for Biblical Immigration to challenge the claims of the Evangelical Immigration Table, which advocates liberal and more flexible immigration policies, has sought to use Scripture to defend restrictions on immigration. In her view, Christians should seek "the whole counsel of Scripture—both of justice to citizens and kindness to guests."[32]

A review of Evangelical church statements and denominational resolutions on immigration reform suggests that most policy analyses use Scripture to illuminate and apply important principles relevant to migration. In addressing immigration, Evangelicals naturally emphasize the key norms of Protestant political ethics discussed earlier, especially the dual nature of citizenship and the demand of justice. In addition, however, Evangelicals emphasize the dignity of persons, hospitality to neighbors, and the need to provide assistance for those in need.

One of the most widely shared Christian convictions is the concept that people matter. They matter because, as Scripture declares, human beings are created in God's image. Genesis 1:27 tells us: "So God created humankind in his image, in the image of God he created them; male and

---

30. National Association of Evangelicals, "Immigration 2009."

31. Mark D. Roberts, "Illegal Immigration: Seeking a Christian Perspective," in *Patheos,* 2010. Available at: http://www.patheos.com/blogs/markdroberts/series/illegal-immigration-seeking-a-christian-perspective/comment-page-1/.

32. For information about Evangelicals for Biblical Immigration, see http://evangelicalsforbiblicalimmigration.com.

female he created them." Because of humans' divine origins, they have infinite worth and are entitled to dignity and respect. Although human beings may differ in their social, economic, political, and intellectual capabilities, as bearers of God's image they are fundamentally equal. The beginning of all Christian social and political thought is thus rooted in the sacredness of persons. M. Daniel Carroll R. (Rodas), an Old Testament professor, observes that the idea that humans are made in God's image is "the most basic conviction for Christians as they approach the challenges of immigration today." He further observes, "Each and every one of those [immigrants] who have come to the United States is God's creation and is worthy of respect."[33]

A second key biblical norm is the need to welcome strangers. Though this principle is seen in both the Old and New Testaments, the need to be hospitable toward strangers is rooted in the early history of Israel. According to Genesis, Abram was forced to leave his native land and to migrate to Egypt. Subsequently, the oppression in that land resulted in the Israelites' departure (Exodus). The experience of being displaced and being an alien in a foreign land was a formative experience for Jews, resulting in important moral teachings.[34] These include: do not oppress an alien (Exod. 22:21); do not mistreat an alien (Lev. 19:33); and love the alien (Deut. 10:19; Lev. 19:34). The New Testament also calls on believers to be hospitable (Rom. 12:13; Heb. 13:2; 1 Pet. 4:9). According to the Free Methodist statement on immigration, the term "hospitality" is best translated from the Greek as "love of strangers."[35]

A third biblical norm is the inclusiveness of God's kingdom. From a Christian perspective, the dignity and glory of persons is based not on the rational or moral nature of humans but on God's unlimited and all-embracing love (*agape*). And because God's love is unconditional and all-inclusive, human dignity is universal, extending to every person regard-

---

33. Carroll, *Christians at the Border*, 67.

34. The Hebrew texts use the word *ger* to refer to the alien status of Abraham and his Jewish people. According to James Hoffmeier, this term, which appears more than ninety-two times in the Old Testament, has been unhelpfully translated as "foreigner," "sojourner," or "stranger." He argues that *ger* refers to aliens who have been accepted by the host nation. It refers to legal aliens. The Hebrew words that apply to those foreign persons who have not been granted permanent residence are *nekhar* and *zar*, which are translated as "foreigners" and "strangers." Hoffmeier argues that this distinction is important in addressing current unauthorized aliens, since *ger* does not apply to those in an unlawful status (Hoffmeier, *Immigration Crisis*, 48–52).

35. "The Free Methodist Position on Immigration."

less of age, race, gender, nationality, or professional status. The apostle Paul powerfully expresses the universality and equality of persons when he writes that "there is neither Jew nor Greek, there is neither slave nor free, there is neither male nor female; for you are all one in Christ Jesus" (Gal. 3:28).

Because of the global, universal nature of the human family, some Christians have regarded the world as a coherent moral community. The Catholic Church in particular has emphasized the unity of the world rooted in the infinite worth of persons. From a moral perspective, what matters is not the independence and prosperity of states but the well-being of persons regardless of their tribal, national, or cultural affinities. The belief in the universality of God's world has led the Catholic Church to give precedence to human rights over state sovereignty.

Finally, Christians emphasize the principle of justice. In the context of immigration policy, justice demands that the practices and laws regulating immigration must not be partial to some groups—they have to be fair to all nations. Additionally, justice domestically means that the rules and practices toward aliens must also be just, meaning that the rules themselves must be fair and appropriate and applied impartially and consistently. Examples of Old Testament admonitions include: to have the same laws for aliens and residents (Lev. 24:22); to not deprive the fatherless and aliens of justice (Deut. 24:17); to apply laws equally to aliens and residents (Num. 15:15); to condemn those who withhold justice from aliens, the fatherless, or the widow (Deut. 27:19); to do what is just and right (Jer. 22:3); and not to deprive aliens of justice (Mal. 3:5). When the prophet Micah asks, "What does the Lord require of you?" he responds, "To act justly, to love mercy, and to walk humbly with your God" (Mic. 6:8).

One of the challenges in pursuing justice in the international community is that political thinkers conceive of justice in a variety of ways. To begin with, the pursuit of justice can be approached either from a global perspective or from a national point of view. In chapter 4, I contrasted two international-relations worldviews—communitarianism and cosmopolitanism—that approach the quest of human dignity from different perspectives. For the communitarian, states are morally significant because they are the means by which human rights are affirmed and protected. For the cosmopolitan, by contrast, the division of global society into states is deeply problematic because such a system perpetuates inequalities among people. These two worldviews give rise to differing conceptions of justice. For the communitarian, justice in the world is a task requiring equity and fairness among the world's member states, a concept I call *international justice*. By contrast, the cosmopolitan justice conceives of justice as among people, not states—which I call *world justice*.

A different way of thinking about justice is by focusing either on procedures or outcomes. I define the first approach as *procedural* justice and the second as *substantive*, or distributive, justice.[36] The first approach is associated with the rightness or fairness of the rules, processes, and institutions of political communities. This approach defines justice not by outcomes of governmental decisions but by the way decisions are reached. According to this view, procedural justice is advanced when rules are applied consistently, impartially, and universally. Such justice is secured not by pursuing particular goals but by ensuring the reliability and credibility of the rule of law. The alternative view, substantive justice, is concerned with desirable outcomes, not with the fairness of the rules themselves. Since this approach focuses on promoting good or right ends, it is often called "social" or "distributive" justice. Whereas Western judicial systems tend to be associated with the first kind of justice, the concern with equitable distribution of social and economic goods has led to the increasing prominence of the social concept of justice.

In addressing immigration, we must include both the procedural and substantive perspectives of justice. If the United States' immigration system is to be perceived as just, its rules must be applied with consistency, uniformity, and impartiality. At the same time, immigration rules must advance the substantive goals that the American people consider important to a just immigration system. Despite the efforts to advance both procedural and substantive justice, the US immigration system is regarded as deficient at both levels. At the procedural level, there is excessive administrative discretion in the application and enforcement of laws. For example, the wide variety of ways in which undocumented aliens have been able to secure legal status has not contributed to a perception of justice. And even though the United States has carried out numerous reforms to ensure greater inclusivity and impartiality, such as the ending of the national-origins quotas in 1965 and the establishment of a diversity visa program in 1990, the reforms have not resulted in the intended outcomes of greater inclusivity.

---

36. Mark R. Amstutz, *International Ethics: Concepts, Theories, and Cases in Global Politics*, 4th ed. (Boulder, CO: Rowman and Littlefield, 2013), 226-27.

The Bible and Political Advocacy

What role should Scripture play in advancing public policies? Should biblical passages be used to justify and promote policy reform? Some Evangelicals have argued that comprehensive immigration reform is justified biblically. An official of the Evangelical Immigration Table, for example, writes, "Scripture is at the center of why I and so many American Evangelicals have become vocal advocates of immigration reform."[37] Most Evangelicals concerned with immigration reform, however, are far more reluctant to justify policy advocacy using the Bible. Some of the immigration studies by Evangelical groups emphasize that Scripture should not be used to advance policy goals. The National Association of Evangelicals' "Immigration 2009" resolution declares, for example, that the Bible does not offer "a blueprint for modern legislation."[38] The CRC immigration study similarly emphasizes the limits of Scripture in making public policy. It observes that God's commands to the ancient Israelites, as recorded in the Old Testament, provide important principles that can help frame contemporary concerns. At the same time, it emphasizes that the church should not "commit the error of adopting God's theocratic blueprint for Israel as though it represents government structures, laws, and policies that must be incorporated in the United States . . . today."[39] According to Carroll, the Old Testament does not offer "a blueprint for action" on immigration concerns.[40] And after examining Jesus' teachings, he says that "there is no explicit teaching on immigration in the Gospels."[41]

Despite the acknowledgment that Scripture should not be used to directly advance specific public policies, most of the Evangelical immigration documents that I examined do just that, implicitly if not explicitly. They do so by using specific biblical texts to emphasize certain themes, such as hospitality and compassion, and by selectively using biblical principles to advance particular policy goals. Indeed, the major shortcoming of Evangelical advocacy is the uneven and unbalanced use of scriptural norms to advance specific public policy goals, such as legalization of unauthorized aliens. But the misuse or selective use of the Bible not only distorts divine revelation but potentially undermines the church's moral authority. To avoid such distortion, some denomi-

---

37. Statement found in Roberts, "Illegal Immigration."
38. NAE, "Immigration 2009." Available at: http://nae.net/immigration-2009.
39. CRC, "Committee to Study the Migration of Workers," 11.
40. Carroll, *Christians at the Border*, 109.
41. Carroll, *Christians at the Border*, 123.

national statements provide a balanced listing of biblical principles but then recommend actions that are consistent with only some of the norms. Another equally serious limitation occurs when the recommended actions are totally divorced from the biblical analysis preceding it. These limitations have been consistently evident in Evangelical declarations that emphasize human dignity, on the one hand, and the rule of law and border security, on the other hand.

The 2011 Southern Baptist Convention resolution on immigration, for example, calls attention to such biblical ideals as human dignity, compassion, and the rule of law, and to governmental norms such as border security and lawful employment practices.[42] Finally, it recommends the legalization of unauthorized aliens, and does so independently of the other pronouncements and without acknowledging the inherent tension between the rule of law and the legalization of those who have violated the law. The "2014 Resolution on Immigration" by the Evangelical Covenant Church, a proposed action that had not been formally adopted as of 2015, similarly demonstrates the gap between biblical principles and policy advocacy.[43] After describing a biblical approach to immigration along with current policy challenges, the resolution calls on members to "advocate for fair and humane immigration laws and policies." Some of the recommended initiatives include fostering greater respect for law and border control; reforming the immigration system to facilitate family reunification; increasing employment-based visas; and providing unauthorized aliens with the means to legalize their status.

The problem here is twofold: first, the call to action does not derive from the biblical foundations that it sets forth; second, the different actions it recommends are inherently in conflict. In particular, the rule of law cannot be easily reconciled with the call to create "a path toward legal immigration status or citizenship for those who qualify and satisfy specific criteria." While there may not be a simple way of reconciling unlawful behavior with border security, a credible denominational initiative should seek to illuminate the inherent tension between competing moral claims and show the relative merits of these claims from a biblical perspective.

Since the Bible is not a manual on politics, religious groups should be

42. SBC, "On Immigration and the Gospel." Available at http://www.sbc.net/resolutions/1213.

43. Evangelical Covenant Church, "2014 Resolution on Immigration." Available at: http://www.covchurch.org/wp-content/uploads/sites/65/2013/03/2014-Resolution-on-Immigration-FINAL-without-Resource.pdf.

reluctant to use Scripture to justify their policy claims, lest such efforts undermine the integrity of the church's witness. To be sure, Scripture calls on people to be compassionate, merciful, and kind to strangers. But biblical principles cannot be translated directly into public policies. Biblical norms do not provide policy guidance on such specific issues as the number of refugees or immigrants that should be admitted annually or the balance between family-based and employment-based visas. And even when one or more biblical principles are applicable to a policy concern, advocacy groups should recognize that policy-making involves more than moral principles. Indeed, public policy-making—whether involving labor, tax policy, or immigration—involves reconciling competing interests of relevant groups and the balancing of short-term and long-term concerns.

In conclusion, over the past several centuries, Christians have developed theological principles and perspectives that can guide believers' reflection and action in public affairs. The Roman Catholic Church has devised the tradition of CST, the most sophisticated and coherent body of political theology, through its encyclicals, pastoral letters, and council declarations. The Protestant churches have also developed a body of foundational principles derived from the various theological strands that emerged from the Protestant Reformation. Though Scripture is the foundation for both Catholic and Protestant political theology, Protestants, especially Evangelicals, are more disposed to justify their thoughts and actions with direct reference to the Bible. But since the Bible is not a manual for political and social life, Christians should use it—as John Bennett suggests at the beginning of this chapter—to provide motives, criteria, perspectives, and limits rather than policy directives.

« 6 »

The Roman Catholic Church
and US Immigration Policy

In 2014, the Roman Catholic Church in the United States had an estimated 76.7 million members—or roughly 22 percent of the country's
population—in some 17,900 parishes. Since Hispanics are the largest percentage of legal and illegal immigrants in the United States, and since Catholicism is the dominant religion of Latin America, Hispanic immigrants
have been a major source of growth for the American church. Of the estimated 50 million Hispanics currently living in the United States, over 29
million are Catholic, representing 59 percent of the Hispanic population
and roughly 40 percent of the Catholic Church's total US membership.[1]
Hispanics are thus very important to the Roman Catholic Church.

Unlike Evangelicals and some Mainline Protestant churches, the
Catholic Church is a centralized religious institution headed by the Holy
See. The pope, with the collective assistance of cardinals, archbishops,
and Vatican staff, provides leadership to the church's bishops and priests
in carrying out their pastoral ministry at the community/parish level. The
pope does this by charting new initiatives, calling for conclaves to address pressing moral and spiritual concerns, appointing new bishops, and
directing the educational ministry of the church by issuing encyclicals
and other teaching documents. The leadership of the American Catholic
Church is provided by the US Conference of Catholic Bishops (USCCB),
a group of 270 active bishops who gather periodically to address issues
of shared concern. Each bishop is responsible for the work of the church
within his diocese, including the ministries of parishes, schools, hospi-
tals, and other humanitarian services.

---

1. USCCB, "Laity and Parishes." Available at: http://www.usccb.org/about/public
-affairs/backgrounders/laity-parishes.cfm.

The work of the USCCB is carried out through numerous specialized committees, each of which is responsible for some area of church concern, such as evangelism, Catholic education, government relations, and international justice and peace. Each USCCB committee is supported by a professional staff. The Committee on Migration and Refugee Services, for example, is supported by professionals who assist bishops in developing and promoting migration initiatives consistent with the values and social teachings of the church. Typically, when the church seeks to influence public affairs, the chairman of the committee will speak on behalf of the USCCB. Although bishops and archbishops may from time to time speak as individuals, the church's influence is enhanced when a committee chairmen speaks on behalf of the church. On truly significant issues, the conference will demonstrate its authority by writing a pastoral letter specifically addressing a particular issue. The significant influence of collective political engagement was dramatically illustrated in the early 1980s, when the USCCB issued a detailed moral assessment of the dilemma posed by nuclear weapons. The pastoral letter, titled "The Challenge of Peace," was the result of a three-year multidisciplinary investigation based on biblical analysis of peacekeeping, the role of just-war theory in the nuclear age, and a moral assessment of the strategy of nuclear deterrence. The bishops' committee on nuclear deterrence prepared two drafts, which were reviewed by the full conference. Only after extensive review was the final letter adopted by the USCCB in 1983. Because of the authoritative nature of the document, the pastoral letter received widespread media coverage and helped shape the moral debate on the role of nuclear weapons in the ongoing Cold War conflict between the United States and the Soviet Union.

In addition to its high level of institutionalization, the Catholic Church is able to address social and political issues more coherently and effectively than other Christian denominations because of the teaching authority of the church. This teaching authority, called the Magisterium, reflects the collective spiritual wisdom developed over time by popes and bishops and provides the moral foundation for more specific church teachings about social, political, and economic life. These more specific teachings—called Catholic social thought (CST)—provide principles that help to structure the moral analysis of contemporary issues.

The Catholic Church and Global Society

Before we address some of the major principles of CST relevant to international relations and, more specifically, to migration, we need to examine how the Catholic Church views the international political system. Historically, the Catholic Church's approach to the international community has been rooted in both Christian theology and its geopolitical role as a temporal institution. Throughout the medieval era, the church's temporal interests, rather than biblical norms, defined how the Church regarded the international community. In the modern era, by contrast, Christian beliefs provide the major pillars for its conception of global order.

For the Catholic Church, Christian beliefs provide the moral basis for viewing the world as a coherent global society. For Christians, the ideal of the universality of the world is based on the message of God's love for all humans rooted in the gospel and in the inherent dignity of all persons. The Vatican's "Compendium of the Social Doctrine of the Church" (2006) declares, "The Christian message offers a universal vision of the life of men and peoples on earth that makes us realize the unity of the human family." As a result, the "Compendium" emphasizes that the world community must be presented "as the concrete figure of the unity willed by the Creator."[2] Although the world has always been divided politically into a variety of governmental units—such as kingdoms, tribes, empires, city-states, duchies, and nation-states—the Catholic Church has emphasized the shared bonds of the universal human family.

The origin of the Catholic Church's teaching on global political unity dates back to the fourth century, when Emperor Constantine made the Christian faith the religion of the Roman Empire. In doing so, he fused religious and temporal power and profoundly influenced subsequent church-state relations. The Constantinian integration of religion and government had several important effects. First, it increased the Catholic Church's concern with temporal political affairs. Throughout much of the medieval era, the Roman Catholic Church not only played a central spiritual and cultural role in Europe; it played a major economic and political role as well. As one of the largest land owners in many regions, the

---

2. Pontifical Council for Justice and Peace, "Compendium of the Social Doctrine of the Church" (The Vatican, 2006), para. 432. Available at: http://www.vatican.va/roman_curia/pontifical_councils/justpeace/documents/rc_pc_justpeace_doc_20060526_compendio-dott-soc_en.html.

Catholic Church had great influence over temporal affairs as it asserted its religious beliefs and temporal claims while also facilitating cooperation and coordination among emperors, princes, and feudal lords. The concern with temporal affairs became especially pronounced in the medieval era, when the popes collaborated with emperors in governing the Holy Roman Empire. According to Brent Nelsen and James Guth, the Catholic Church ruled over Western Christendom despite the political fragmentation of feudalism, the weakness of the Holy Roman Empire, the rising power of nation-states, and the ongoing resistance from secular authorities.[3]

A second result of the Constantinian fusion of spiritual and temporal authority was the concept of the world as a universal community. As I noted above, the Christian faith gave strong impetus to the notion of universalism. But with the integration of temporal and spiritual affairs, theological universalism was supplemented with the claims of natural law and the universality of the law. Indeed, the Roman conception of universal empire, in turn, influenced how Catholic Church officials conceived of the temporal world in which they were to carry out their religious vocation. Thus, one legacy of the Constantinian integration of church and state was that it further reinforced not just the ideal of a unitary world but also the need for a global order that ensured peace and prosperity for all of its subparts. In short, the Catholic Church came to view the world as a temporal, unitary, transnational community. According to church leaders, the world was not simply a disparate collection of empires, kingdoms, and city-states; rather, it was a coherent moral society over which they had a divinely sanctioned responsibility.

A third Constantinian influence on the Catholic Church concerns organization and law. As its responsibilities in temporal and spiritual affairs expanded, the Church necessitated increased institutionalization. The institutions that emerged were patterned after the Roman *imperium* and were headed by a papal government that was supported by a papal court (*curia*). Although the hierarchy of pope, bishops, and priests provided a unified system of organization, the primary justification for the structure was theological. It provided a way of ensuring apostolic succession—that is, continuity in the carrying out of the ministry first entrusted to the apostles. The fusion of spiritual and temporal authority

---

3. Brent F. Nelsen and James L. Guth, *Religion and the Struggle for European Union: Confessional Culture and the Limits of Integration* (Washington, DC: Georgetown University Press, 2015), 49.

also contributed to a related development, namely, the emergence of canon law. When Constantine made Christianity the religion of the Roman Empire, the principles and laws governing the church were given the force of public law. And as the church expanded its rules through papal decrees, synodical decisions, and council edicts and declarations, there was an increasing need to integrate these actions in a systematic way. The result was the development of canon law, which originally applied chiefly to church governance but in time provided spiritual norms governing society at large.

The Reformation brought about sweeping cultural, political, economic, and religious changes as it encouraged broader participation, empowered lay leaders, and fostered decentralization. Unfortunately, it also spawned bitter fighting between Catholics and Protestants in the late sixteenth and early seventeenth centuries, culminating in the Thirty Years' War (1618-1648). Though this war was fought chiefly in Germany, it involved other European powers as well, including Sweden, Denmark, France, Austria, and Spain. The war, which claimed more than 20 percent of the German population, ended in 1648 with a series of treaties collectively known as the Peace of Westphalia. This accord specifically affirmed that sovereign leaders had the right to decide their nation-state's official religion, and thus it increased the secularization of political authority and hastened the decline of the Roman Catholic Church's influence over political affairs.[4]

Even though Westphalia brought respite from religious wars, the Catholic Church adamantly opposed the accord. Realizing that the peace treaty undermined universal Catholic temporal authority, Pope Innocent X issued a bull condemning it as "null, void, invalid, iniquitous, unjust, damnable, reprobate, inane, empty of meaning and effect for all time."[5] For the Roman Church, the rise of state sovereignty was not simply an affront to the Catholic Church's temporal influence but also an outright challenge to its historic conception of a unitary global order. As a result, throughout the seventeenth, eighteenth, and nineteenth centuries the Catholic Church continued to regard state sovereignty as contrary to

4. It is important to note that the idea of political leaders determining the religion of a state did not arise with Westphalia. In the Peace of Augsburg, signed in 1555 between Lutheran and Catholic leaders, secular supremacy was affirmed in the principle of *cuius regio, eius religio* ("where you come from decides your religion"), implying that within that region no other can be tolerated. See Nelsen and Guth, *Religion and the Struggle*, 74.

5. Quoted in Daniel Philpott, *Revolutions in Sovereignty: How Ideas Shaped Modern International Relations* (Princeton, NJ: Princeton University Press, 2001), 87.

the natural order established by God. As late as the nineteenth century, the Catholic Church still banned the writings of Hugo Grotius, an early defender of the sovereign state and the father of international law. Beginning in the mid-twentieth century, the church began to reluctantly embrace political liberalism and democracy while still holding to the ideal of a global world order based on principles grounded in a divine system of natural law. Daniel Philpott writes that in spite of the Catholic Church's commitment to freedom and participatory government, it has remained opposed to "the absolutely sovereign state as an idolatrous claimant to godlike status, an affront to a moral order and to a natural law, whose authority lies ultimately far outside the orders of the state."[6]

Given the Church's bias favoring a coherent moral international community over a decentralized system of nation-states, it is not surprising that Roman Catholics have historically been reluctant to acknowledge the rights and responsibilities of states. And because of their focus on the universality of the global family, they have similarly been reticent to celebrate the considerable achievements of modern democratic states in reducing poverty, improving overall living conditions, increasing human freedoms, and protecting human rights through the rule of law.

This short overview of the Catholic Church's history highlights how Catholicism and Protestantism developed two different concepts of global society. While both traditions assumed that the "heavenly city" was manifested by the invisible body of believers, each drew different conclusions about the temporal church and the unity of the world. For Roman Catholics, the church was not simply a spiritual expression of the body of Christ in the world but also a physical manifestation, expressed in the Vicar of Christ, the pope. Furthermore, Catholics affirmed not simply the ideal of an international moral community but also sought to express that ideal through claims of human equality, social inclusiveness, and universalism. Although Catholics have rarely supported world government, they have been strong advocates of transnational institutions that qualify the sovereignty of states.

Protestants, by contrast, have been far more supportive of spiritual and political fragmentation. For Protestants, the invisible church can be unified even if the visible church is expressed in a variety of institutions. Moreover, not only do Protestants see no need for universal political rule, but they are comfortable with a fragmented, decentralized political system that curbs sin through countervailing authority, such as

---

6. Philpott, *Revolutions in Sovereignty*, 262.

checks and balances in domestic politics or the balance of power among states. In other words, they believe that state sovereignty can contribute to a humane world. Nelsen and Guth put it this way: "Christendom was important to Protestants, but preserving Christendom did not require the preservation of a *single* visible, worldwide church—or a single visible empire. Christian governance could survive at the local or national level; it was not political union that mattered but spiritual union as ordered by divine providence."[7]

Despite the Vatican's past reluctance to support democracy and the nation-state, in the modern era the Catholic Church has come to terms with both participatory modes of government and the modern sovereign state. For the Catholic Church, the acceptance of the nation-state is rooted in the belief that the modern state is a vehicle to advance communal peace and justice. According to the Vatican's "Compendium of the Social Doctrine of the Church," the rights of nations are nothing but "human rights fostered at the specific level of community life."[8] The compendium goes on to declare that nations have a fundamental right to existence and to their own languages and cultures, through which people can express and promote their common life. It then highlights the need for states to work cooperatively in pursuing shared goals. "The international order requires a *balance between particularity and universality*, which all nations are called to bring about, for their primary duty is to live in a posture of peace, respect and solidarity with other nations" (para. 152; italics in original).

Catholic Social Thought and Migration

In chapter 5, I described some important features of the tradition of Catholic social thought. I emphasized that this tradition, rooted in Scripture, natural law, and church teachings, comprises a well-developed set of principles on which to structure the church's moral reasoning on social and political affairs. In the following I specifically examine some of the CST principles that are most relevant to the practice of human migration. The three moral norms that most directly impact immigration are human dignity, common good, and solidarity. Two subsidiary principles are also

7. Nelsen and Guth, *Religion and the Struggle*, 75.
8. "Compendium of the Social Doctrine of the Church," para. 157. Hereafter, paragraph references to the "Compendium" appear in parentheses within the text.

relevant to the analysis of migration—the preferential option for the poor and the dignity of work.

Human dignity

The foundation of CST is the inviolable dignity of every human as a person created in God's image. The sacredness of human life is the foundation for a moral vision of national and international political life. Because all persons bear the image of the Creator, they are fundamentally equal and entitled to dignity, which is expressed through claims of human rights. According to the Catholic Church, the proclamation of human rights in the modern era is "one of the most significant attempts to respond . . . to the demands of human dignity" (para. 157). Human rights apply not simply to persons but also to peoples, who have the collective right of self-determination and political autonomy. Nations are simply an expression, according to the Catholic Church, of "'human rights' fostered at the specific level of community life" (para. 157).

Common good

Since human beings are social by nature and can find fulfillment only through association with others, maintaining strong communal bonds is essential to human dignity. The common good of community life is found when individuals and groups seek the shared welfare of members of society, whether at the group, national, or international level. According to Catholic Church teaching, the common good reflects "the sum total of social conditions which allow people, either as groups or as individuals, to reach their fulfillment more fully and more easily." It is important to stress that the common good does not consist in the addition of particular goods for each member of a society. Rather, it is a shared good because "it is indivisible and because only together is it possible to attain it, increase it and safeguard its effectiveness" (para. 164).

Solidarity

Like the common good, this principle is rooted in the social nature of persons and their equal dignity. It affirms the need to view the different social classes, ethnic groups, business sectors, and political groups of society as parts of an interdependent whole. Pope Benedict XVI roots this principle in the parable of the Good Samaritan. He says that whereas the idea of "neighbor" was used in biblical times to refer to one's countrymen and foreigners who had settled in a single country, in the modern era this is no longer the case. Now the correct conception is: "Anyone who needs me, and whom I can help, is my neighbor."[9] According to the Catholic Church's CST, solidarity is both a social principle and a moral virtue. It is a social principle because human life is realized in association with others—whether at the local, national, or international level—and at the same time it is a moral virtue because expressing concern and meeting the needs of others is not an automatic byproduct of human life. Rather, to care for groups and peoples that are not in one's particular community requires a manifestation of uncommon love and compassion for human beings. The solidarity principle applies to the shared well-being within a neighborhood, city, region, country, and international community. During his pontificate, John Paul II repeatedly emphasized the importance of solidarity between developed and developing nations.

The preferential option for the poor

This principle, first developed by the Latin American Bishops' conference in Puebla, Mexico, in 1979, affirms that God has a special concern for persons who are poor, vulnerable, and oppressed. A moral test for society is how it treats those who are vulnerable and poor. When the norm first emerged, it was associated with liberation theology, which had deeply influenced the Conference of Latin American Bishops (CELAM). As a result, the norm was viewed as part of class conflict between the rich and the poor. In the mid-1980s, the Vatican challenged key elements of CELAM's liberation theology, especially its Marxist socioeconomic overtones, and this resulted in a gradual shift in the meaning of the preferential option principle. As it has been accepted by the Catholic Church, the principle is now viewed as an expression of communal justice, solidarity, and the common good. It highlights the need to prioritize those who

9. Quoted in Donald Kerwin, "Rights, the Common Good, and Sovereignty in Service of the Human Person," in Donald Kerwin and Jill Marie Gerschutz, eds., *And You Welcomed Me: Migration and Catholic Social Teaching* (Boulder, CO: Rowman and Littlefield, 2009), 104.

are most vulnerable in society. Since God has no favorites, this principle does not connote a preference for one group over another or an optional course of conduct. Rather, it reflects, as Donald Kerwin has pointed out, "the universality of God's love which compels action on behalf of those whose rights have been violated or imperiled."[10]

The dignity of work

Work is an economic activity that helps sustain life. Labor is not only necessary to meet human needs but also a moral activity that affirms the inherent worth of persons. Indeed, the Catholic Church regards labor as a form of service and creativity that allows participation in the ongoing work of "God's creation."[11] The challenge for nations and businesses is to create the conditions that foster job creation in order to develop and use people's gifts and abilities to create goods and services that enhance the quality of life. Government officials, employers, and employees all have an important role in creating conditions that foster the common good through economic development.

Each of these CST principles provides important insights and perspectives on how the church should approach the issue of migration. The norm of human dignity calls attention to the infinite worth of all persons, regardless of their nationality, ethnicity, religion, or legal status. Because migrants are God's children, their well-being is a priority to the church. Furthermore, since humans are social by nature, establishing and maintaining strong communal bonds is essential. Solidarity involves not only persons we know but also strangers, including foreign migrants. The common good emphasizes the need for an inclusive community that pursues the shared well-being of all persons. Whether at the local, national, or global level, the common good must always take into account the needs and wants of all persons, including migrants. The fourth principle, the preferential option, emphasizes the need to give priority to those who are most vulnerable and oppressed. From a global perspective, this means that refugees and asylum seekers should have the greatest moral claim among migrants. Finally, since work is not simply a means to sus-

10. Kerwin, "Rights, the Common Good," 98.
11. "Forming Consciences for Faithful Citizenship: A Call to Political Responsibility from the Catholic Bishops of the United States" (Washington, DC: United States Conference of Catholic Bishops, 2007), 15.

tain life but also to enhance human dignity, the church is called to defend migrants who leave their homelands to find work in order to meet basic needs. Catholic bishops claim that many unauthorized aliens come to the United States to find work but that they are also frequently fleeing war and economic devastation.[12]

Applying Catholic social teaching

In addition to these five principles, the Catholic Church's view of migration is significantly influenced by its cosmopolitan view of global society. As Drew Christiansen has observed, the Church takes a "universalist view of international relations," conceiving the world as a human family.[13] As a consequence, human rights are not dependent on citizenship but on the fundamental and inherent dignity of all persons. As Pope Paul II observed to the International Catholic Migration Commission on July 5, 1990, "[human] rights are not based primarily on juridical membership in a determined community, but, prior to that, on the dignity of the person."[14] While a universalist perspective reinforces transnational human rights claims, it must necessarily confront the political realities of a politically fragmented global order. Thus, if the church is to contribute to the moral analysis of migration, it must confront the regulatory role of sovereign states.

In a short teaching document titled "Catholic Social Teaching on Immigration and the Movement of People," the Catholic Church offers a succinct framework for assessing migration. It identifies three principles that synthesize Catholic teaching on migration: (1) the right to migrate; (2) the right of a country to control migration; and (3) the need for justice and mercy in regulating borders.[15] The first principle affirms that "people have the right to migrate to sustain their lives and the lives of their fam-

12. USCCB, "Welcoming the Stranger Among Us: Unity in Diversity," November 15, 2000.

13. Drew Christiansen, SJ, "Movement, Asylum, Borders: Christian Perspectives," *International Migration Review* 30 (Spring 1996): 10.

14. "Speech of Pope John Paul II to the General Assembly of the International Catholic Migration Commission," July 5, 1990. Available at: https://cliniclegal.org/sites/default/files/cst_passages.pdf.

15. USCCB, "Catholic Social Teaching on Immigration and the Movement of People." Available at: http://www.usccb.org/issues-and-action/human-life-and-dignity/immigration/catholic-teaching-on-immigration-and-the-movement-of-peoples.cfm.

ilies." The second claim asserts that "a country has the right to regulate its borders and to control immigration." Since the first and second principles are likely to come into conflict, the third principle declares that a country "must regulate its borders with justice and mercy." According to the Catholic Church, a country must not be concerned solely with its own interests but must also be concerned with the common good of all. The document states, "A sincere commitment to the needs of all must prevail."

The social teachings of the Church not only provide principles and perspectives to guide reflection and analysis about immigration; they also offer a basis for critiquing existing practices and proposed initiatives. Donald Kerwin, the executive director of the Center for Migration Studies, a Catholic migration think tank in New York City, has identified a number of policy initiatives and practices that he believes are contrary to the norms of CST.[16] For example, he suggests that the efforts by federal, state, and local governmental institutions to deny humanitarian assistance to migrants are inconsistent with the Catholic Church's mission to care for those in need. In addition, he argues, the efforts to use the "rule of law" as a way to "marginalize" immigrants offend the Church's social teaching and mission. In a bold but gross overstatement, Kerwin claims that "attempts to criminalize the work or mere presence in the United States by persons without immigration status . . . do not honor the rule of law."[17] A third kind of immigration initiative that challenges CST is the use of derogatory terminology to classify migrants. According to Kerwin, terms like "illegal aliens" or "criminal aliens" are morally unacceptable, and he says that it is "sacrilegious" to call God's children "illegal." Elsewhere he writes, "To people of faith, nobody can be illegal."[18] Kerwin claims that categorizing migrants in this way tends to dehumanize them and to expose them to ridicule and hatred.[19]

16. Donald M. Kerwin, "Catholic Church and Immigration," in Judith Gans, Elaine M. Replogle, and Daniel J. Tichnor, eds., *Debates on US Immigration* (Los Angeles: Sage Reference, 2012), 434.

17. Kerwin, "Catholic Church and Immigration," 434.

18. Donald Kerwin, "The Long Journey of Faith Communities on Immigration," *The Huffington Post*, May 18, 2015. Available at: http://www.huffingtonpost.com/donald-kerwin/the-long-journey-of-faith-communities-on--immigration_b_7295372.html.

19. Kerwin's critique fails to acknowledge the radical distinction between the two kingdoms—the City of God and the City of Man. In the City of God, all humans are welcome, but in the earthly city, membership in a state is based on fulfilling legal preconditions. People who bypass migration rules in entering the United States have done so unlawfully and are irregular or unauthorized aliens.

US Catholic Bishops and Immigration Reform

US Catholic Bishops have issued numerous pastoral letters and teaching documents on immigration in the new millennium. Some of these were issued by individual bishops for use in their own dioceses, such as "I was a Stranger and You Welcomed Me," written by Bishop Anthony Taylor of Little Rock, Arkansas.[20] A number of letters were written by groups of bishops, including "Traveling Together in Hope," written by Wisconsin bishops;[21] "Family Beyond Borders," written by bishops of the border region of Texas, New Mexico, and Mexico;[22] "You Welcomed Me," a pastoral letter by bishops from Arizona;[23] and "Immigration and Our Nation's Future," written by Colorado bishops.[24] Arguably, the most important document on immigration by the US Catholic Church is "Strangers No Longer: Together on the Journey of Hope" (SNL), written by American and Mexican bishops in 2003. The letter is important because it provides perspectives and principles that have been used by the USCCB in its analysis and advocacy of immigration reform in subsequent years.

The Bishops' Pastoral Letter on Immigration

The pastoral letter offers reflections on migration based on the Old and New Testaments and on the Catholic Church's social doctrines. It then proposes five principles that should structure moral reflection on immi-

20. Bishop Anthony B. Taylor, "I Was a Stranger and You Welcomed Me . . . ," A Pastoral Letter on the Human Rights of Immigrants, November 5, 2008. Available at: http://www.ethicsdaily.com/photos/Bishop_Taylor_s_Pastoral_Letter_on_Immigration.pdf.

21. "Traveling Together in Hope," A Pastoral Letter on Immigration from the Catholic Bishops of Wisconsin, December 12, 2011. Available at: http://www.wisconsin catholic.org/statements/WCC%20Immigration%20Letter--ENGLISH.pdf.

22. "Family Beyond Borders," An Open Letter from the Bishops of the Border Region of Mexico, Texas, and New Mexico, November 28, 2013. Available at: http://www .justiceforimmigrants.org/documents/family-beyond-borders.pdf.

23. "You Welcomed Me," A Pastoral Letter on Migration Released on the Feast of Our Lady of Guadalupe, December 12, 2005. Available at: http://dphx.org/wp-content/uploads/2015/09/PL-You-Welcomed-Me-121505.pdf.

24. "Immigration and Our Nation's Future: A Pastoral Letter on Immigration," October 2, 2013. Available at: http://www.coloradocatholicherald.com/ArticleDetails/tabid/1249/ArticleID/1206/IMMIGRATION-AND-OUR-NATIONS-FUTURE-A -Pastoral-Letter-on-Immigration-English-Text-and-Audio.aspx.

gration: (1) persons have the right to find opportunities [work] in their own countries; (2) persons have the right to migrate to support themselves and their families; (3) sovereign nations have the right to control their borders; (4) refugees and asylum seekers should be afforded protection; and (5) human dignity and the rights of undocumented migrants should be respected.[25]

A quick review will show why these ideas offer an incomplete and inadequate framework on which to structure moral reasoning about migration.

The five principles

The first principle—that people should be able to find fulfillment in their homelands—is a central assumption of liberal political thought and a reasonable expectation of all modern constitutional states. From a human rights perspective, the task of government is to maintain political order through the rule of law and to foster economic prosperity. (Indeed, this principle is so basic that it could have been omitted altogether.)

The second principle—that people have a right to find work in foreign lands—is based on the bishops' assumption that "all the goods of the earth belong to all people." The bishops declare, "When persons cannot find employment in their country of origin to support themselves and their families, they have a right to find work elsewhere in order to survive. Sovereign states should find ways to support this right" (SNL, 35). This is a bold claim, more attuned to modern human rights law than to biblical political ethics. The bishops justify economically based migration on the basis of economic inequalities brought about by globalization. They justify the claim for economic migration as follows: "In the current conditions of the world, in which global poverty and persecution are rampant, the presumption is that persons must migrate in order to support and protect themselves and that nations who are able to receive them should do so whenever possible" (SNL, 39).

The third principle—the right of states to regulate borders—is not a fundamental CST principle but a prudential norm arising from the re-

25. "Strangers No Longer: Together on the Journey of Hope," A Pastoral Letter Concerning Migration from the Catholic Bishops of Mexico and the United States, 2003. Available at: http://www.usccb.org/issues-and-action/human-life-and-dignity/immigration/strangers-no-longer-together-on-the-journey-of-hope.cfm. Hereafter, page references to this pastoral letter appear in parentheses within the text.

alities of a decentralized global order of independent states. While it is appropriate for the Catholic Church to acknowledge the legal right of sovereign states to regulate their domestic affairs, including their territorial boundaries, the more fundamental moral principle is the need to recognize the legitimacy of government and the need to obey legitimate authority. Government, after all, is also a divinely ordained institution, called to maintain order and promote justice within its territorial jurisdiction. From an immigration perspective, international justice can only be advanced when states fulfill their legal and moral obligations toward other member states and fulfill their constitutional responsibilities toward their own people. Regulating borders is a legitimate governmental responsibility. Like all moral responsibilities, it is not an absolute claim but one that is advanced by balancing the needs and interests of its own members with the needs and interests of migrants. While the bishops give lip service to border regulation, their real concern is with the rights of migrants to cross borders, whether they are authorized by government officials or not. Indeed, to the extent that they address border regulation, their concern is not with securing the border but with ensuring that unauthorized migrants are treated with dignity and afforded due process rights. The bishops' focus is not on the rule of law but on how to enhance human dignity and foster transnational solidarity. For the most part, the bishops critique current US border practices without suggesting alternatives. The unremitting concern is on the welfare of migrants, not the nurturing of humane, law-abiding nations.

The fourth principle of providing protection to refugees—persons fleeing their own homelands because of persecution and rampant violence and destruction—is undoubtedly the most morally compelling norm. To meet the needs of refugees, states must first determine which migrants are refugees and then determine how they should share the responsibility for caring for them, either through financial assistance or resettlement. The challenge of allocating responsibility for the care of refugees has been graphically illuminated in 2015 and 2016 as tens of thousands of migrants from Syria, Iraq, Afghanistan, Somalia, and other collapsed states have sought refuge in Europe. Although European Union member states sought to devise a common policy toward this crisis, their leaders had been unable to resolve distributional responsibilities among member states as of mid-2016. The challenge of regulating unlawful migration along the United States' southwestern border is considerably less acute. While poverty and crime are prevalent in some Latin American countries, especially El Salvador, Honduras, and Guatemala, the political and economic conditions in Latin America are much less threatening to human rights than those in war-torn Middle East and African states. Mexico, with an average per capita income of nearly $10,000, is classified by the World Bank as an upper-middle-class society. Since Mexico has a reasonably functioning state with a modernizing economy, migrants from Mexico are unlikely to be classified as refugees.

The final principle—human rights—is a universal claim that applies to all persons in all countries, regardless of nationality, legal status, religious beliefs, ethnicity, or social status. As a result, the call to protect the rights of unauthorized aliens is redundant, contributing little to the moral assessment of migration. When we address the subject of unauthorized aliens, the issue is not whether such persons are entitled to equal and fair treatment but how to respond to a person's unlawful presence in a foreign state.

The bishops' recommendations

Using Scripture, CST, and especially the five principles noted above, the bishops' pastoral letter proceeds to offer numerous recommendations they believe will contribute to a more just immigration system. Following are some of the most important suggestions.

1. *Addressing root causes.* The bishops argue that the Mexican and US governments must address the root causes of migration (SNL, 59–63). Since the ideal is for people to be able to secure a reasonable standard of living, the bishops believe that much contemporary migration is a result of economic necessity. Such necessity is fueled by widespread poverty and the existence of significant economic inequalities within and among states. As a result, more resources need to be addressed to foster development in the sending states. But not all sending states are low-income countries. As noted above, Mexico is a modernizing middle-income country with a GNP per capita income far above countries like Bolivia, Haiti, Honduras, Nicaragua, and most African countries.

2. *Family-based immigration.* The bishops argue that the existing system of family preferences is unacceptable because the US immigration ceilings result in long delays waiting for immigrant visas (SNL, 64–67). To ensure that family unity is affirmed, the bishops argue that the family-based system should be reformed to ease the waiting times for visas. But as I noted in chapter 3, the long delays for unification of Mexican families is a result of the generosity of the US system. The United States has argu-

ably the most generous family-unification policy in the world. One way to resolve the frustration arising from long wait times is to limit family unification to the nuclear family—a subject the bishops do not touch.

3. *Legalization of unauthorized aliens.* The bishops claim that close to one-half of all Mexican-born persons living in the United States are undocumented. To resolve this unacceptable condition, the bishops propose that unauthorized aliens be granted legal status—a move they believe would help "to stabilize the labor market in the United States, to preserve family unity and to improve the standards of living immigrant communities" (SNL, 68–71). The call for legalization, which the bishops believe would be beneficial to both Mexico and the United States, has been subsequently reconceived by the USCCB as "earned legalization," which would require aliens to establish eligibility, pass background checks, and pay a fine. Although such a proposal is not amnesty, it is a conditional amnesty in which the original illegality is overcome through time in residence coupled with meeting specified preconditions. But this initiative, rather than solving the problem of unlawful entry, would simply sustain it. For if such a policy were to become law, it would undermine existing immigration laws and become the de facto policy for future migrants.

4. *Employment-based immigration.* The bishops conclude that the United States "needs Mexican laborers to maintain a healthy economy" (SNL, 72). According to the pastoral letter, the current US immigration system provides inadequate opportunities for Mexican laborers to work in the United States either on a permanent or a temporary basis. As a result, the bishops recommend that the current employment-based preference system should increase work opportunities for permanent as well as short-term employment (SNL, 72–77). Any reforms should ensure that the workers' rights are protected and that their wages and benefits are adequate.

5. *Enforcement.* While the bishops acknowledge that the US government has a legitimate right to intercept illegal migrants attempting to cross the border, they believe that some of the border policies have had the effect of "undermining the human dignity of migrants and creating a confrontational and violent relationship between enforcement officers and migrants" (SNL, 79). The letter notes that increased border security in certain sectors has driven migrants to more remote areas for unlawful border crossing, resulting in many deaths. This fact leads the bishops to offer the following innocuous recommendation: "Care should be taken not to push migrants to routes in which their lives may be in danger"

(SNL, 89). The bishops provide no specific suggestions concerning how the US Border Patrol can halt illegal entry. Indeed, the thrust of their analysis is not to ensure border control but to protect the lives and human rights of all migrants.

6. *Due-process rights.* The bishops claim that the Illegal Immigration and Immigrant Responsibility Act (1996) is a problematic law that has resulted in unjust family separations. As I have noted in chapter 2 above, that law increases the penalties for unauthorized migration by forcing those who have remained in the United States unlawfully to leave the country for three or ten years. The bishops recommend that Congress reexamine this statute. They are troubled by the policy of expedited removal, which allows immigration officials to detain and deport illegal aliens without appearing before an immigration judge. In addition, they are troubled by the fact that aliens who seek to enter the United States unlawfully are detained not because they are criminals but because they sought to enter unlawfully. According to the US Supreme Court, such persons must be treated humanely even though they do not enjoy the rights of citizens. That is why the federal government does not provide legal counsel to aliens in its immigration courts.

Assessing the pastoral letter

What are we to make of the "Strangers No Longer" pastoral letter? Is the biblical and moral analysis compelling, and are the policy suggestions helpful in designing a more humane and just US immigration system? Does the bishops' moral analysis contribute to a more informed debate among Catholic parishioners about comprehensive immigration reform?

I have already noted that the immigration principles highlighted by the pastoral letter are themselves insufficient to guide a careful moral overview of immigration policy. Why, for example, didn't the bishops address the problem of human sin? Isn't unlawful migration a sin? And isn't the economic exploitation of migrants a manifestation of sinful greed? Furthermore, why did the letter not address the legitimacy of government and the imperative to obey just laws? And why didn't the bishops address the Christian ideas of mercy and forgiveness, especially in view of their advocacy of legalizing unauthorized aliens? Finally, why didn't the bishops acknowledge the social and economic goods arising from the common life in America? Doesn't the solidarity principle involve obligations to one's country? Shouldn't a pastoral letter on the ethics of migration have recognized citizens' dual responsibilities to their own fellow nationals and to foreigners?

The pastoral letter suffers from several shortcomings. First, the bishops' policy analysis and recommendations are insufficiently grounded in biblical ethics and moral principles. What is striking about the letter's recommendations is how little they relate to biblical norms and the quest for justice: a discontinuity exists between the letter's moral analysis and its policy prescriptions. The recommendations, most of which touch on technical and political concerns, seek to advance a more open US immigration system. But the decision concerning how many migrants to admit, and on what basis, is not simply a moral judgment but a political decision, one that needs to be made by elected government officials based on prudential considerations. Of course, clergy can help structure the policy debate about how to advance a just immigration system. But the bishops' competence is in biblical and moral analysis, not a public-administration or public-policy analysis. By promoting particular policy reforms, the bishops have entered into the contentious terrain of political decision-making—an area of prudential judgment in which clergy do not have expertise.

A second, related limitation of the pastoral letter is the failure to emphasize moral education and to help structure the moral debate about immigration. Had the bishops sought to contribute to the public policy debate on immigration, they could have illuminated biblical norms and moral principles that should guide the analysis of immigration. But rather than seeking to structure the policy debate by illuminating how transcendent principles apply to immigration, the bishops seem more eager to directly advance particular policies, a practice that is ordinarily carried out by interest groups. But the church is not simply a political interest group; rather, it is a community of believers who are called to fulfill a religious mission of proclaiming redemption from sin. Only the church can fulfill its redemptive witness in society. The late Richard John Neuhaus provides a clear and compelling statement of the church's central mission in society:

> The first political task of the Church is to be the Church. That is, Christians must proclaim and demonstrate the Gospel to all people, embracing them in a sustaining community of faith and discipline under the Lordship of Christ. . . . Communal allegiance to Christ and his Kingdom is the indispensable check upon the pretensions of the modern state. Because Christ is Lord, Caesar is not Lord. By humbling all

secular claims to sovereignty, the Church makes its most important political contribution by being, fully and unapologetically, the Church.[26]

To the extent that the bishops have been excessively concerned with policy advocacy, it detracts from the church's more fundamental responsibility, namely, teaching political morality to the laity. Interestingly, the US bishops themselves have acknowledged the church's pivotal role in "forming consciences" through its teachings. In 2007 the US Conference of Catholic Bishops issued a study titled "Forming Consciences for Faithful Citizenship," which emphasizes the church's responsibility to teach moral values that should shape people's individual and public lives. The study declares, "Clergy and lay people have complementary roles in public life. We bishops have the primary responsibility to hand on the Church's moral and social teaching. Together with priests and deacons, assisted by religious and lay leaders of the Church, we are to teach fundamental moral principles that help Catholics form their consciences correctly, to provide guidance on the moral dimensions of public decisions, and to encourage the faithful to carry out their responsibilities in political life."[27] But in addressing immigration concerns, Catholic bishops have not been content to focus on their pastoral and teaching ministry; instead, they have pursued a more activist strategy in seeking to directly influence US public policies. Rather than seeking to provide moral education to parishioners, they have sought to advance specific public-policy reforms.

A third shortcoming of the pastoral letter is the unbalanced way it assesses illegal migration. Fundamentally, the SNL letter approaches the challenge of unlawful migration as an American problem, one that is to be resolved by modifying existing US laws, statutes, and practices. According to Mark Ensalaco, the bishops tend to absolve the Mexican government of its moral duties toward its own people and to absolve Mexican Catholics of their moral obligations to develop a more just Mexican society. "If the bishops choose to stand in solidarity with migrants," he writes, "perhaps it is better to stand with them in an authentic struggle for justice in Mexico, a struggle guided by the very social teaching that the bishops

---

26. Richard John Neuhaus, "Christianity and Democracy: A Statement of the Institute on Religion and Democracy" (Washington, DC: The Institute on Religion and Democracy, 1981), 1.

27. "Forming Consciences for Faithful Citizenship: A Call to Political Responsibility from the Catholic Bishops of the United States" (Washington, DC: USCCB, 2007), 5.

invoke in their appeal for comprehensive immigration reform."[28] This partiality is illustrated by the letter's condemnation of the xenophobic and racist attitudes of anti-immigrant groups, the human rights abuses by government agents, or the mistreatment of unaccompanied minors. But while the letter critiques American failures, it is silent about the role of indigenous conditions that foster illegal migration. Ensalaco notes that while the death of children in the desert is shameful, "the real shame belongs to Mexican families who permit their children to undertake a dangerous journey through the desert, or with Mexican authorities who fail to police their own northern border in order to protect children from abuse by 'bandits.'"[29]

Finally, the bishops' assertions on migration are problematic in maintaining stable, humane nation-states. As we have seen before, people have the right of emigration but no corresponding right of immigration. Since emigration and immigration are two sides of the same coin, some critics argue that if people have a right to leave their homeland, they must also have the commensurate right to enter another country. The Catholic ethicist Drew Christiansen makes this point: "A right to emigrate is vacuous if there is no corresponding right to immigrate. Official Catholic social teaching is unambiguous on this issue. The reasons that justify emigration equally justify immigration, and 'grave requirements of the good, considered objectively' permit making exceptions to this rule."[30] Furthermore, the emphasis on the right to immigrate is problematic because by declaring that people have a "right" to enter another country in search of a better standard of living, it fosters unrealistic expectations about the transnational movement of people. More significantly, the idea of unregulated migration not only undermines state sovereignty, a core pillar of the Westphalian order, but calls into question the state's ability to establish guidelines to ensure that the rate of migration will not exceed a country's capacity to assist immigrants in integrating and assimilating into the host nation. Ethically, states must be welcoming to persons in need, but statecraft must be guided not simply by compassion but must

28. Mark Ensalaco, "Illegal Immigration, the Bishops, and the Laity: 'Strangers No Longer,'" in Todd Scribner and J. Kevin Appleby, eds., On "Strangers No Longer": Perspectives on the Historic US Mexican Catholic Bishops' Pastoral Letter on Migration (New York: Paulist Press, 2013), 253.

29. Ensalaco, "Illegal Immigration," 269.

30. Drew Christiansen, SJ, "Sacrament of Unity: Ethical Issues in Pastoral Care of Migrants and Refugees," in Bishops' Committee on Migration, USCCB, Today's Immigrants and Refugees: A Christian Understanding (Washington, DC: USCCB, 1988), 87-88.

also pursue the common good of the nation. Such a task must balance the needs of citizens with those migrants who wish to resettle in the new society.

The Catholic Church's Contribution to the Immigration Debate

Given its commitment to human dignity and global solidarity, the Catholic Church has played an important role in advancing human rights throughout the world. During the Cold War, church leaders repeatedly challenged political regimes that undermined human rights and provided support to groups whose well-being was threatened by military regimes and nongovernmental groups. In the post–Cold War era the Catholic Church has continued its important task of proclaiming the inherent worth of all persons, regardless of nationality, ethnicity, or legal status. In addressing contemporary challenges posed by the millions of migrants who are fleeing war, destitution, and religious persecution, the church has continued to be a beacon of hope. Reminding leaders of the inherent dignity of all people has been, and remains, the most important political task of the church.

Although the Catholic Church celebrates the rights of persons and the universal solidarity of the international community, it has been reticent to acknowledge the important role of the nation-state in protecting human rights and advancing economic prosperity. For example, when the US bishops address migrants' needs in the "Strangers No Longer" document as well as in other pastoral letters, they treat American society and its institutions as a market, a place where strangers work and pursue their economic interests, not a society where people share common bonds. But, as CST has made clear, work is not simply an economic activity but a means for human flourishing and a way by which people use their abilities to advance the common good of a nation. The letter fails to acknowledge the legitimate obligations of citizens toward their own society. Instead, it celebrates the responsibilities toward strangers. Fulfilling communal responsibilities is neither nativist nor selfish but arises from the desire to advance the well-being of the nation. The common good of the nation is essentially made up of a community's patrimony, its shared traditions, and its common values and ideals. If the common good of a nation is to be preserved, it needs to be nourished, and this can only be done if membership is regulated.

If immigration policy is to be assessed from an ethical perspective, it is important to recognize the moral legitimacy of both the nation and the world. As citizens of our particular national community, we owe special responsibilities to our fellow citizens, but as human beings who are a part of global society, we owe obligations to strangers. Therefore, as we assess immigration policy, it is important to acknowledge the dual responsibilities to our particular communities and to the world at large. Peter Meilaender writes, "We are called to recognize the image of God in every human being, and we owe something to each person simply by virtue of his or her humanity. But we also stand in particular relationships to certain persons for whom we bear special responsibilities: sons and daughters, brothers and sisters, friends and neighbors, fellow citizens. These special relationships channel our potentially endless obligations and make them practicable."[31] It is thus important, as we seek to devise an ethical immigration policy, to balance the competing obligations to neighbors and strangers. This means that the particular demands of democratic citizenship must be reconciled with the universal responsibilities toward all persons in global society.

Fundamentally, the bishops want a more open and flexible immigration system. Their recommendations, which are shared by most secular pro-immigration interest groups, call for increased immigration for families as well as employment for those migrants, and they favor a more lenient approach to law enforcement. Although they affirm the right of states to regulate immigration, they are opposed to strict enforcement of immigration laws because they regard migration as a way of meeting human needs and improving human welfare. But correcting the flaws in the existing legal order is not an easy task. Just because a law is passed to advance a particular social goal does not mean that the statute will necessarily contribute to the desired end.[32] The art of policy-making is difficult because it requires bargaining skills, competence in reconciling moral principles with competing political demands, democratic accountability, and the ability to get bureaucratic institutions to effectively implement the government's decisions. Since clergy are unlikely to possess the orga-

31. Peter C. Meilaender, "Immigration: Citizens and Strangers," *First Things* (May 2007).

32. For example, many of the Great Society welfare initiatives of the mid-1960s, which were designed to uplift the socioeconomic life of inner-city minorities, not only failed to ameliorate living conditions but spawned new social problems as well. Similarly, the 1996 Illegal Immigration and Immigrant Responsibility Act, which was designed to curb illegal immigration by increasing the penalties for unlawful entry, not only failed to reduce illegal immigration but contributed to its significant rise.

nizational skills and political judgment necessary to advance policy goals, the most important contribution that they can offer is the nurturing of values and perspectives that contribute to the desired moral goals.

Citizens, interest groups, political parties, and political leaders are, of course, entitled in a democratic polity to express their opinions and to advance laws and policies through open debate. However, the church is not a political advocacy organization but a community of believers. Following St. Augustine's differentiation of the role and responsibilities of the heavenly city and the earthly city, the church needs to guard against conflating these two realms. Failure to distinguish the two realms will not only harm the church but also deprive the state of authentic moral wisdom. Jesus articulated the challenge of defining spiritual and temporal responsibilities with his admonition to "render to Caesar the things that are Caesar's and to God the things that are God's" (Matt. 22:21). What Jesus teaches in that answer to those trying to trip him up is that Caesar has rights, but these are limited. Caesar is not God; only God is God. As a result, Caesar has no rights over the things that belong to God. Since Jesus is silent about what exactly belongs to either Caesar or God, believers must figure out what things belong to each realm. This is difficult, challenging work.

When the Catholic Church recommends specific public policies such as those in the 2003 joint pastoral letter, is that advocacy consistent with the "two kingdoms" theological framework? There is no simple answer to this question. The quest for a more just approach to migration must necessarily use morality to critique existing policies and to structure possible alternatives in light of the analysis. However, abstract moralizing without addressing the specific problems is unlikely to advance a more just immigration system. At the same time, policy recommendations that are not justified with careful moral reasoning based on biblical teachings are likely to be regarded simply as political preferences of interest groups. Moreover, excessive policy advocacy could undermine the church's authority as a moral teacher. According to Archbishop Charles Chaput, "the church has no special claim to policy competence. Her task is offering basic principles for her people to apply in daily life. The more specific and complex her statements grow, the more they invite criticism and the more prone they become to charges of partisan bias."[33]

Clergy will no doubt claim that their moral teaching can only be ef-

---

33. Charles J. Chaput, *Render unto Caesar: Serving the Nation by Living Our Catholic Beliefs in Political Life* (New York: Doubleday, 2008), 209.

fective if the ideas and principles are applied to specific political decisions or policies. But there can be little doubt that the bishops' fundamental concern is to carry out a sustained advocacy campaign to liberalize US immigration policies and legalize unauthorized aliens. Soon after issuing the SNL pastoral letter, the USCCB initiated a national campaign for immigration reform. The initiative, titled "Justice for Immigrants," is a society-wide advocacy campaign to convince Congress to pass comprehensive immigration reform.[34]

In recent years the USCCB has expanded its campaign for immigration reform. Although the US bishops and many dioceses have carried out a variety of educational initiatives on migration concerns, the main focus has been on advancing major changes in immigration legislation. Thus, when the US Senate began addressing comprehensive immigration reform in early 2013 using a bipartisan framework developed by eight leading Senators, the Catholic Church intensified its advocacy. Since that framework called not only for legalizing unauthorized aliens but also for granting them a pathway to citizenship, the USCCB similarly decided to call for reform that included both legalization and citizenship.

In his testimony on immigration reform before the Senate Judiciary Committee on February 12, 2013, Archbishop José Gomez, the chairman of the USCCB, claimed that it was essential to regularize the large number of unauthorized aliens and to give them a means of applying for citizenship. He began his testimony by declaring that "the current immigration system, which can lead to family separation, suffering, and even death, is morally unacceptable and must be reformed."[35] Although the archbishop reiterated several of the recommendations discussed in the 2003 pastoral letter, the centerpiece of his testimony was his call for making citizenship possible for unauthorized aliens. He declared, "A main feature of any comprehensive immigration reform measure should be a path to citizenship that permits undocumented immigrants of all

34. The major objectives of the "Justice for Immigrants" campaign are: (1) to educate the public ... about Church teaching on migration and immigrants; (2) to create political will for positive immigration reform; (3) to enact legislative and administrative reforms based on the principles articulated by the bishops; and (4) to organize Catholic networks to assist qualified immigrants to obtain the benefits of the reforms. Available at: http://www.justiceforimmigrants.org/index.shtml.

35. USCCB, "Testimony of the Most Reverend José H. Gomez, Archbishop of Los Angeles and Chairman, USCCB, before the Senate Judiciary Committee on Comprehensive Immigration Reform" (February 12, 2013), 3. Available at: http://www.usccb .org/about/migration-policy/upload/CIR-Testimony.pdf.

nationalities in the United States the opportunity to earn permanent residency and eventual citizenship." He further argued that the USCCB was opposed to legalization while withholding access to LPR status and eventual citizenship, since such an initiative would create a permanent underclass in the United States. Finally, Archbishop Gomez highlighted several benefits that would result from placing unauthorized aliens on a path to citizenship: (1) keeping families together and improving the well-being of US-born children, (2) recognizing and maintaining the economic contributions of the undocumented, (3) improving wages and working conditions for all workers, (4) helping to bring US immigration policy in line with US economic policy, and (5) making us [the United States] more secure.[36]

What is extraordinary about the testimony of the chairman of the USCCB is how involved the Catholic Church leadership is in the specifics of immigration policy. There is little in the testimony to suggest that the speaker was a clergyman responsible for ministering to the spiritual life of its members. There is no evidence that the archbishop is seeking to apply CST to the ongoing immigration debate. Indeed, all of the recommendations could have been offered by a secular humanist concerned with promoting a more liberal migration system. To be sure, integrating morality and political action is a difficult task, especially in confronting a complex, multifaceted topic like immigration reform. But if the Catholic bishops are to help members of Congress and the lay public understand how a more just and compassionate immigration policy can be advanced, they should do so by providing moral education.

If the above critique of the USCCB's advocacy of immigration reform is valid, then the Catholic Church has neglected its primary public function of teaching morality ("forming consciences") and has instead pursued policy advocacy. And even when the Catholic Church has sought to highlight biblical and CST principles, it has neglected to integrate the morality with the different elements of immigration policy. If the Church's ethical analysis of immigration is to be credible, it must, at a minimum, provide an authoritative description of the problem and then identify and apply relevant moral norms to the issue. Since many moral values are relevant to most social and political issues, applied political ethics must necessarily illuminate how competing moral claims can be reconciled in advancing proximate justice. For example, since human dignity and the rule of law norms are potentially in conflict in migration,

36. Gomez, "Testimony," 7–8.

the pastoral letter could have shown how these two norms might be integrated. Similarly, since the right to migrate is in tension with sovereignty, the bishops could have used their considerable theological and moral resources to illuminate how to reconcile these claims in advancing just immigration. Instead, the bishops assert the right to regulate borders but then recommend, without biblical or moral justification, the legalization of unauthorized aliens—an action contrary to the sovereignty norm. This recommendation may be a prudent or even necessary action, but the bishops fail to show how this recommended action is justified in terms of biblical morality.

In conclusion, while the Catholic Church has the most developed social and political theology among Christian churches, it has not used its considerable resources to advance a campaign of moral education on just global migration in the contemporary international system. The campaign for US immigration reform has focused on policy advocacy, not education. Unlike its extraordinary US bishops' pastoral letter on nuclear deterrence and arms control, which modeled a sophisticated integration of biblical and moral principles with the intractable issue of nuclear deterrence, the Catholic Church's approach to US immigration policy fails to accurately represent the complexity of the moral dilemma involved. Instead, its call for a more flexible and humane policy, one that is welcoming to strangers regardless of whether they arrived legally or not, is unpersuasive because it lacks the careful integration of the three elements of rigorously applied theological ethics: competent definition of a problem; delineation of relevant biblical and moral principles; and the application of moral principles to policy issues. Given the Catholic Church's eagerness to advance immigration reform, the advocacy campaign has contributed little to the policy debate and called into question the bishops' moral authority as well.

When churches become excessively involved in the specifics of political affairs, they run the risk of neglecting their primary redemptive mission. The late Avery Cardinal Dulles observed, "In the sociopolitical area the Church's mission is not to make pronouncements on the technical aspects of politics, economics, and the social sciences, but to illuminate the moral and religious dimensions of social questions so that the faithful may better form their consciences."[37] In *Mere Christianity*, C. S. Lewis trenchantly makes a similar point:

37. Avery Cardinal Dulles, SJ, *Magisterium: Teacher and Guardian of the Faith* (Naples, FL: Sapientia, 2007), 64.

The clergy are those particular people within the whole Church who have been specially trained and set aside to look after what concerns us as creatures who are going to live forever: and we are asking them to do a quite different job for which they have not been trained [when we ask them to provide political advice]. The job is really on us, on the laymen. The application of Christian principles, say, to trade unionism and education, must come from Christian trade unionists and Christian schoolmasters; just as Christian literature comes from Christian novelists and dramatists—not from the bench of bishops getting together and trying to write plays and novels in their spare time.[38]

38. C. S. Lewis, *Mere Christianity* (New York: HarperCollins, 2002), 75.

« 7 »

Evangelicals and US Immigration Policy

Historically, Evangelicals have been more reluctant to get involved in political affairs than either mainline Protestants or Roman Catholics. What is striking, therefore, is the increased political engagement of contemporary Evangelicals in public-policy debates about global issues, such as religious liberty, climate change, and environmental protection.[1] In recent years the issue that has galvanized the greatest support among Evangelical leaders has been immigration reform. This chapter examines the role of Evangelicals in the policy debate over US immigration.

Although there is general consensus about the nature of Roman Catholicism and mainline Protestantism, the nature of Evangelicalism is far more elusive. As I portray Evangelicals here, they are a distinct group of orthodox Christians who believe the good news that Jesus, the Son of God, has atoned for human sin and offers salvation.[2] According to theologian Alister McGrath, the Evangelical faith is based on four central beliefs: (1) Scripture is the ultimate authority in matters of spirituality, doctrine, and ethics; (2) the death of Jesus Christ on the cross is the only source of salvation; (3) conversion or "new birth" is a life-changing experience; and (4) a commitment to sharing the Christian faith, especially through evangelism.[3] Historian David Bebbington provides a similar conceptualization. In his view, four core convictions and attitudes characterize the Evangelical faith: (1) conversion—the priority of salvation;

1. For an overview of the rise in Evangelical global engagement, see Mark Amstutz, *Evangelicals and American Foreign Policy* (New York: Oxford University Press, 2014), especially chapters 6-8.

2. Since I assume that Evangelicals are a distinct group of Christians, I follow the suggestion of the 2008 "Evangelical Manifesto" and capitalize the term.

3. Alister E. McGrath, *Christianity: An Introduction* (Oxford: Blackwell, 1997), 331.

(2) biblicism—the belief that all necessary spiritual truth is found in the Bible; (3) activism—the belief that faith needs to be expressed through service to God, including sharing the gospel with others; and (4) crucicentrism—the belief that Christ's death on the cross provides the means by which people can be reconciled to God.[4] While both definitions give priority to Scripture, conversion, and salvation, Bebbington emphasizes the activist nature of Evangelicals, while McGrath emphasizes evangelism. Based on McGrath's and Bebbington's conceptualizations, I examine Evangelicalism here as a movement that emphasizes three beliefs: the primacy of the Scriptures as the final authority for religious faith; the need for conversion through the personal acceptance of Jesus's atonement on the cross; and the imperative of sharing the "good news" of the gospel through evangelism.

It is a challenging task to identify who is an Evangelical; it is especially difficult to estimate the size of the American Evangelical population. Using survey data from a variety of sources, the Institute for the Study of American Evangelicals estimates that the number of Evangelicals in the United States is roughly 30 percent of the US population, or about 100 million Americans.[5] Robert Putnam and David Campbell, in their exhaustive study of American religion titled *American Grace*, similarly claim that Evangelicals are the largest religious tradition in the United States, accounting for about 30 percent of the US population.[6]

Evangelical Political Ethics

Evangelicals, building on Reformation teachings, emphasize the sufficiency of Scripture and the capacity of individuals to understand the gospel and accept it by faith. In practice, Evangelicals look to the Bible not only to nurture faith but also to guide everyday life, including public-affairs concerns. Many Evangelicals assume that Scripture is an adequate guide not only for religion but also for public life. Political theorist Jay Budziszewski writes, "Although all traditional Christians

---

4. David W. Bebbington, *Evangelicalism in Modern Britain: A History from the 1730s to the 1980s* (London: Unwin Hyman, 1989), 2-17.

5. Institute for the Study of American Evangelicals, "How Many Evangelicals Are There?" Available at: http://www.wheaton.edu/ISAE/Defining-Evangelicalism/How-Many-Are-There.

6. Robert D. Putnam and David E. Campbell, *American Grace: How Religion Divides and Unites Us* (New York: Simon and Schuster, 2010), 16.

believe in the truth and authority of Scripture, Evangelicals surpass all others in their determination to study and follow it. Their first thought on almost every subject is, 'What does the Bible say?'"[7] However, the challenge for Evangelical political thinkers, he notes, is not that the Bible fails to address government and politics but rather that "the Bible does not provide enough by itself for an adequate political theory."[8] Thus, when Christians seek to ground political action solely on the Bible, they inevitably pursue what Budziszewski terms "inflationary policies"—that is, drawing conclusions from Scripture that are unwarranted.[9] While the Bible must remain the foundation of Christian political ethics, Evangelicals need to acknowledge that Scripture alone is insufficient to develop a comprehensive Christian approach to domestic and international political ethics.

Because of its "biblicist" tradition, along with its decentralized, fragmented nature, Evangelicalism has not developed a body of moral teachings comparable to Roman Catholic social thought. Since it is a Christian movement that is based on core religious beliefs and held together by weak institutions, it has not established a coherent body of biblically based social and political teachings. To the extent that Evangelicalism has devised a system of political and social ethics, its dominant feature is an emphasis on personal spirituality over collective social action. Richard Mouw writes that a major shortcoming of Evangelicalism is its exclusive focus on personal religion. Jesus, he observes, is not simply a savior but also a king.[10] Ronald Sider attributes the limited political influence of Evangelicals to the underdeveloped nature of Evangelical political ethics. In his book *The Scandal of Evangelical Politics*, he argues that Evangelical political action in domestic and international affairs has been a "disaster"—a failure due to the absence of a "biblically grounded, systematic approach to the complicated task of politics."[11]

Although Evangelicals have not developed a political theology, they do have a distinctive approach to public affairs based on their past teachings and actions. Their approach, which builds on the Protestant political

7. J. Budziszewski, *Evangelicals in the Public Square: Four Formative Voices on Political Thought and Action* (Grand Rapids: Baker Academic, 2006), 20.

8. Budziszewski, *Evangelicals in the Public Square*, 23.

9. Budziszewski, *Evangelicals in the Public Square*, 27-30.

10. Richard J. Mouw, *Abraham Kuyper: A Short and Personal Introduction* (Grand Rapids: Eerdmans, 2011), 87.

11. Ronald J. Sider, *The Scandal of Evangelical Politics: Why Are Christians Missing the Chance to Really Change the World?* (Grand Rapids: Baker Books, 2008), 19.

theology that I sketched in chapter 5, has a number of distinctive features. These include the primacy of the spiritual realm, a focus on personal responsibility, and the need for a limited state.

The primacy of the spiritual realm

The primacy of spiritual development is a direct consequence of Evangelicals' belief that the basis of the moral life is God's gift of salvation. Because of human sin, a humane and just politics is possible only where individuals are rightly related to God and to each other. Spiritual regeneration is thus a precondition to a humane politics. Although Evangelicals value human rights and individual responsibility as important elements of personal agency, they give priority to the inward spiritual condition of persons over the outward manifestations of behavior. Carl F. H. Henry, one of the early leaders of the neo-Evangelical movement, captures the centrality of the gospel to social change: "The evangelical task primarily is the preaching of the gospel, in the interest of individual regeneration by the grace of God, in such a way that divine redemption can be recognized as the best solution of our problems, individual and social."[12]

The priority of individual responsibility

A second element of Evangelical political ethics is the importance of personal responsibility. Since sin is personal, Evangelicals believe that redemption from sin is only possible when one accepts divine grace. Salvation occurs when individuals accept God's gift through faith and pursue spiritual maturity via individual habits and practices that nurture a deeper reliance on God and a more faithful fulfillment of his Word. In *The Cost of Discipleship*, theologian Dietrich Bonhoeffer reflects on the radical individualism of the Protestant faith:

> Through the call of Jesus men become individuals. Willy-nilly, they are compelled to decide, and that decision can only be made by themselves. It is no choice of their own that makes them individuals: it is

---

12. Carl F. H. Henry, *The Uneasy Conscience of Modern Fundamentalism* (Grand Rapids: Eerdmans, 1947), 88.

Christ who makes them individuals by calling them. Every man is called separately, and must follow alone.[13]

Given Evangelicalism's emphasis on personal spirituality, the movement places a high priority on personal responsibility in social and cultural life. This does not mean that social and political institutions are unimportant but rather that the development of just policies and institutions is possible only through the moral actions of persons. Furthermore, since responsibility is maximized when individuals are fully accountable, Evangelicals tend to prefer decentralized organization over centralized government initiatives, not because they are necessarily more effective or efficient but because they are more consistent with their view of human beings: individuals are morally accountable to God, to self, and to other persons. The transformational impact of moral leadership is illustrated, for example, in the lives of William Wilberforce and Charles Colson. Wilberforce, an early nineteenth-century member of the British Parliament, led a political campaign against the slave trade; Colson, a former White House official, helped bring about significant reform in the American penal system.

The need for a limited state

A third feature of Evangelical ethics is a deep skepticism toward government and the belief that its role needs to be constrained. The need to limit political authority is derived from three fundamental biblical truths: the dignity of persons, human sinfulness, and the sovereignty of God. Since human beings are created in the image of God, they are entitled to dignity and respect. This means that governments may not trample on human rights. In particular, they may not make unlimited claims on their subjects nor circumscribe people's freedom of conscience. Moreover, since humans are prone to sin and the misuse of power and wealth, governmental officials must be held accountable. In democratic societies, such accountability is maintained through periodic elections and institutions that constrain power through checks and balances and separations of powers. The third truth—that God is sovereign—suggests that the state cannot make unlimited claims. Because temporal power is under divine judgment, the authority of the state must be limited. Given the natural

---

13. Dietrich Bonhoeffer, *The Cost of Discipleship* (New York: Macmillan, 1961), 84.

tendency for power to become more centralized, maintaining a limited government is a never-ending challenge. While constitutional provisions can help to sustain a limited government, the rule of law, a pluralistic culture, and strong mediating institutions such as unions, professional associations, and churches can also play a pivotal role.

If the church is to help keep government morally accountable, it must remain separate and distinct from the state. And to do so, it must refrain from engaging in partisan politics. As Alexis de Tocqueville noted long ago, "the church cannot share the temporal power of the state without being the object of a portion of that animosity which the latter excites."[14] In his important statement "Christianity and Democracy," Richard John Neuhaus observes, "The first and final assertion Christians make about all of reality, including politics, is 'Jesus Christ is Lord.'" Neuhaus goes on to note that because the church's major task is to proclaim this message, it must maintain a critical distance from all actual or proposed temporal initiatives. "Christians betray their Lord," he writes, "if, in theory or practice, they equate the Kingdom of God with any political, social or economic order of this passing time."[15]

Avoiding partisan politics does not mean that the church should avoid public affairs. Rather, it suggests that Christians should bring biblical perspectives to bear on political problems and policy disputes while avoiding excessive political entanglement. The fundamental task of Evangelical political engagement is to illuminate spiritual values that can contribute to greater human dignity and foster a more just and humane world. Such a strategy can only work, however, if believers follow St. Paul's admonition to not be conformed to this world but instead to be transformed by the renewal of mind and body in Christ (Rom. 12:2).

The Rise of Evangelical Political Engagement on Immigration

Evangelical leaders began addressing US immigration policy in the twenty-first century. An important factor in fostering a concern for immigration issues was President George W. Bush's call for major reform in the US immigration system. Although this initiative failed to gain nec-

14. Alexis de Tocqueville, *Democracy in America*, trans. Henry Reeve (New York: Appleton, 1904), 1:334.

15. Richard John Neuhaus, "Christianity and Democracy: A Statement of the Institute on Religion and Democracy" (Washington, DC: Institute on Religion and Democracy, 1981), 1.

essary support from Congress, the policy debate in Bush's second term contributed to a growing interest among Evangelical leaders on this issue. During President Barack Obama's first term in office, Evangelicals expanded their political engagement on immigration, instituting an advocacy campaign for comprehensive immigration reform. After the US Senate passed a comprehensive immigration bill (S744, Border Security, Economic Opportunity and Immigration Modernization Act) in mid-2013, Evangelical groups redoubled their support of immigration reform.

Why did Evangelical leaders take up the cause of immigration reform? What explains the widespread support among Evangelical leaders of churches, nongovernmental organizations, and educational institutions for immigration reform? A review of Evangelical leaders' declarations and statements suggests four reasons for their immigration concerns. First, Evangelicals assumed that the American immigration system was a threat to migrants' human dignity. According to Richard Land, the former head of the Southern Baptist Convention's Ethics and Religious Liberty Commission (ERLC), Evangelicals are involved in immigration reform because the issue involves core moral values. Russell Moore, who replaced Land as head of the ERLC, observes that repairing the immigration system is not just a legal, political, or economic issue. "It's a moral issue," he declared, "and it's been a stain on our country for too long."[16] Similarly, Rev. Samuel Rodriguez, a California pastor and head of the National Hispanic Christian Leadership Conference, says, "At the end of the day this is not a political issue but rather one of a moral and spiritual imperative . . . an issue of justice firmly grounded on biblical truth." Rodriguez, in fact, claims that immigration reform is "a Christian issue."[17]

A second reason why Evangelicals have taken up immigration is because they believe that reform is necessary to fulfill the biblical commandment to be compassionate and caring to "strangers." Jim Wallis, the progressive Evangelical founder of *Sojourners* magazine, says, "We don't think a faith-based argument exists against immigration reform, at least if you're reading the Bible closely. God's passionate, abiding concern for immigrants and foreigners, strangers and travelers—and for our neigh-

16. Tom Strode, "Moore: ERLC Committed to Immigration Reform," May 31, 2013. Available at: http://mail.erlc.com/article/moore-erlc-committed-to-immigration-reform.

17. Jeffrey Scott Shapiro, "The Evolution of Evangelicals on Immigration," *Washington Times,* June 20, 2013. Available at: http://www.washingtontimes.com/news/2013/jun/20/the-evolution-of-evangelicals-on-immigration/?page=all.

bors—is obvious to anyone reading through Scripture."[18] To bolster the claim of welcoming unauthorized aliens, the Evangelical Immigration Table (EIT), a coalition of Evangelical leaders supporting immigration reform, notes that the Hebrew Bible mentions immigrants (Hebrew *gēr*) ninety-two times.[19]

A third reason Evangelicals have taken up the cause of immigration is the belief that existing rules are unnecessarily complex and unfair, resulting in excessively long delays in bringing families together. American business leaders, especially in service, construction, and other businesses that are reliant on unskilled labor, have profited from the low-wage labor of migrants, which in turn has fueled a rise in unauthorized border crossings when the government has failed to increase the number of visas to meet the business demand. As a result, the immigration system sends conflicting messages: it welcomes workers but it makes legal entry difficult, providing visas only to those who are patient and fortunate. Even when a person receives a temporary or permanent visa, family members are not automatically allowed to join the worker. Indeed, major problems in implementing family unity result from the delays involved in uniting relatives. Some backlogs extend beyond twenty years. In his 2009 testimony before the Senate Subcommittee on Immigration, Border Security, and Refugees, Rev. Leith Anderson, president of the National Association of Evangelicals (NAE), declared that the backlog in family reunification petitions was immoral, resulting in much suffering and encouraging people to work around federal laws. Anderson went on to say that "laws must serve the good of society and create law and order and the when they do not, they need to be changed"—thereby implying that the existing system was unjust and needed reform.[20]

Finally, Evangelicals have become involved in immigration reform because they believe that immigrants, including those residing without government authorization, comprise a growing portion of their congregations. A Pew Research Center survey suggests that in 2013, 16 percent of Hispanics in the United States were Evangelicals, reflecting an increase of 4 percent since 2010. By contrast, though more than half of all His-

---

18. Jim Wallis, "The Bible's Case for Immigration Reform," *Los Angeles Times*, August 8, 2013.

19. See EIT's website: http://evangelicalimmigrationtable.com.

20. Statement of Leith Anderson, Hearing on Faith–Based Community Perspectives on Comprehensive Immigration Reform, Senate Judiciary Subcommittee on Immigration, Border Security, and Refugees (October 8, 2009). Available at: https://www.judiciary.senate.gov/imo/media/doc/10-08-09%20Anderson%20testimony.pdf.

panics (55 percent) were Catholic in 2013, the percentage of Catholics had declined from the 67 percent in 2010, reflecting a dramatic loss of 12 percent.[21] According to some observers, Evangelical concern with immigration is thus fueled in part by the missional opportunities among Latinos. Evangelical leaders believe that by supporting immigration reform, especially advocacy of illegal aliens, they can better meet the needs of immigrant members and strengthen church growth.

Although each of these factors has contributed to the Evangelical concern about immigration, the dominant political dynamic propelling immigration reform is the question of what to do with aliens that are living in the United States without governmental authorization. To a significant degree, Evangelical engagement has been motivated by the need to care for unauthorized aliens and to provide a means by which they can gain legal status. Evangelical groups favored the 2013 Senate immigration bill (S744) because it provided a pathway to legalize millions of unauthorized aliens. But as of 2016, immigration reform remains intractable because political groups have been unable to overcome the resistance in the public toward granting unauthorized aliens a means to legalize their status.

Evangelical Teachings on Immigration

Since Evangelicals comprise more than forty US denominations, no organization ensures the coherence of the movement or speaks on its behalf. Perhaps the most unifying and representative organization is the National Association of Evangelicals, an association of Evangelical denominations established in the early 1940s. Since it is the most representative organization of American Evangelicals, I begin my analysis by surveying relevant NAE resolutions. Second, I examine the declarations of the Southern Baptist Convention (SBC), the largest Evangelical denomination. Finally, I examine the initiatives of the Christian Reformed Church, since the denomination has devoted significant resources to the immigration debate.

---

21. Emma Green, "The Catholic Church Isn't Doing So Well with Hispanic-Americans," *The Atlantic* (May 7, 2014). Available at: http://www.theatlantic.com/national/archive/2014/05/the-catholic-church-isnt-doing-great-with-hispanic-americans/361709/.

The National Association of Evangelicals (NAE)

When the NAE wishes to express its concerns about a domestic or international public-policy concern, it typically issues a one- or two-page declaration. It rarely provides an extended analysis of a problem or illuminates how biblical and theological principles apply to the issue of concern. In addressing US immigration and the plight of refugees, the NAE has followed this tradition of brevity.

Since the end of the Cold War, the NAE has issued three resolutions on immigration—in 1995, 2006, and 2009. The first, titled "Compassion for Immigrants and Refugees," calls on Christians to express God's love and compassion toward immigrants and refugees. It declares, "While we recognize the right of nations to regulate their borders, we believe this responsibility should be exercised with a concern for the entire human family in a spirit of generosity and compassion." Accordingly, the declaration calls on the US federal government to ensure that its refugee and immigrant admissions policies are "reasonable and just." The second resolution, issued in October 2006, renews the call for border security, the rule of law, and compassion for migrants. The resolution declares, "As a people of faith we support immigration reform that reflects human dignity, compassion, and justice integral to a nation under God." The "Immigration 2009" resolution, which is more than twice the length of the previous statements, is radically different in character, marking a significant departure from the previous NAE resolutions.[22]

The two-page resolution is divided into three relatively equal sections: "Biblical Foundations," "National Realities," and "Call to Action."[23] The first section acknowledges that all humans are made in the image of God and that Christians are called to show compassion and hospitality to migrants. It further declares that God has established nations and that laws should be respected. In addition, it declares that immigration policies should affirm human dignity and "demonstrate biblical grace to the foreigner." Furthermore, while the resolution acknowledges that the Bible does not offer a blueprint for modern laws, it betrays this truth by proceeding to offer specific policy suggestions in its call to action.

The second section acknowledges that the United States is a country

22. NAE, "Immigration 2009." Available at: http://nae.net/immigraton-2009/.
23. Although the "Immigration 2009" resolution was adopted overwhelmingly by the NAE board of directors, only fourteen of forty member denominations had formally adopted the document as of 2013.

of immigrants and that the significant increase in migration has led to numerous problems. "The challenge today," the resolution declares, "is to determine how to maintain the integrity of national borders, address the situation with millions of undocumented immigrants, devise a realistic program to respond to labor needs, and manifest the humanitarian spirit that has characterized this country since its founding." The fundamental "national reality" is that the United States is not admitting an adequate number of aliens to meet the country's economic needs. As a result, many migrants have entered the country illegally, not only to advance their own economic interests but also to provide cheap labor to US businesses. The resolution states, "Due to the limited number of visas, millions have entered the United States without proper documentation or have overstayed temporary visas." In assessing the NAE resolution, Peter Meilaender and I have questioned the religious leaders' competence to assess the government's visa policy. We write,

> But how many visas would be "enough," and how would one decide that question? By considering US demand for foreign workers? Or the number of foreign workers seeking to come here? Does it make a difference whether we are considering skilled or unskilled labor? How do we weigh the benefits to American consumers, in the form of cheaper goods and services, against the costs to American labor, in the form of wage competition? Or how should we allocate visas among workers, family members, and refugees? All of these difficult but critical questions are simply buried beneath the bland assumption that we are not admitting "enough" immigrants.[24]

The third section, "Call to Action," offers several policy recommendations, including: ensuring that the Border Patrol emphasizes respect for human dignity; facilitating the entry of a "reasonable number of immigrant workers"; reconsidering (and, by implication, increasing) the number of visas available for family reunification; reevaluating the impact of deportation on families; providing a qualified amnesty for illegal aliens; protecting the civil rights, especially with respect to fair labor practices, of all those present in the United States; and enforcing immigration laws "in ways that recognize the importance of due process of law, the sanctity of the human person, and the incomparable value of

24. Mark Amstutz and Peter Meilaender, "Public Policy and the Church: Spiritual Priorities," *The City* (Spring 2011): 4–17.

family." The NAE's fundamental message is captured in the following declaration: "We believe that national immigration policy should be considerate of immigrants who are already here and who may arrive in the future and that its measures should promote national security and the general welfare in appropriate ways."

When we take these suggestions together, it is clear that the authors of the NAE statement believe that a more expansive and flexible immigration system is needed, one that will facilitate "earned legal status for undocumented aliens" and will give greater priority to family reunification. Interestingly, the document is silent about how the widespread presence of illegal aliens in the country undermines the rule of law, and little is said about the financial burdens that they impose on the citizenry for social, medical, and educational services. Even the two recommendations that concede the need to monitor the border and enforce the laws emphasize the need to protect the human rights of those seeking entry rather than border security.

A serious shortcoming of the NAE declaration is that it fails to illuminate how biblical and moral principles apply to the challenges of immigration reform. To be sure, the resolution emphasizes the inherent dignity of persons and—after noting that migration was common in biblical times—emphasizes the need for compassion toward strangers. It also pays lip service to "the rule of law." But human dignity, compassion, and rule of law are not the only biblical principles relevant to immigration. More important, the NAE statement fails to illuminate how biblical norms can help structure the moral analysis of immigration. Instead of showing how competing and conflicting values and interests might advance a just immigration policy, the NAE statement offers simplistic assertions, such as "an evaluation of recent immigration cannot be reduced to economics and national security issues" or "policies must be evaluated to reflect that immigrants are made in the image of God and demonstrate biblical grace to the foreigner."

To the credit of the authors of the NAE resolution, the statement acknowledges that the Bible does not "offer a blueprint for modern legislation." Even though the statement concedes that the Bible is not a manual for public policy, it nevertheless claims that its concerns and recommendations are "guided by Scripture." But given the failure to morally critique the immigration system's shortcomings, there is little integration of biblical analysis with the recommended actions. For instance, the NAE statement urges the US government to "establish a sound, equitable process toward earned legal status for currently undocumented immigrants," but

173

it provides no biblical or moral basis on which to advance such a recommendation. Similarly, the statement urges that "immigration enforcement be conducted in ways that recognize the importance of due process of law, the sanctity of the human person, and the incomparable value of family." But since the resolution does not identify law-enforcement shortcomings, it is unclear what the NAE is suggesting—and why.

Given its brevity, the NAE resolution oversimplifies a complex issue and fails to illuminate fundamental tradeoffs among competing values. Tradeoffs include competing moral claims: refugees versus immigrants; family-based migration versus employment-based migration; migrants' rights versus citizens' rights; and mercy and forgiveness for unauthorized aliens versus strict legal enforcement. As a result, the resolution contributes little to the moral analysis of this public-policy concern. Furthermore, because of the resolution's brevity, the document fails to identify and explain relevant biblical principles or to show how they apply to the various dimensions of immigration policy.

The Southern Baptist Convention (SBC)

The SBC, the largest Evangelical denomination, is a network of some 46,000 churches with more than 15 million members. Although it is not a member of the NAE, the SBC shares with the NAE member churches a deep commitment to biblical faith, personal salvation through Christ, and a commitment to evangelism. The SBC holds an annual meeting in which delegates address leadership and organizational issues. At the same time, delegates typically adopt eight to ten one-page resolutions that address common spiritual, cultural, and social concerns. Resolutions in recent conventions have addressed topics such as transgender identity, government-sponsored casinos, the sanctity of human life, the persecuted church, and racial reconciliation. In addition, the SBC adopted resolutions addressing the immigration issue during the 2006 and 2011 meetings.

The 2006 resolution, titled "On the Crisis of Illegal Immigration," observes that the US government has failed to regulate its southern border and to enforce immigration laws, including laws governing the employment of aliens. And because of the unclear and tenuous position of undocumented aliens, the resolution acknowledges the danger that some employers might seek to exploit workers. Because of the many economic, political, and social problems arising from unlawful migration, the SBC resolution calls on the federal government to address the immigration crisis. In particular, it calls on the federal government to strengthen border security and increase enforcement of immigration laws, including the laws governing the employment of aliens. The resolution also calls on Christians to follow biblical principles in caring for migrants and calls on churches to "act redemptively" in meeting the needs of immigrants in their communities.

The 2011 resolution, titled "On Immigration and the Gospel," addresses similar themes to those covered in the 2006 statement.[25] But where the earlier resolution emphasizes the rule of law and the lack of government enforcement, the 2011 resolution emphasizes the care and well-being of migrants. After highlighting some of the problems with contemporary migration, the resolution urges churches to teach and model the gospel of Jesus Christ, highlighting the inclusive nature of the church and condemning bigotry and harassment of persons. Like the earlier resolution, the 2011 statement calls for strengthening borders and holding businesses accountable for hiring legal workers. Most startling, however, is its recommendation that the US government, after securing its borders, implement "a just and compassionate path to legal status ... for those undocumented immigrants already living in our country." Since this initiative is conditional on migrants fulfilling "appropriate restitutionary measures," the resolution also declares that "this resolution is not to be construed as support for amnesty for any undocumented immigrant." The resolution concludes by emphasizing that though SBC members might disagree about how to achieve a just and humane immigration policy, they are united in their belief that the gospel of Jesus Christ is open to all who believe.

Like the NAE statement, the two SBC resolutions highlight biblical principles related to migration and express social, political, and legal concerns arising from illegal migration. Besides emphasizing border security and the need for enforceable rules, the SBC resolutions recommend a pathway to legalization and citizenship for unauthorized aliens. Such a proposal may be politically prudent and socially desirable, but church leaders do not offer a rationale for such an initiative on either biblical or moral grounds. Instead, they advance legalization simply as a prudential measure to meet human needs. Evangelicals could have argued that the mercy and forgiveness of sins, which are central elements of the Chris-

---

25. SBC, "On Immigration and the Gospel." Available at: http://www.sbc.net/resolutions/1213.

tian faith, justify overriding existing policies, provided that aliens fulfill "restitutionary" measures as an expression of their assumed guilt. But the SBC resolution does not use theological arguments to justify the call for normalization. Rather, it follows the views of most groups advancing immigration reform by encouraging legalization through the payment of a fine, undergoing a background check, and paying back taxes.[26]

The Christian Reformed Church (CRC)

The Christian Reformed Church, a member of the NAE, is a denomination of more than one thousand congregations and about 250,000 members. In 2007 the synod of the CRC established a commission to study the issue of migration of workers as it relates to the church and to offer suggestions as to how the church might "advocate on behalf of those who are marginalized." The commission issued its report in 2009, and it was adopted by the church's 2010 synod.[27]

The thirty-three-page report, perhaps the most comprehensive analysis of immigration by an Evangelical denomination, is an important study because it seeks to integrate biblical analysis with the challenges posed by contemporary migration. About a third of the report is devoted to an overview of immigration policies of the United States and Canada, with the bulk of it devoted to biblical and theological perspectives on immigration. The report concludes with recommendations on how the church should carry out its educational ministry, advocacy, and humanitarian work.

The report begins its assessment of current US immigration concerns by noting that many migrants from poor countries "try to make a new beginning in the greener pastures of the United States" (CRC, 4). The commission report alleges that many migrants cross the border illegally because of the limited number of visas and the long delays in securing them. However, once migrants enter the country illegally, they are unable to regularize their status without returning to their home country.

---

26. A further difficulty with the legalization proposal is that the adoption of "earned legalization" undermines existing laws and establishes a new de facto policy, one that allows unauthorized aliens who have lived in the shadows for many years to normalize their status.

27. CRC, "Committee to Study the Migration of Workers." Available at: www.crcna .org/sites/default/files/Migration.pdf. Hereafter, page references to this document appear in parentheses within the text.

Although the call for comprehensive immigration reform among most advocacy groups is fueled by a desire to provide a means to regularize the status of unauthorized aliens, the CRC report does not explicitly endorse amnesty.

Based on teachings from the Old and New Testaments, the report presents a biblical framework on how to treat aliens and strangers. Some of the key elements of this framework include giving priority to the claims of vulnerable people, welcoming and caring for strangers, emphasizing the inclusiveness of the human community, and meeting the needs of neighbors who live nearby. The report also highlights several important theological principles that should guide the church and the state in addressing immigration issues. First, the church must be inclusive, keeping its doors open for all persons regardless of ethnicity, wealth, or legal status. The report declares, "The church today carries forward the love of God for the strangers as revealed in the Old Testament and the love of God for all the vulnerable strangers in our midst as incarnated by Christ Jesus the Lord in the New Testament" (CRC, 24). Second, while the claims of the church are universal, the boundaries of the state are limited. As a result, states have the responsibility to create and enforce immigration laws. The church, by contrast, has a responsibility to show love and compassion to all immigrants regardless of how they arrived (CRC, 30). Third, since government is responsible for the affairs within its own territorial boundaries, it is responsible for controlling borders and for establishing policies based on citizens' interests. While a nation may give preferential treatment to its own people, it should not neglect the needs of foreigners. Finally, the report emphasizes the legitimacy of the state and the need to obey government. Christians must always acknowledge the supremacy of divine authority; furthermore, obedience to lawful authority, while conditional, is a biblical imperative.

The commission concludes its biblical and theological analysis by affirming four core *principles*: (1) all persons are created in God's image and entitled to dignity; (2) Christians are to welcome strangers in their midst and to give special care to those who are in greatest need; (3) the church is an inclusive community of persons who profess faith in Christ; and (4) while believers must respect governing authorities, citizenship in the kingdom of God demands that believers show love and compassion to neighbors and "advocate for laws that will mandate the just and humane treatment of immigrant peoples" (CRC, 31).

The CRC study recommends four *initiatives*: first, it calls on the church's "Office of Social Justice and Hunger Action to help institute 'fair, just, and equitable laws' for unauthorized aliens; second, it encourages people to seek to change immigration laws and practices that "appear to be unduly harsh or unjust"; third, it seeks to reduce the number of unauthorized aliens by expanding the opportunities to legalize their status; and fourth, it calls for more just treatment of imprisoned unauthorized aliens.

Despite the study's lengthy biblical and theological analysis about migration, this analysis does not lead to a dispassionate assessment of the US immigration system. As a result, the recommended actions are not explained or justified in terms of the report's theological analysis or a critique of current government practices. For example, the CRC report calls for a reform of laws that "appear unduly harsh or unjust," but it does not inform us about which practices are inconsistent with biblical justice. In addition, the report calls for more humane treatment of aliens who are imprisoned, but the suggestion is not based on an assessment of existing detention practices. Finally, the report calls for increased opportunities for unauthorized aliens to legalize their status, but it provides no moral rationale for this policy suggestion. The report declares, "Christians are right to advocate for immigration policies within a given nation that will be more just, fair, and generous, and that will assist the nation in welcoming more strangers as citizens, not fewer" (CRC, 26). Christian citizens are entitled to advance their policy interests and concerns, but when a church seeks to do so it should provide a clear biblical or moral rationale for its desires. But the report does not explain why increased migration advances justice for citizens and migrants or why the unauthorized aliens should be granted a path to citizenship.[28]

What are we to make of the Evangelical teachings on US immigration? Based on our review of the NAE and SBC declarations and the denominational study by the CRC, it is clear that the Evangelical teachings offer strong support for human dignity, compassion for migrants, and a concern for family unity. Like those espousing the social teachings of the Catholic Church, Evangelicals emphasize the fundamental worth and equality of all persons and de-emphasize the contribution of nation-states in advancing human dignity. While Evangelicals acknowledge

28. Moreover, the call to "welcome more strangers as citizens" is not consistent with immigration policies. No immigrant is guaranteed citizenship. The process to become a citizen is a lengthy one. Aliens are typically admitted as immigrants and are eligible to apply for citizenship after spending five or more years as a legal permanent resident (LPR). Many LPRs, however, do not apply for citizenship.

the reality of the Westphalian system and declare their support for the regulation of territorial borders, their teaching is completely one-sided. They promote compassion and mercy and seek to advance a more liberal and flexible immigration system. The one-sided approach is most evident in Evangelicals' support for the legalization of unauthorized aliens for the sake of mercy. But the task of government is not simply to be compassionate but to advance justice, both within its own territorial boundaries and in the world at large. Evangelicals' one-sided perspective neglects justice, secured by government not through love and compassion but through the making and enforcing of just laws. Such laws must necessarily protect the rights and interests of citizens and incorporate the needs and interests of migrants.[29] In sum, Evangelical teachings are ethically compelling but politically incomplete.

Evangelical Advocacy of Immigration Reform

In 2012, progressive Evangelical leaders decided to establish a political alliance to promote comprehensive immigration reform. This informal initiative, known as the Evangelical Immigration Table (EIT), sought to mobilize Evangelicals to support immigration reform based on six principles: (1) respect for human dignity; (2) protection of the unity of the immediate family; (3) respect for the rule of law; (4) security of national borders; (5) fairness to taxpayers; and (6) legalization of unauthorized aliens. The EIT defines legalization as establishing "a path toward legal status and/or citizenship for persons who qualify and wish to become permanent residents." It further declares that "a just and fair immigration system should include, for those who want it and qualify, clear steps to citizenship. This call is rooted in our biblically informed commitment to human freedom and dignity."[30] Although the first five EIT principles are widely supported by the American people, the last one is problematic, not only because it is inconsistent with principles 3 and 4 but also because

---

29. The most important international expression of states' transnational obligations is the emergence of the principle of "Responsibility to Protect" (R2P). According to this principle, when states are unable or unwilling to protect the human rights of their own people, the right of sovereignty gives way to the international community's responsibility to protect persons.

30. See EIT, "Statement on Citizenship." Available at: http://evangelicalimmigration table.com/cms/assets/uploads/2013/10/Table-Statement-on-Citizenship-.pdf.

it calls into question the predictability and stability of the rules made by the US government.

In seeking to advance immigration reform, Evangelicals have emphasized two biblical principles—human dignity and compassion. For example, Russell Moore, the head of the Southern Baptist Convention's Ethics and Religious Liberty Commission, argues that the United States needs to reform its immigration system in order to respect "the God-given dignity of every person." Since the Hebrew Bible teaches that Israelites, who were once aliens in a strange land, were morally obligated to treat aliens in their own land with compassion, religious leaders have concluded that US citizens should similarly treat aliens with love and compassion. Indeed, migrants should be welcomed into American society. Matthew Soerens and Jenny Hwang Yang, two World Relief employees, have published a book on immigration reform with a title that captures this sentiment: *Welcoming the Stranger*.[31]

But human dignity, compassion, and inclusiveness provide a weak foundation for pursuing immigration reform. As a result, if Evangelical leaders want to contribute to a more just and humane immigration policy, they will need to delineate how compassion and the rule of law can be reconciled. To begin with, ethical analysis must identify and apply fundamental moral precepts relevant to citizenship, migration, and the concerns posed by illegal migration. Since the demand for permanent admission into the United States is much greater than the number of immigrant visas supplied by immigration authorities, officials select only some applicants for admission using the legal guidelines established by the Immigration and Nationality Act of 1965.[32] Although compassion and generosity are important interpersonal moral virtues, they cannot serve as the foundation of a legal system that seeks to treat all persons equally and with dignity. In particular, they cannot serve alone in resolving the plight of unauthorized aliens. In addressing this problem, government must weigh the competing claims of human dignity and the rule of law and seek to reconcile them in the service of national and global justice.

The EIT has succeeded in recruiting the support of leading Evangelical organizations, religious leaders, pastors, and college presidents. In-

31. Matthew Soerens and Jenny Hwang Yang, *Welcoming the Stranger: Justice, Compassion and Truth in the Immigration Debate* (Downers Grove, IL: InterVarsity, 2009).

32. While the high demand for visas is evident by the significant number of migrants who seek employment-based and family-based visas, the best illustration of high demand for visas is the more than ten million applicants annually for the 55,000 diversity visas that are distributed by a lottery.

deed, in the annals of Evangelical political advocacy, few initiatives have received as much broad support among leaders as has the EIT. While the EIT works to gain support for immigration reform through seminars and workshops at colleges and denominational gatherings, its main focus has been lobbying Congress. When the US Senate was considering a major reform initiative (S.744), the EIT mobilized hundreds of pastors and religious leaders to lobby for the legislation. And following the passage of the Senate bill in mid-2013, the EIT launched a broad media campaign, targeting key congressional districts in states such as North Carolina, Ohio, Oklahoma, and Texas. It also sought to increase political pressure for further legislative action via a ninety-two-day Pray for Reform campaign.[33] However, the House of Representatives, controlled by Republicans, refused to take up the Senate bill.

While the EIT has gained the tacit support of leading Evangelical pastors and leaders, it has been much less successful in mobilizing parishioners. Mark Tooley, the head of the Institute on Religion and Democracy, has noted that the EIT has succeeded with the "grasstops" but failed with the "grassroots."[34] According to Jonathan Merritt, "the Evangelical movement on immigration has been mostly top-down and not bottom-up. It has failed to do the difficult work of convincing and mobilizing (or at least neutralizing) the millions of Evangelical churchgoers and voters."[35]

What explains the limited support for comprehensive immigration reform among the Evangelical church members? One issue is that most Americans do not consider immigration a priority. Public opinion polls have found that issues such as the economy, jobs, health care, terrorism, budget deficit, taxes, and energy are all considered more important.[36] Additionally, surveys consistently show that among religious groups,

---

33. Since the EIT is not a legal entity, it is not allowed to collect and disperse funds. As a result, the National Immigration Forum (NIF), a secular advocacy organization, has served as the sponsoring organization for the EIT. Since the NIF has received support from billionaire George Soros, a number of Evangelicals expressed deep concern about the affiliation of the EIT with the NIF. The popular Christian author Eric Metaxas withdrew his name from the EIT when he learned of EIT's affiliation with Soros's funding.

34. Mark Tooley, "Evangelical Grassroots versus 'Grasstops,'" *The American Spectator*, July 31, 2013.

35. Jonathan Merritt, "Why Evangelicals' Push for Immigration Reform Isn't Working," Religion News Service, July 23, 2013.

36. Pew Research Center, "Few Say Religion Shapes Immigration, Environment Views," September 17, 2010. Available at: http://www.pewforum.org/2010/09/17/few-say-religion-shapes-immigration-environment-views/.

Evangelicals are the least likely to support immigration reform and the legalization of unauthorized aliens. A 2013 Public Religion Research Institute (PRRI) poll, for example, found that 56 percent of Evangelicals supported legalization of unlawful aliens, but a year later, the same (PRRI) poll found that that support had declined to 48 percent—an eight-point drop.[37] The survey also found that the value of welcoming the stranger, a norm emphasized by Evangelicals, was viewed as less important than promoting national security, keeping families together, protecting human dignity, ensuring fairness to taxpayers, and enforcing the rule of law.[38] Among Evangelicals, even the call to "love the stranger" was not considered decisive. According to a poll of Evangelical voters, only 11 percent of respondents believed that this moral responsibility involved giving legal status to illegal immigrants, while 78 percent interpreted the principle as treating illegal immigrants humanely while still enforcing the law.[39]

A second and more important reason for EIT's limited influence in mobilizing support for reform that is substantive is that Evangelical leaders have not made a persuasive biblical and theological case for immigration reform—and, more specifically, for legalizing unauthorized aliens. Since Americans consider illegal migration the central issue of immigration reform, an effective immigration campaign should necessarily be rooted in an authoritative argument about how to address and resolve the legal status of irregulars.[40] But like the USCCB, Evangelical leaders have failed to develop a comprehensive theological account of how to reconcile the rule of law with compassion to strangers. Instead, they have presented a variety of principles and ideas that collectively offer a one-sided perspective based on mercy and forgiveness while disregarding justice and the rule of law. Bill Blankschaen writes that the

37. Lauren Markoe, "Evangelicals See 8-point Drop in Support for Immigration Reform," Religion News Service, June 11, 2014. Available at: http://www.religionnews .com/2014/06/10/evangelicals-see-8-point-drop-support-immigration-reform/.

38. Public Religion Research Institute, "Citizenship, Values, and Cultural Concerns: What Americans Want from Immigration Reform," March 2013, 35. Available at: http://www.prri.org/research/2013-religion-values-immigration-survey/.

39. Pulse Opinion Research, "National Poll of Evangelical Voters' Biblical Views and Moral Priorities on Immigration Policy," February 2014. Available at: https://www .numbersusa.com/content/files/PulseSurvey_Evangelicals.pdf.

40. John C. Green, "Religion and Immigration: A View from the Polls." Available at: http://www.washingtonpost.com/r/2010-2019/WashingtonPost/2013/11/07/Editorial -Opinion/Graphics/religion_and_immigration.pdf.

EIT has "fixated on mercy to the exclusion of justice."[41] But mercy is not superior to or more important than justice. Indeed, both are central to a Christian worldview. Because of the incompleteness and partiality of the EIT campaign, the advocacy campaign fails to resonate with rank-and-file believers, who not only support mercy but also expect people to obey the law.

A third reason for the limited success of the EIT in the area of immigration reform is that the overuse of Scripture to bolster policy claims can undermine the moral analysis of complex public-policy issues such as immigration. Christians, of course, look to Scripture for important principles and teachings to inform attitudes and values about immigrants. But the use of Scripture to assess such issues as a numerical ceiling for migrant workers or refugees or the plight of unauthorized aliens living in the United States reflects an overreliance on biblical revelation to address those public-policy concerns. In a 2015 public opinion survey of Evangelicals, only 12 percent of the respondents said that the Bible influenced their views on immigration. Even more surprising, the survey found that church affiliation had even less impact, influencing only 2 percent of parishioners' views on immigration.[42]

The gap between Evangelical leaders and the rank-and-file churchgoers in the pew was evident when the NAE board adopted the "Immigration 2009" resolution. Despite its adoption, only eleven of the more than forty member denominations subsequently endorsed the statement. And given the perception that the NAE action had endorsed amnesty for undocumented aliens, some church groups felt compelled to declare publicly that the NAE statement had not done so. When the SBC adopted its immigration reform resolution in 2011—in a statement that endorsed conditional legalization for undocumented aliens—it was sufficiently concerned about misunderstanding and potential opposition from conservative members that it declared that the resolution was "not to be construed as support for amnesty for any undocumented immigrant." When Jonathan Merritt, a religion observer, examined polling of Evangelicals in 2013, he concluded that Evangelical elites had grown

41. Bill Blankschaen, "The Isolationist Immigration Gospel of the Evangelical Immigration Table," July 26, 2013. Available at: http://www.patheos.com/blogs/faith walkers/2013/07/why-i-disagree-with-the-isolationist-gospel-of-the-evangelical -immigration-table/.

42. Bob Smietana, "Evangelicals Say It Is Time for Congress to Tackle Immigration," LifeWay Research, 2015. Available at: http://www.lifewayresearch.com/2015/03/11/ evangelicals-say-it-is-time-for-congress-to-tackle-immigration/.

increasingly supportive of immigration reform, while "the Evangelical masses continued to lag behind."[43]

Finally, Evangelicals have been historically more conservative theologically and politically than other Christian groups. For example, while public opinion surveys by the Pew Research Center found that 54 percent of Evangelicals viewed immigrants as a burden to the country, the percentage for Mainline Protestants and Catholics was 43 percent and 44 percent, respectively. This finding is reinforced by other surveys.[44] Lyman Kellstedt and Ruth Melkonian-Hoover write, "In our continuing and in-depth analysis of public opinion data on religion and immigration attitudes we have found that white evangelicals have been, and continue to be, the most opposed to immigration reform among religious groups. This finding has been present consistently over the past twenty years in dozens of surveys from polling organizations including the Pew Research Center, the Public Religion Research Institute (PRRI), the General Social Surveys, and the American National Election Studies."[45]

In response to the partiality of the EIT's biblical message, Kelly Monroe Kullberg initiated an alternative immigration movement with the goal of challenging some of EIT's claims. Called Evangelicals for Biblical Immigration (EBI), this ad hoc movement seeks a more complete approach to immigration rooted in "the whole counsel of Scripture." EBI's website declares, "While pro-amnesty Evangelicals are selectively quoting Scriptures, EBI looks at the whole of Scripture."[46] Regrettably, EBI has provided few biblical and theological resources to bolster its claims. Even more dubious is the claim that the Bible can provide a sufficient basis for devising immigration policy. Both the EIT and the EBI suffer from an excessive eagerness to use Scripture to advance political ends. Mark Tooley, president of the Institute on Religion and Democracy, provides wise counsel when he observes, "Evangelical elites, when speaking politically for ecclesial bodies, should stick with issues to which Scripture and Christian tradition speak most directly. As representatives

43. Jonathan Merritt, "Evangelicals and Immigration: Crunching the Numbers," Religion News Service, August 1, 2013. Available at: http://jonathanmerritt.religionnews.com/2013/08/01/evangelicals-and-immigration-crunching-the-numbers/.

44. Michael Lipka, "Catholic Leaders Urge Immigration Reform," Pew Research Center, September 6, 2013. Available at: http://www.pewresearch.org/fact-tank/2013/09/06/demographics-play-role-in-catholic-leaders-push-for-immigration-bill/.

45. Lyman A. Kellstedt and Ruth Melkonian-Hoover, "White Evangelicals and Immigration Reform," *The Christian Post*, April 19, 2015.

46. http://evangelicalsforbiblicalimmigration.com.

of mostly democratic polities, they should strive to represent a consensus view within their churches. Otherwise they will create resentment among their members and are likely not to be taken seriously by policymakers or, ultimately, the media."[47]

Assessing Evangelicals' Political Advocacy

A major strength of Evangelical engagement on immigration is its concern with the inclusion of immigrants into American society. In particular, they have expressed concern for the plight of unauthorized aliens living in the shadows of society. Believing that all humans are entitled to dignity, Evangelicals have emphasized the need to treat all migrants, regardless of their legal status, with love and compassion. In many communities, churches provide humanitarian relief, and some churches have established centers that offer low-cost legal aid to immigrants. World Relief, NAE's humanitarian relief arm, has played an important role in assisting tens of thousands of refugees to integrate into local communities and has also provided migrants with language training, legal assistance, and basic living necessities. But meeting human needs and treating migrants with dignity and compassion is one thing; seeking to reform existing immigration policy, which is the concern of the SBC, the NAE, and several of its member denominations, is a radically different and more challenging task.

Evangelical political advocacy for immigration reform suffers from several shortcomings. First, it overemphasizes social inclusion—"welcoming the stranger"—and deemphasizes obedience to lawful authority, that is, rendering to Caesar the things that belong to Caesar. Inclusion is a hallmark of the church, but the international community is a society of states, each with its own laws, customs, and social practices. Because the kingdom of Christ is a universal community, the church can exist without boundaries. But the state is responsible to control the affairs within its territorial boundaries. Without sovereign control, there is no state; without a state, no law enforcement is possible. Not surprisingly, citizens regularly make border security a priority. For example, a 2013 survey by the PRRI found that the moral values Americans considered most important in carrying out immigration reform were national security (84 percent), family unity (84 percent), protecting human dignity

47. Tooley, "Evangelical Grassroots versus 'Grasstops.'"

(82 percent), and fairness to taxpayers (77 percent). Only 50 percent of Americans considered following the biblical norm of "welcoming the stranger" important.[48]

A related limitation of Evangelicals' strategy is the moral priority given to compassion over justice. While the church is guided by love, the purpose of government is to advance justice through the impartial application of law. Some Evangelical leaders claim that the current policies are unjust because too few visas are available for family reunification or because the waiting time for such visas impedes family unification. But these leaders fail to explain how giving precedence to the millions of undocumented aliens is consistent with public justice, especially when millions of migrants have followed existing rules and waited patiently for an opportunity to come to the United States. Some leaders have argued that undocumented aliens have entered the country not to violate the law but simply to care for the needs of their families. Such a perspective assumes that the quest for better living conditions justifies unlawful entry. But if the rule of law is to be sustained, individuals must obey laws. Some pro-immigrant advocates argue that the immigration system is broken and that many of its parts contribute to injustice. But until new laws are adopted, people must obey existing rules and follow established procedures.

Third, Evangelicals' advocacy underestimates the political costs of disregarding the laws governing admission. For example, in his 2009 testimony to a US Senate subcommittee, Leith Anderson, president of the NAE, minimized unlawful entry into the country by declaring that "undocumented immigrants who have otherwise been law-abiding members should be offered a pathway to citizenship."[49] Richard Land has similarly minimized illegality by claiming that the US government and American people need to accept some responsibility for the plight of undocumented workers: "The 12 million undocumented workers are a testament to our federal government's disrespect for its own immigration laws under both Democrat and Republican administrations."[50] Land ar-

48. Public Religion Research Institute, "Citizenship, Values and Cultural Concerns: What Americans Want From Immigration Reform," 2013, 34. Available at: http://public religion.org/site/wp-content/uploads/2013/03/2013-Immigration-Report-Layout-For-Web2.pdf.

49. Leith Anderson, Hearing on Faith-Based Community Perspectives on Comprehensive Immigration Reform, Senate Judiciary Subcommittee on Immigration, Border Security, and Refugees (October 8, 2009). Available at: https://www.judiciary.senate.gov/imo/media/doc/10-08-09%20Anderson%20testimony.pdf.

50. Richard Land, "God and Immigration Reform," USA Today, August 15, 2010.

gues that applying laws retroactively is wrong and unfair. But contrary to Land, delayed accountability for avoiding border inspection is not simply the result of governmental officials' failure to enforce the law but a consequence of people entering and living "in the shadows." The problem of unlawful migration would not exist if aliens did not enter or remain in the United States in willful disregard of US federal law.

Fourth, Evangelical leaders tend to disregard the unintended effects of legalization of unauthorized aliens. Advocates of comprehensive immigration reform correctly assume that the existence of an underground, unauthorized community is problematic. But the challenge is how to reduce the number of unauthorized aliens without further undermining the rule of law. Social scientists note that disregarding or limiting the consequences of harmful and unlawful behavior will only perpetuate unwanted behaviors. This phenomenon, known as "moral hazard," was demonstrated in the 1986 immigration law that provided amnesty to some 3 million illegal aliens. The 1986 statute failed to halt unlawful entry. Indeed, by 2005 the total number of unlawful migrants had risen to more than 12 million.

A fifth shortcoming of Evangelicals' advocacy campaign is the willingness to encourage forgiveness for unlawful behavior. In emphasizing the need for compassion and mercy for the irregular migrants, NAE president Anderson declared that "the process of redemption and restitution is core to Christian beliefs, as we were all once lost and redeemed through love of Jesus Christ."[51] To be sure, Evangelical leaders championing legalization have claimed that their initiative is not amnesty but rather a process of "earned citizenship."[52] What is less clear, however, is why Evangelicals have championed mercy over legal accountability and forgiveness over justice. Molly Worthen offers a plausible explanation. She argues that whether or not unauthorized aliens are viewed as criminals or victims trapped in an unjust system will depend on how one views sin and responsibility. If sin is conceived of chiefly as individual wrongdoing, then one is likely to emphasize personal culpability for unlawful entry. If, on the other hand, unlawful behavior is viewed as a result of a flawed, unjust immigration system, then guilt shifts from the indi-

51. The failure to control unlawful migration was due in part to the government's unwillingness to secure the border and to ensure compliance with the required verification of an employee's legal status.

52. For example, Land argues that the restitutionary process is not a gift but a conditional grant based on payment of back taxes, a security screening, and appropriate fees. See Land, "God and Immigration Reform."

vidual to the impersonal structures and institutions.[53] But the problem for Evangelicals in adopting the structural explanation for guilt is that it is inconsistent with the theological pillars of Evangelicalism discussed earlier in this chapter. As I have observed above, Evangelicals emphasize that sin is centered in the desires and actions of individuals, not the injustices of political and economic structures. Accordingly, God's grace is available not to collectives but to persons who are penitent and willing to acknowledge their sin. The collective justification for wrongdoing is not only inconsistent with Evangelical thought but is, on the contrary, in line with the progressive "social gospel" advocated by Walter Rauschenbusch and other Protestant liberals a century ago.

In the final analysis, Evangelical advocacy of immigration reform is problematic because it overemphasizes political action and neglects political ethics. Rather than seeking to carry out a campaign of moral education on the political theology of migration, Evangelical groups have behaved like a political interest group. By focusing on policy reform, however, Evangelical denominations and associations have deprived society—and in particular, its church members, citizens, and public-policy officials—of the church's teaching of biblical morality. When churches pursue advocacy, as Evangelical church leaders have done, they not only neglect an opportunity to highlight biblical teachings in their area of professional competence; they also speak about areas of public affairs in which they have limited competence. Thus, when preachers get overly involved in public-policy concerns such as immigration reform, they run the risk of undermining their own spiritual and moral authority. Finally, since politics is always a divisive and contentious arena, when church leaders seek to advance specific policy reforms, they run the risk of introducing division within their congregations.[54]

In conclusion, Evangelical groups have contributed to the public-policy debate on US immigration by raising awareness of the system's shortcomings and calling for significant reforms in existing statutes. Fundamentally, Evangelical leaders have used Scripture to call for a more liberal and flexible immigration system. In justifying such changes, Evangelicals have emphasized biblical teachings that highlight the uni-

53. Molly Worthen, "Love Thy Stranger as Thyself," *The New York Times*, May 11, 2013.

54. A lesson of mainline Protestant political advocacy during the Cold War era was that the initiatives of church leaders rarely represented the views of the rank and file. Indeed, most denominational public policy resolutions reflected the more progressive views of church leaders rather than the more moderate views of parishioners.

versality of human dignity, the need for compassion toward people in need, and the need to welcome strangers (foreigners). For the most part, church declarations and denominational statements have set forth biblical principles relevant to migration from the perspective of a cosmopolitan world rather than from the existing system of nation-states. While leaders have acknowledged states' rights to regulate borders, their declarations and analyses focus on the need to welcome and care for migrants. There is little or no moral analysis of the competing and conflicting moral claims of citizens and migrants or of the relative merit of family-based and employment-based migration. They even neglect the subject of how to weigh the claims of refugees against those of regular migrants. For the most part, the immigration initiatives of Evangelicals have focused on policy advocacy, not moral education. This is regrettable because the most important contribution churches can make to policy debates is at the moral level. Political interest groups can seek to advance their particular interests through advocacy. But churches have a unique contribution to make in the world of public affairs. That contribution is moral education, not political advocacy. As decision-makers continue to weigh the merits of how best to strengthen the American immigration system, Evangelical groups can make a unique contribution to the policy debate by illuminating biblical norms, identifying key ethical issues, and showing how proximate justice can be advanced.

Other Protestant Churches
and US Immigration Policy

Historically, Protestant Christianity has shaped the values, traditions, and cultural norms of the American people. When the Puritans first settled in New England in the early seventeenth century, they brought with them their religious beliefs and moral values, which helped to define the nation's nascent identity. The moral-cultural system that emerged prioritized values such as human frailty, personal spiritual redemption, human liberty (especially religious freedom), individual responsibility, distrust of centralized institutions, and the need for governmental accountability. In the late eighteenth century, the founding fathers, in designing the political institutions of the new nation, relied heavily on Protestant assumptions about human nature, personal responsibility, liberty, and individual rights. As America evolved and matured institutionally throughout the nineteenth and twentieth centuries, Protestant Christianity continued to influence the evolution of the nation's social, cultural, and political life.[1]

However, despite Protestantism's profound early impact on the United States, Protestant churches had begun to decline by the 1970s, and by the beginning of the new millennium, they had lost more than one-third of their membership and much of their religious and cultural influence. According to the Pew Research Center, 14.7 percent of US adults were affiliated with the major Protestant churches in 2014, while Evangelicals accounted for 25.4 percent and Catholics 20.8 percent.[2]

1. Joseph Bottum, "The Death of Protestant America: A Political Theory of the Protestant Mainline," *First Things* (August/September, 2008).

2. David Masci, "Compared with other Christian groups, Evangelicals' Dropoff is Less Steep," Pew Research Center, May 15, 2015. Available at: http://www.pewresearch.org/fact-tank/2015/05/15/compared-with-other-christian-groups-evangelicals-dropoff-is-less-steep/.

This chapter examines the nature and role of Mainline Protestant churches in the immigration debate.[3] In the first part of the chapter I briefly sketch the significant role of Protestant religious beliefs and values on the nation's development. Next, I briefly discuss some key elements of Mainline political ethics. Third, I examine how Mainline churches have addressed immigration concerns, focusing specifically on several significant denominational initiatives. In the final section, I analyze how the Lutheran Church Missouri Synod (LCMS) has addressed this issue. Although the LCMS is a major Protestant church (with more than two million members), it is not a part of the Mainline nor is it associated with the National Association of Evangelicals. Rather, it is a Protestant church that hews to an orthodox interpretation of Scripture and to a conservative perspective on cultural, social, and political issues. I focus on the LCMS's approach to immigration issues because of the careful theological study that the denomination issued in 2012 regarding immigration reform.

Protestant Religion and American Society

Protestant religion—especially manifested through Congregational, Episcopalian, Methodist, and Presbyterian churches—has influenced American society in two fundamental ways. First, the Protestant faith has helped to nurture fundamental values for the American nation through the dissemination of religious beliefs, ideals, and values. Protestant Christianity, in effect, has provided the political theology justifying the ideals and institutions of the American political experiment in self-government. In his book *Who Are We? The Challenges to America's National Identity*, the distinguished political scientist Samuel P. Huntington argues that the foundation of the United States' identity is found in the cultural and religious roots of Protestantism.[4] He claims that Protestant values—such as the inherent worth of persons, individual responsibility, religious freedom, and dissent—provided the moral basis for the Found-

3. Although there are more than thirty different Protestant denominations in the United States, the largest ones comprise the "Mainline." These include the following church groups: the American Baptist Church, the Episcopal Church, the Evangelical Lutheran Church of America (ELCA), the Presbyterian Church USA (PCUSA), the United Church of Christ (formerly the Congregational Church), and the United Methodist Church.

4. Samuel P. Huntington, *Who Are We? The Challenges to America's National Identity* (New York: Simon and Schuster, 2005).

ing Fathers' core political ideals. These core beliefs, which he terms the American creed, are important but insufficient to unify and sustain a nation. For Huntington, the more important source of communal bonding is culture. In the American context, this source is the Anglo-Protestant culture, an amalgamation of religious beliefs and cultural norms that bind people together.

Second, Protestant values helped structure public affairs. One manifestation of Protestantism's public role was the emergence of a civil religion that relied on religious language to define and justify political action. While Protestant churches may have, at times, been overly engaged in public life, their role in defining and structuring the dominant values and political morality of the American people cannot be denied. Even though the churches had different theological beliefs and organizational practices, the leading Protestant denominations contributed to a common moral-cultural order, providing a vocabulary and political morality that helped structure the conceptualization of important domestic and international public affairs.[5] Through their public witness, Protestant churches advanced Christian ideals and provided moral guideposts on public-policy concerns. According to Joseph Bottum, "Protestantism helped define the nation, operating as simultaneously the happy enabler and the unhappy conscience of the American republic—a single source for both national comfort and national unease."[6]

In view of the historical legacy of Protestantism in American society, one of the most important but surprising developments in the late twentieth century was the dramatic decline in the size and influence of the major Protestant churches. In 1960, Mainline Protestant denominations accounted for 25 percent of all church members; by 2003 this percentage had fallen to 15.[7] Membership fell among all Mainline churches, with the

5. To a great degree, the significant influence of Protestant churches in American public life was facilitated by their inter-denominational cooperation. Such cooperation was made possible by the establishment of the Federal Council of Churches in 1908 and its successor organization, the National Council of Churches (NCC), in 1950.

6. Bottum, "Death of Protestant America."

7. This decline is evident in the large and rapid fall in church membership in the principal Protestant denominations, including Methodist, Episcopalian, Presbyterian, and Lutheran churches. While the National Council of Churches (NCC)—with thirty-six denominations—continues to claim some 100,000 congregations with about 45 million members, this membership estimate grossly overstates the size of the Mainline. To begin with, many churches overstate their membership because they include persons who were legitimately added to the membership list but who have stopped attending or have moved away. (The counting of church members is difficult since there are no widely

most precipitous declines experienced by the United Methodist Church (from 11 million members to 8.2 million), the Episcopal Church (from 3.6 million members to 1.9 million), and the Presbyterian Church USA (from 3.2 million members to 2.4).[8] As Kenneth Woodward wrote in a feature article in *Newsweek* in 1993, Mainline churches were "running out of money, members and meaning."[9] The fall in Mainline membership resulted in dramatic changes in the National Council of Churches, the association of Protestant denominations. In its heyday in the 1960s, the NCC boasted a staff of more than six hundred persons in its New York City headquarters, the so-called "God-box" on Riverside Drive. But by 2015, the NCC had a staff of fewer than ten and had all but disappeared from public life.

The most important result of the Mainline's collapse was not the decline in membership but the loss of cultural and social influence. Protestant preachers and theologians previously had significant influence on American cultural life in the mid-twentieth century, but by the beginning of the twenty-first century, Mainline Protestant churches had lost nearly all influence in American public life. Unlike earlier times, Mainline churches were no longer able to play an important role in structuring moral reasoning on political affairs. According to Bottum, the collapse of the Mainline, which he calls "the central fact of our time," is important because Protestant institutions have lost their credibility to influence the moral-cultural ethos undergirding the American nation. In his words, "the Mainline has lost the capacity to set, or even significantly influence, the national vocabulary or the national self-understanding."[10]

One of the major consequences of the decline of the Mainline has been the reduced number of public-policy initiatives undertaken by churches. Where Protestant denominations had been deeply involved in addressing domestic and foreign-policy concerns in the 1960s and 1970s, in the new millennium Mainline churches have by and large devoted few resources to public affairs. Their chief concern is no longer how to influence national social and political life but rather how to stem

---

accepted standards for membership. It is easy to add the names of family members who join a local church. But it is unclear how membership totals are affected when church members move, simply stop attending, or their children move on.)

8. Walter Russell Mead, "God's Country?," *Foreign Affairs* 85 (September/October 2006): 36.

9. Kenneth L. Woodward, "Dead End for the Mainline? The Mightiest Protestants Are Running Out of Money, Members and Meaning," *Newsweek*, August 9, 1993, 46–48.

10. Bottum, "Death of Protestant America."

membership decline. As a result, most Protestant denominations have devoted fewer resources to the US immigration debate than either Catholics or Evangelicals.

Mainline Political Ethics

Liberal Protestants, like Evangelicals, build their political ethics on the Protestant political theology as I have presented it in chapter 5. Where Evangelicals reinforce orthodoxy by emphasizing the spiritual demands of the kingdom of God, Mainline believers emphasize the temporal responsibilities in the "City of Man," making social justice a priority. Additionally, where Evangelicals emphasize the authority and sufficiency of Scripture, Mainline Protestants emphasize the role of reason in addressing temporal concerns of political community. Finally, Mainline ethics gives priority to global, universal concerns over those of groups and nations. The following is a brief examination of each of these distinctive features.

The importance of the City of Man

As I have noted above, while Protestant theology emphasized the all-embracing sovereignty of God over all creation, it also emphasized the radically different way that the divine will was carried out in the "City of Man" and the "City of God." These two realms, which are frequently associated with the state and the church, have radically different purposes, involve different structures, and represent different human responsibilities. Although Protestants have historically developed a variety of theologies to interpret the nature and role of the two kingdoms, the modern division between the Protestant Mainline and Evangelicals provides a stark divergence in priorities. Whereas Evangelicals emphasize the spiritual domain, Mainline churches give greater emphasis to temporal responsibilities. For liberal Protestants, salvation is not simply redemption from sin but also the restoration of broken societies, the renewal of peace, and the pursuit of justice within and among human communities. From the Mainline perspective, the task of the church is not simply to proclaim the gospel but to bear witness through teaching and service of God's love for all humans—a task that inevitably requires reflection and action in the social and political sphere. While love can be expressed through acts of charity, it also demands service in the social, economic, and political realms of society.

The priority of social justice

One of the consequences of liberal Protestantism's emphasis on temporal concerns is the shift in priorities from individual sin to social sin, from personal redemption to collective salvation. This alternative approach gives priority to human progress by contributing to public policies that advance human dignity and social justice. In *Christ and Culture*, H. Richard Niebuhr identifies various ways that Christians have historically sought to relate culture (the temporal realm of social, political, and cultural life) to Christ (the spiritual realm). One of these traditions views citizenship in the heavenly kingdom and the temporal state as being harmonious. As Niebuhr observed, the followers of this tradition of the "Christ of culture" "feel no great tension between church and world, the gospel and social laws, the workings of divine grace and human effort, the ethics of salvation and the ethics of social conservation or progress."[11]

To a significant degree, Mainline political ethics has been influenced by this progressive tradition. Rather than emphasizing the tension between the demands of faith and the responsibilities of temporal citizenship, liberal Protestants have sought to advance social progress. For them, the church's task is not simply to nurture personal spirituality but to advance social justice within communities. But as theologian Stanley Hauerwas has noted, in the attempt to control society, Christians have too readily accepted the prevailing liberal ideas of society and have failed to teach and model Christian values and practices. In effect, the church has failed to be the church. Indeed, Hauerwas calls into question the efforts of Christians to advance justice, not because he opposes justice but because he assumes that Christians' concept of justice is rooted in the presuppositions of liberal societies rather than in divine revelation. He writes, "Out of an understandable desire to be politically and socially relevant, we [Christians] lose the critical ability to stand against the limits of our social orders. We forget that the first thing as Christians we have to hold before any society is not justice but God."[12]

---

11. H. Richard Niebuhr, *Christ and Culture* (New York: Harper Torchbooks, 1951), 83.

12. Stanley Hauerwas, *After Christendom? How the Church Is to Behave if Freedom, Justice, and a Christian Nation Are Bad Ideas* (Nashville: Abingdon, 1991), 68.

The important role of reason

According to J. Philip Wogaman, a Methodist pastor and professor of Christian ethics, one of the major tensions in Christian ethics is between divine revelation and human reason. He says that the biblical perspective "would seem to suggest that serious thought about ethics must employ both revelation and reason, although the meaning of revelation, the nature of reason, and the proper way to employ the two together have been elaborated in very different ways through Christian history."[13] Although Protestantism emphasizes the centrality and authority of Scripture in addressing spiritual life, Christians have historically held a variety of views about the manner and degree that reason should supplement biblical revelation. Whereas Evangelicals have emphasized the sufficiency of Scripture, liberal Protestantism relies heavily on reason not only to interpret biblical revelation but also to guide and inspire human behavior. For Mainline believers, the quest for justice and human rights, for example, is defined primarily as human initiatives based on human reason. Thus, where Evangelicals tend to justify their political and social initiatives with Scriptural references, Mainline Protestants tend to define and justify their political advocacy through reason instead of revelation.

The priority of global identity

A fourth element of Mainline political ethics is the priority given to universalism over group identity. The primacy of global responsibilities is expressed by the Mainline's emphasis on such concerns as protecting and promoting international human rights, caring for the needs of foreign peoples suffering from poverty and oppression, promoting international peace, and protecting the global commons from environmental degradation. Since all persons are morally entitled to dignity, some Mainline churches claim that universal bonds should take precedence over the particular tribal, national, and ethnic subdivisions of the world. According to Wogaman, the tension between group identity and universalism is one of six major issues in Christian ethics.[14] The tension arises from the fact that God selected a nation (the Jewish people of Israel) to illu-

13. J. Philip Wogaman, *Christian Ethics: A Historical Introduction* (Louisville: Westminster/John Knox, 1993), 5.
14. Wogaman, *Christian Ethics*, 6.

minate love, righteousness, moral accountability, and redemption from sin while also sending his son, Jesus, to redeem humans from sin through his death and resurrection. A Presbyterian report on immigration titled "Transformation of Churches and Society through Encounters with New Neighbors" (1999) defines this tension as follows: "God's love knows no boundaries, yet nation-states draw boundaries very tightly to limit the entrance of 'outsiders.' Christ overcomes the walls of hostility, which divide peoples, yet nation-states divide people according to national membership and use fences, walls and armed forces to keep peoples separated. Christians live with and within this tension."[15] In view of the tension between nation and the world in biblical revelation, how should Christians conceive of the church—as a denomination or a worldwide society of believers? Even if subordinated to the universal claims of global society, what is the place of the nation, ethnic groupings, and religious affiliations? While these subgroups are important, the primary community is global society—a view rooted in the universality and equality of all persons. Because of the importance of universalism, Christian churches in general and Mainline congregations in particular emphasize the need for freedom of movement among the world's countries and the need to respond with compassion towards migrants seeking refuge or desiring a better standard of living.

Mainline Protestantism and US Immigration

Since the 1990s, the largest Protestant churches have been politically engaged with regard to US immigration concerns to varying degrees. Although some churches have issued short reports and declarations, few denominations have examined the challenges of immigration from a biblical perspective. For the most part, the primary concern of the Mainline has been a policy that would increase immigration and facilitate the legalization of unauthorized aliens. They have not sought to inspire or guide *theological* reflection on immigration; rather, their chief concern has been to advance immigration reform *politically*. Below I briefly sketch some of the most important church initiatives, focusing on the reports by

15. General Assembly, PCUSA, "Transformation of Churches and Society through Encounters with New Neighbors." Available at: http://www.pcusa.org/media/uploads/ _resolutions/encounter-with-new-neighbors-1999.pdf. Hereafter, page references to this document appear in parentheses within the text.

the Presbyterian Church (USA), the Episcopalian Church, and the Evangelical Lutheran Church of America (ELCA).

The Presbyterian Church (USA)

The PCUSA periodically addresses migration issues pertaining to refugees, asylum, and immigration law. At its 206th General Assembly (1989), the biennial conference of Presbyterian leaders, pastors, and laypersons, the delegates adopted a resolution that called for Presbyterians to "work and pray for a just and compassionate US immigration policy."[16] At the 211th General Assembly (1999), the official delegates approved an important study titled "Transformation of Churches and Society through Encounters with New Neighbors" (TCS, 1). The TCS report, which was the work of the church's Advisory Committee on Social Witness, was written to assist Presbyterian churches in addressing rising immigration concerns. In endorsing the TCS report, the General Assembly resolution states that the Christian faith provides an opportunity to break down barriers and heal divisions while fostering churches that are more inclusive. The resolution declares, "Whereas fears may incline us to self-protectiveness, faith in the promise of God in Christ can launch our churches into adventurous encounters with new neighbors that will transform churches and energize us for more expanded ministry."

The TCS report provides a brief historical overview of US policy toward refugees, asylum seekers, and immigrants, and it highlights important theological and ethical convictions that have guided the church's teachings on immigration. Some of theological tenets examined include: (1) the need to care for basic human needs; (2) the inherent worth of persons because they are created in God's image; (3) the confession that Jesus Christ as Lord transforms "strangers" into neighbors; (4) the responsibility to challenge and shape immigration policy; (5) the need to pursue justice for migrants; and (6) the challenge for believers to reconcile the competing responsibilities to Christ and the nation (TCS, 14–18). The report's concluding section describes principles that should guide individual thought and action on immigration policy, including: (1) eliminating discrimination and racism; (2) adhering to international human rights laws; (3) protecting the legal rights of refugees, asylum seekers, and

---

16. "Presbyterian Policy on Immigration." Available at: https://www.pcusa.org/site_media/media/uploads/oga/pdf/immigration-resolution-2006.pdf.

immigrants; (4) ensuring a generous immigration policy; and (5) ensuring that immigration law is enforced humanely (TCS, 18-22). The report also includes a study guide to encourage group discussion and moral reflection on immigration concerns.

From a social perspective, the report encourages individuals and groups to welcome migrants: "God is opening up profound opportunities for churches to make friends with new neighbors in our communities," it declares (TCS, 8). Therefore, the report's gist is that Christians should be especially loving and compassionate in welcoming these neighbors into their communities and churches. Perhaps some churches have neglected the biblical message of inclusiveness and need to be reminded of the need to show love and nondiscrimination in their collective witness to society. And it is clear that some groups exhibit xenophobia and distrust of aliens—as demonstrated by the anti-immigrant movements throughout American history. While such sentiments continue to be periodically expressed by some American groups, the limitations of contemporary immigration policy derive not from anti-immigrant sentiments but from the system's inherent shortcomings (as I have discussed in chapter 3).

From a public-policy perspective, an important shortcoming of the TCS report is its failure to assess the limitations of the existing immigration laws and practices in light of biblical and theological principles. Although some believers may need to be reminded to be caring and compassionate toward strangers, the most important need in advancing a more just immigration system is robust moral analysis. Given the church's competence in biblical teaching, the report could have illuminated biblical norms, shown how to reconcile competing responsibilities to church and state, and provided ethical principles for reforming existing immigration policies. Regrettably, the study provides few resources or perspectives on either how to balance competing citizenship claims or how to assess the moral claims of migrants and citizens. If Christians are to assist in creating a more humane immigration system, they have to do so both as members of the universal church and as members of particular political communities.

In adopting the TCS study, the Presbyterian General Assembly formally endorsed the report's principles and policy recommendations and provided additional advocacy initiatives. The additional recommendations included more generous admissions of refugees, support for due-process rights for migrants, opposition to the militarization of the nation's borders, and the repeal of parts of the Illegal Immigration Reform and Immigration Responsibility Act (1996), a law that sought to curb illegal immigration via increased sanctions and expedited removal.[17] The recommendations were all consistent with the church's emphasis on establishing a more flexible and generous immigration system that de-emphasized the distinction between legal immigration and unauthorized migration.

In 2004, the PCUSA General Assembly approved an additional report on immigration. Titled "Comprehensive Legalization Program for Immigrants Living and Working in the United States," the new study sought to address the problem arising from the presence of a growing number of unauthorized immigrants in the United States. The 2004 report acknowledges that because of the gap between the availability and demand for visas, a significant backlog has emerged. Since unauthorized aliens are not permitted to regularize their status without leaving the country, many migrants choose to live and work in the shadows. As a result, the study suggests that immigration reform is necessary, though it should avoid excessive concern with border security, since such a focus might inhibit Christians in their love of strangers. "Our only true security," the report declares, "is to be found in God, not in constructing walls that separate us from others."[18]

Instead of focusing on border security, the report argues, Christians should support giving legal status to unauthorized migrants. In justifying such legalization, the report makes an extraordinary claim: that irregular aliens have ignored immigration law "because they no longer have confidence in the justice and effectiveness of this law."[19] If laws are unjust and ineffective, it is the prerogative of citizens to change the laws. But until the change is carried out through legitimate institutions, the existing law must be regarded as binding. The report does not provide a biblical or moral justification for legalization. Instead, the study's biblical and theological analysis focuses on theological "insights" that emphasize solidarity and inclusion rather than justice and the rule of law.

In 2012, the 220th General Assembly adopted two resolutions updating the church's advocacy on immigration concerns. The first calls

17. It is illuminating that the TCS report incorrectly calls the 1996 law the Immigration Reform and Immigration Responsibility Act (IRIRA). The correct title is Illegal Immigration Reform and Immigration Responsibility Act (IIRIRA), which better reflects the fundamental aim of the law, which was to address the rise in unauthorized migration.

18. PCUSA, General Assembly (2004), "Comprehensive Legalization Program for Immigrants Living and Working in the United States," 5.

19. PCUSA, "Comprehensive Legalization Program," 6.

on church leaders and congregations to make the welfare of immigrants and unauthorized migrants a priority. The second, titled "On Advocating for Comprehensive Immigration Reform," sets forth ideas on making the US immigration system more effective and just. The recommendations, many of which were developed by the American Immigration Lawyers Association, include the following: (1) make family unity a priority; (2) permit unauthorized aliens to legalize their status; (3) eliminate long detention for migrants; (4) ensure that legal enforcement is humane; and (5) ensure that workers' rights are protected.

The Episcopal Church

At the 2006 General Convention of the Episcopal Church, conference delegates approved a short report on immigration, "The Alien among You," which called on Christians to welcome strangers and encouraged Episcopal Church members to support comprehensive immigration reform. According to the report, the US immigration system was not working well and needed significant revisions. Although there was no biblical or theological analysis, the Episcopal Church nonetheless adopted a resolution endorsing the following immigration reform guidelines:

1. undocumented aliens should be able to pursue permanent residency;
2. legal workers should be allowed to enter the United States to meet labor needs;
3. family members should be permitted to reunite with lawful relatives;
4. legal due process should be granted to all persons;
5. enforcement of border security and immigration policies should be "proportional and humane."[20]

At its 2010 General Convention, the Episcopal Church released an important theological study on immigration titled "The Nation and the Common Good: Reflections on Immigration Reform" (NCG study).[21] The study is noteworthy because it explores the relationship of temporal

20. Episcopal Church, General Convention, 2006, "The Alien among You." Available at: http://madreanna.org/immref/alien.pdf.

21. House of Bishops, Episcopal Church, "The Nation and the Common Good: Reflections on Immigration Reform," September 21, 2010. Available at: http://www.episcopalchurch.org/notice/house-bishops-issues-pastoral-letter-along-theological-resource-%C2%93-nation-and-common-good-refl.

responsibilities within a nation to the broader spiritual responsibilities of membership in the universal church. The NCG study examines the interrelationship of church and state from the perspective of the Anglican theological tradition. Using the writings of Richard Hooker, a sixteenth-century Christian political thinker, it explores how the Anglican tradition provides insights concerning how Christians should view citizenship in the nation and within the church. Whereas most Protestants have emphasized a deep chasm between the church and the state, Hooker argued for close cooperation between the two realms. According to the NCG report, the Anglican tradition regards the nation-state "as an essentially moral enterprise, in which a relatively diverse collection of people from different local regions, speaking different local dialects, belonging to different classes and harboring different religious views, are expected to achieve common ground."[22] While expressing solidarity with members of one's nation is vital, it is also important that commitments not be confined to the nation. Rather, compassion and care, impelled by God's love, must be extended to migrants and to peoples from other nations.

Since the church must always be an inclusive, welcoming community, Christians are called to follow Jesus by expressing love and compassion to strangers. The NCG study declares that, in addressing the problems arising from unauthorized aliens, the church's "starting point" must involve advocacy "for every undocumented worker, each one of whom is someone for whom Christ died."[23] This does not mean, however, that Christians must necessarily support legalization, especially if some citizens believe that such action would condone illegality. The report declares that, to the extent that Episcopalians rely on the Anglican tradition of church-nation alliance and take responsibilities to the nation seriously, it is important that Christians pay as much attention to the claims of fellow citizens as they do to the claims of unauthorized migrants. Thus, while Christians must make humanitarian concerns a priority, resolving the status of unauthorized aliens is challenging because the needs of citizens must also be taken into account. The report explains the importance of citizens' concerns as follows:

> The claim of the vulnerable is always a strong claim, and undocumented workers are unquestionably vulnerable. Yet so is the claim of those with whom we have entered into covenant as fellow citizens, if,

22. Episcopal Church, "The Nation and the Common Good."
23. Episcopal Church, "The Nation and the Common Good."

indeed, we, as Episcopalians, regard the modern nation as a collection of more or less diverse communities and individuals who have agreed to engage with one another as equals and, insofar as they are fellow citizens to love one another. Those who are related to each other by such a covenant have a prior claim on one another. This is so because they depend on one another for the fulfillment of the common goal, which the national covenant is meant to serve.

When the Episcopal Church released the NCG study, it also issued a pastoral letter on immigration.[24] It is interesting that while the study provides a nuanced theological reflection on immigration, the brief pastoral letter sets forth a set of policy reforms that do not necessarily emerge from the study's analysis. Some of the principal church concerns on immigration include: (1) condemnation of "inhumane" law enforcement against unauthorized aliens; (2) opposition to racism and racial profiling of unauthorized aliens; and (3) passively accepting the labor of undocumented workers without accepting responsibility for them. In particular, the letter calls for the creation of a more just immigration system that involves a path to citizenship for unauthorized workers, greater concern for family unification, and an effective system for temporary or seasonal guest workers.

In 2010, the Episcopal Diocese of Maryland also released a pastoral letter on immigration reform titled "Welcoming the Stranger."[25] Written by the diocese's two bishops, it provides biblical principles for assessing migration and offers several recommendations on how to establish a more humane system. In particular, the letter recommends that unauthorized migrants living in the United States be permitted to become citizens. The bishops make a bold claim: "People who have come here to overcome poverty, to escape war, or to fulfill economic demands in this country should be able to become permanent members of our society." The bishops provide no theological, moral, or prudential rationale for this recommended action. The only apparent justification is the recognition that migrants have become part of American society and want to remain

24. Episcopal Church, "A Pastoral Letter from the House of Bishops." Available at: http://www.episcopalchurch.org/notice/house-bishops-issues-pastoral-letter-along -theological-resource-%C2%93-nation-and-common-good-refl.

25. Eugene Taylor Sutton and John L. Rabb, "Welcoming the Stranger: A Pastoral Letter Addressing the Need for Comprehensive Immigration Reform." Available at: http://www.collegeforbishops.org/assets/1145/2010-09-02-pastoral-ltr-immig-english .pdf.

in the country. The bishops declare, "We need their contribution, and we should welcome their presence and receive them as fellow citizens." But simply welcoming aliens who have disregarded immigration law is morally problematic. To be sure, the American immigration system has many limitations, but those limitations do not necessarily justify unlawful behavior.

Individual citizens are, of course, entitled to advocate whatever measures they believe will advance a more humane immigration system. But when a denomination speaks on a public-policy issue, as the Episcopalian House of Bishops and the Maryland Diocese did by way of their pastoral letters, it should do so by providing theological justification. Regrettably, the Episcopal Church has failed to do so. The NCG study provides invaluable theological insights into church and state, but this careful analysis is not integrated into the pastoral letters issued by the House of Bishops and by the Maryland Diocese.

The Evangelical Lutheran Church of America (ELCA)

The Lutheran church in America was established by immigrants from northern Europe in the mid-nineteenth century. However, the Lutheran church was not created as a single, unified denomination but rather as a variety of distinct church groups (synods), each representing immigrants from a particular country or region. Although Lutheranism held core beliefs in common, rooted in the authority of Scripture and affirmed in the Augsburg Confession of 1530, synods tended to develop distinct beliefs and practices that frequently resulted in divisions among Lutheran churches.[26] At the beginning of the new millennium, the three major Lutheran churches in the United States were the Evangelical Lutheran Church in America (ELCA), the Lutheran Church Missouri Synod (LCMS), and the Wisconsin Evangelical Lutheran Synod (WELS). The

---

26. The Missouri Synod Lutheran Church was founded in 1847 by German immigrants to Missouri; this was followed by the creation of Wisconsin Evangelical Lutheran Synod (WELS) in 1850, and the Augustana Evangelical Lutheran Church in 1860 by Swedish immigrants. Subsequently, other Lutheran church groups were established, including the Danish-American Lutheran Church in 1872 (later named the United Danish Evangelical Church), the Finnish Evangelical Lutheran Church in 1890, and the Norwegian Lutheran Church in 1917. In 1918, three German-American synods merged to establish the United Lutheran Church in America (ULCA), and in 1930 the Iowa Synod and the Buffalo Synod merged to form the American Lutheran Church (ALC).

ELCA (with about 3.8 million members) is a progressive Mainline church that is a part of the National Council of Churches (NCC); the LCMS (with about 2.3 million members) is a more theologically conservative denomination and not considered part of the Mainline; the Wisconsin Synod (with about 380,000 members) is also a theologically conservative denomination and, like the LCMS, is not a member of the NCC. Here I address immigration concerns of the ELCA. In the next section I examine the work of the LCMS.

The ELCA, a denomination with deep nineteenth-century immigrant roots, has frequently expressed concern for immigrants. In 1969, the Lutheran Council in the United States issued a statement describing important denominational objectives for a fair and generous immigration system. The key objectives included offering a generous admission to new migrants, using nondiscriminatory criteria in selecting immigrants, and providing reasonable access to citizenship to all aliens admitted for permanent residence. To promote a generous immigration system, the Council urged, among other things, that priority be given to family reunification, skilled workers, and refugees.[27]

In 1998, the ELCA's Church Council released an immigration message that was designed as a teaching aid for congregations.[28] The nine-page statement describes the important role of migrants to the economic development of the United States and explains why hospitality to migrants is imperative, why refugees should receive priority by governmental authorities, and why the church must support fair and generous immigration laws. The statement urges Christians to offer support to detained aliens, to make the care of unaccompanied children a priority, and to provide immigration services through congregations.

As the political debate on immigration reform was becoming more prominent in American society in the new millennium, in 2009 the ELCA adopted a policy resolution designed to influence the policy reform. Titled "Toward Compassionate, Just, and Wise Immigration Reform," the eight-page statement sets forth theological principles that should guide immigration policy. It highlights two principles: that all people are created in God's image and that government should serve the common good. The resolution acknowledges that government plays an important

27. ELCA, Division for Church in Society, "A Message on . . . Immigration," 1998, 6-7. Available at: http://download.elca.org/ELCA%20Resource%20Repository/ImmigrationSM.pdf.
28. ELCA, "A Message on . . . Immigration."

role "in facilitating orderly migration and integration, and in preventing migration that might be dangerous or harmful to host communities."[29] Since not all laws are necessarily just, the resolution reminds Christians that they should constantly monitor governance in light of the pervasiveness of sin. "The ELCA's posture toward governing authorities," the resolution declares, "is one of critical respect—respectful of their role to serve the common good, yet critical of unjust and harmful ideologies, structures, and processes."

In the second and third sections, the resolution assesses current US immigration policy and describes key moral concerns about immigration. According to the resolution, the five major issues that should influence policy are: (1) the reuniting of families and integrating the marginalized; (2) protecting workers' rights; (3) establishing just and humane law enforcement; (4) revitalizing refugee resettlement; and (5) assessing the root causes of forced migration.[30] A year after releasing the 2009 resolution, Mark Hanson, the presiding bishop of the ELCA, issued a pastoral letter calling on parishioners to support immigration reform. He justified his call for action based on the truth of God's unlimited love. He observed that the biblical witness is clear: "The distinctions that so often divide humankind are overcome in Christ. By grace through faith on account of Christ we are joined together in a radically inclusive community."[31] For Bishop Hanson, the universal bonds among all people override the political divisions among states.

In assessing the ELCA 2009 resolution, political scientist Peter Meilaender highlights the document's chief limitation, which is also evident in the bishop's pastoral letter, namely, the lack of an adequate theory of the state and a discussion of the purposes of government.[32] While people of good will can agree that countries should treat migrants compassionately, the challenge for government is to devise rules that can result in justice. Since the number of persons who want to immigrate to the United States far exceeds the number government authorities allow in (roughly a million persons per year), the challenge is to devise rules that are sup-

29. ELCA, "Toward Compassionate, Just, and Wise Immigration Reform," 2009, 2. Available at: http://download.elca.org/ELCA%20Resource%20Repository/Immigration_ReformSPR09.pdf?_ga=1.134439793.148149688.1417053813.

30. ELCA, "Toward Compassionate . . . Immigration Reform," 6-7.

31. Bishop Mark Hanson: Time for Immigration Reform, July 20, 2010. Available at: http://day1.org/2211-bishop_mark_hanson_time_for_immigration_reform.

32. Peter C. Meilaender, "Ethics without Political Science," *Journal of Lutheran Ethics* 10 (April 2010).

ported by the American people and are fair and humanely enforced. Welcoming strangers is not a sufficient basis for policy-making. Biblical values and theological principles alone are insufficient to undertake the task of immigration reform, which is why political ethics requires not only knowledge of morality but also domestic politics and international relations. As Meilaender notes, if you want to produce adequate Christian reflection on public policy, you need both ethics and political science.

In sum, Mainline Protestant churches have produced few documents that illuminate the theological and political ethics of immigration. With a few exceptions, they have been more concerned with political advocacy than with moral teaching. And because of their declining influence in American society, they have sought to advance their immigration concerns by cooperating with other religious groups.[33] But these advocacy initiatives have had little impact on either their own church members or the politicians in the branches of government responsible for making and enforcing immigration policies.

The Lutheran Church Missouri Synod Approach to US Immigration

A very different approach to the immigration debate is reflected in the careful theological work of the Lutheran Church Missouri Synod. In view of growing concern among LCMS congregations about how to address immigration issues, in 2008 the president of the denomination formally requested that the church's Commission on Theology and Church Relations (CTCR) prepare a study to assist its members in assessing immigration concerns from a biblical perspective.[34] After careful deliberations over four years, the CTCR released its study, titled "Immigrants

---

33. They have carried out the reform agenda through the Interfaith Immigration Coalition (IIC), a religious advocacy alliance that seeks to promote comprehensive immigration reform. The major aims of the IIC have been to legalize unauthorized aliens living in the United States and to facilitate the integration of migrants into American society. As an advocacy organization, the coalition has sought to advance immigration legislation that takes into account the following concerns: (1) factors that force migrants to emigrate; (2) legalization of undocumented aliens (including a pathway to citizenship); (3) giving priority to family unification; (4) providing protection to refugees; (5) protecting workers' rights; (6) humanitarian enforcement of immigration policies; and (7) providing aid to facilitate assimilation and care of migrants.

34. The CTCR is a small group of church officials, theologians, and church members that is designed to represent the denomination's membership.

among Us: A Lutheran Framework for Addressing Immigration Issues"
(IAU).[35] The IAU report does not set forth the denomination's view on
US immigration or provide policy advice to church members; rather, its
aim is to serve as a "framework" or teaching tool for the laity. The IAU
report states its aim as follows: "The main goal of the present study is to
offer some biblical and confessional principles and guidelines to LCMS
lay members, congregations, and church workers as they reflect—individually or corporately either as members of the church or as citizens or
residents of the nation—on their Christian responsibilities towards their
immigrant neighbors" (IAU, 8).

"Immigrants among Us" is an extraordinary achievement. Owing to
the care and depth with which this study was undertaken, it stands as a
model of how to assess a complex public-policy concern from a biblical
perspective. Indeed, of all the church pronouncements and studies on
US immigration that have been published in the past two decades, the
Missouri Synod's report represents the most sophisticated and nuanced
integration of biblical analysis with the challenge posed by contemporary immigration concerns, including the problem of unlawful migration.
Therefore, I devote the remainder of this chapter to a description and
assessment of the IAU report.

The IAU Report

The IAU report is divided into five parts. Parts 1 and 2 examine Christians' twofold responsibility to love their neighbors and obey civil authorities. Part 3 uses the Lutheran teachings on dual kingdoms to explore
the tension between obligations to the heavenly realm and duties in the
temporal sphere. Since fulfilling spiritual and temporal obligations is always carried out with reference to particular individuals or groups, part 4
examines how Christians should approach their responsibilities in both
realms through people's individual work or roles in society. The implication of the analysis is that fulfilling temporal and spiritual responsibilities
on immigration issues will vary among diverse vocations. As a result, the
approach and responsibilities of, say, an immigration officer, a citizen,
or a pastor will differ because their callings are different. Finally, part 5

---

35. The "Immigrants among Us" report is available at: http://www.lcms.org/
Document.fdoc?src=lcm&id=2194. Hereafter, page references to this document appear
in parentheses within the text.

offers principles and guidelines for church workers as they confront immigration issues within their congregations.

In part 1, the IAU report examines how Scripture addresses aliens in both the Old Testament and New Testament. According to the study, Scripture provides a clear message about how God's people should treat aliens—with love and compassion. Although IAU acknowledges that the Bible does not provide public-policy advice on immigration, it nevertheless offers a framework that should guide believers' attitudes toward strangers. The report declares, "The biblical data invite us to see immigrants as our neighbors. . . . Above all, the people of God are to love the alien because this is the will of the Lord, who loves, provides for, watches over, and hears in heaven the cry of the alien" (IAU, 15). The report declares emphatically that "we are bound by Scripture to love our neighbor, including the immigrant in our midst" (IAU, 18). While love of neighbor is a biblical imperative, the IAU report emphasizes that it would be wrong to conclude that Scripture gives precedence to the care of aliens over the rule of law. The IAU study states, "While biblical mandates to love and welcome the stranger in our midst as our neighbor stand as God's law, we cannot ignore the demands that civil laws place upon citizens and immigrants alike in the contemporary US and international contexts" (IAU, 12). In sum, while the prophetic and apostolic teachings of Scripture affirm the need to love strangers and aliens, the Bible does not address immigration law. As a result, Scripture does not give direct guidance on immigration laws or policies (IAU, 18).

Part 2 of the IAU report—titled "God's Law, Civil Law, and the Neighbor"—examines how Christians should fulfill their temporal obligations to the state while also fulfilling the call to love strangers. According to IAU, the Bible instructs Christians to obey government authority. In particular, the report declares, "While Scripture does not offer a specific position on immigration law, it does bind Christians to obey the civil authorities, including laws dealing with immigration" (IAU, 21).[36] The report summarizes the dual responsibility to love others and obey government as follows:

> The commands to love our neighbor (including the alien) and to obey civil authority are both included in the law of God and, therefore,

---

36. According to Martin Luther, the prohibition of murder involved the promotion of our neighbor's life, while the commandment to honor one's father and mother involved submission to the authorities God has established.

Christians are required to fulfill their demands. Because both mandates are comprehended in the divine law, fulfilling them is itself a matter of love. In this sense, love of one's immigrant neighbor . . . and obedience to civil servants . . . are not antithetical to one another, for the immigrant is not the only neighbor Christians are called to love. There is also the neighbor citizen or resident of a nation, who may or may not be as vulnerable or needy as the immigrant neighbor in every case, but whose well-being is also a matter of concern for both the government and for Christian citizens. (IAU, 26)

At the same time, the report acknowledges that Christians are to disobey civil authority when it is contrary to God's law. If a Christian considers a civil law to be in conflict with divine revelation, the Christian should carry out his or her disobedience in a nonviolent manner and be prepared to bear the potential penalties for such behavior. Since discerning when a civil law is inconsistent with God's law is challenging, Christians are likely to disagree among themselves concerning "the degree of godliness and justice of particular immigration laws." As a result, when addressing complex ethical public-policy concerns, including those dealing with immigration law, Christians should exercise care in judging each other's responses and to demonstrate charity toward others. The report further states that disagreements about how to reconcile disagreements about immigration policies should not compromise Christians' "unity in Christ." According to the IAU report, "there can be a reasonable spectrum of opinions and a variety of debate positions concerning what is—and what is not—just, good, reasonable, orderly, and peace building for society in current immigration law" (IAU, 33).

Part 3 of IAU, "Living in God's Two Realms," examines immigration issues in light of the Lutheran doctrine of the two kingdoms. According to this doctrine, God uses the church in the spiritual realm to reconcile sinners to himself through the preaching of the gospel, while he uses government in the temporal realm to restrain sinful behavior and to ensure a fundamental order in society. The IAU report emphasizes that it is important not to confuse the work of each realm. Confusion of the two realms occurs when "obedience to government and civil law concerning the legal status of immigrants interferes with the church's responsibility to proclaim the gospel to them and do the works of mercy that flow from the gospel for them without regard to their legal status." It also occurs when "the church's zeal to proclaim the gospel among the nations in her midst interferes with the government's responsibility to regulate and enforce immigration laws according to what is reasonable and just" (IAU, 51). Since discerning how to fulfill obligations in both the spiritual and temporal realms is unlikely to result in consensus among believers, it is important that Christians should "exercise civility" when addressing public-policy concerns they disagree on. Above all, the report emphasizes the need for repentance and forgiveness when policy disputes become a source of division within the church.

Part 4 examines the role of "vocation" in fulfilling obligations toward one's neighbors. When we fulfill this calling, two important issues arise. The first one is the question, Who is my neighbor? Second, what are the responsibilities arising from one's different vocations or roles in society? Because Christians are involved in various social groups and communal endeavors, they tend to develop "neighborly" ties with people at work, at church, in their neighborhoods, and in various social and professional associations. They also develop ties with fellow citizens. As a result, loving one's neighbor is a challenge at various levels and in a variety of contexts. But since love must be manifested concretely, the report emphasizes that loving our neighbor must begin with our families and those who are in closest proximity to us. This does not mean that we can neglect persons who do not live in close proximity. Rather, the challenge is to fulfill responsibilities to those nearby while also keeping in mind the needs of those in distant communities. The report declares, "While no Christian is able to do good in equal measure to every neighbor, we never ought to assume that God would have us exclude anyone from the love of neighbor to which we have been called" (IAU, 41).

The second important issue involves the diverse responsibilities arising from people's different vocations. A father, for example, has a special responsibility toward his own children that the family's pastor does not. Similarly, a Border Patrol agent has special duties in enforcing immigration laws, while a pastor must serve all persons, regardless of their legal status, and must refrain from confronting unlawful behavior. In short, people's work or vocation will impose different responsibilities on them as they carry out their respective duties.

The significance of the IAU report

As I have observed above, the LCMS study on US immigration is a noteworthy analysis of theological ethics relevant to immigration concerns. Unlike most church resolutions on immigration, which offer pronouncements about how Christians should view migrants and how US policies should be reformed, the bulk of the IAU report is devoted to biblical and theological analysis. The church study focuses on two imperatives—love of neighbor and obedience to the authorities—and illuminates the different tasks and responsibilities that arise in the spiritual realm and in the temporal realm. But what makes the report compelling is that it highlights the inherent tension between the two imperatives (love and obedience) and the two kingdoms (spiritual and temporal). The conflict between the polarities of love and obedience and church and state is evident throughout the report, and the following statement succinctly captures the complexity in fulfilling dual responsibilities as members of the body of Christ and as citizens:

> On the one hand, the desire to proclaim the Gospel and do the work of mercy can foster an unwillingness to deal with immigration laws. As we consider what the Bible says about God's command to love the aliens in our midst, we should also take seriously God's command to obey the authorities. On the other hand, the desire to promote the rule of law can foster an uncritical, passive, and even idolatrous attitude towards government and civil law that does not lead to a serious consideration of a potentially unjust state of affairs. Here the Christian should take seriously God's command to love the immigrant neighbor, but also seek to be well informed on the state of current civil law on immigration and its potential problems and injustice, precisely for the sake of respect for God's law in general and for the rule of law in particular. Lutheran theology helps us to avoid extremes. (IAU, 45)

In contrast to the Evangelical and Mainline denominational declarations on immigration, and to the Catholic pastoral letter "Strangers No Longer," the Missouri Synod's "Immigrants among Us" is a significant contribution to Christian reflection on immigration. Its importance lies not in its views on US immigration but in the biblical and theological resources that it offers to assist believers in assessing migration from a Christian perspective. As the report's subtitle suggests, IAU provides a biblical "framework" for addressing immigration concerns, not policy advice. What parishioners need and desire from the church is not guidance on how to resolve the shortcomings of current US immigration laws and practices; rather, they need biblical and theological resources that can help structure reflection about immigration, especially unlawful immigration. Regrettably, few denominations have developed a framework of theological ethics that can assist believers in fulfilling their responsibilities as followers of Christ and as citizens of a state.

The IAU report is noteworthy for several reasons. First, the document is a teaching resource: its aim is to equip the laity to carry out its temporal responsibilities while fulfilling the command to love neighbors. It carries out this function by illuminating biblical and theological principles and by avoiding the specifics of US immigration law and practice. By concentrating the analysis on political and theological ethics, the report provides a biblical framework that can assist individuals, groups, and congregations in assessing contemporary US immigration and confront some of the challenging situations posed by unlawful migration. As a teaching instrument, the report does not provide answers to the complex problems arising from flawed laws and unlawful behavior. But it offers a perspective on how to address questions such as the following: How should a Christian respond to a fellow Christian who is hiring migrants who are not authorized to work in the United States? How should a church administrator deal with an undocumented worker who cleans the church? Can an undocumented Christian worker serve as a youth pastor?

A second strength of the IAU study is that it avoids political advocacy. As I have noted earlier, most churches involved in the immigration political debate have been at the forefront of seeking a more flexible and liberal immigration policy. The dominant message of Christian churches—whether Evangelical, Mainline, or Catholic—has been that Scripture calls on Christians to welcome strangers. This truth has then been translated by most Christian advocacy groups into a call for legalization of undocumented aliens. That advocacy is problematic because it is rarely justified by biblical or even moral analysis. Furthermore, since church groups rarely provide a careful analysis of the justice or injustice of current immigration laws and practices, their advocacy rarely reflects a singular desire to resolve the legal status of unauthorized aliens, even if such action results in unjust consequences—either intended or unintended. By avoiding advocacy and focusing on moral teaching, the LCMS report provides a more important and more lasting impact within the church by highlighting the competing biblical obligations to God and to Caesar.

From a public-policy perspective, the major shortcoming of the IAU report is that it fails to address the justice or injustice of existing immigration laws and practices; indeed, the study neglects them. The failure to address US immigration policy, however, is not an omission but a result of the limited design of the IAU, which aims to provide a theological perspective on immigration issues. The aim of the LCMS study is not to advance a more just immigration system or to repair the system's current shortcomings. Rather, the goal of IAU is to assist parishioners in assessing immigration concerns from a Christian worldview. Obviously, the church could prepare additional teaching resources that could aid Christians in assessing US immigration policies. But to do so would require an expansive description and analysis of current immigration policy, followed by a moral assessment of the system using the framework set forth in IAU. In the meantime, the LCMS has provided an invaluable aid in setting forth a framework that can be applied not only to immigration law but also to other public-policy issues.

In conclusion, Mainline Protestant churches have sought to address the inadequacies of the US immigration system by publishing studies and carrying out a modest advocacy campaign. Because of the Mainline churches' limited current influence in American society, their campaign has had little impact. Unlike the Evangelicals, however, a number of Protestant churches have issued helpful theological studies of the moral challenges in devising a more just and effective immigration system. The Episcopal Church's 2010 theological study is especially helpful in illuminating the challenges in reconciling a state's commitment to the rule of law with the need to respond with compassion to the needs of unauthorized migrants.

Even more helpful in describing the competing moral claims of citizens and migrants is the Lutheran Church Missouri Synod's report "Immigrants among Us," which reflects the most careful theological study of immigration that I have examined. While the report does not offer policy recommendations on how to advance a just immigration system, it does provide something more important and more consistent with the church's primary vocation, namely, moral and theological education. By avoiding simplistic platitudes about migration, the report highlights the different responsibilities assigned to the church and the state. Unlike denominational resolutions that proclaim the right of immigration based on the universality of the church, the LCMS does not resolve the tensions between the dual membership in and the responsibilities to the kingdom of Christ and the state. Instead, it provides biblical teachings that illuminate the never-ending task of "rendering to Caesar the things that are Caesar's, and to God the things that are God's."

« 9 »

Strengthening the Christian Witness on Immigration

Up to this point, I have described and assessed the role of Christian churches in the contemporary policy debate on US immigration. My analysis of the political engagement of Christian churches and groups on this public policy issue has been influenced by the belief that the church and the state involve distinct realms, each with its own tasks and responsibilities. Guided by Augustinian presuppositions, I have suggested the church's primary task is to proclaim the gospel (the good news of personal salvation through Christ's atonement) and to illuminate how believers should carry out their spiritual responsibilities in the temporal city. The state, by contrast, is charged with the responsibility of making and enforcing laws in order to maintain social order and advance public justice. Whereas the domain of the City of God is universal, the City of Man remains fractured into diverse political communities. Additionally, while the City of God is guided by love, the City of Man relies on coercive force to ensure compliance with its laws.

The history of US immigration policy over the past century underscores the difficulty of establishing just and humane immigration policies that are subject to the competing, conflicting, and shifting interests of major political groups. Historically, the major political contestants involved in immigration policy have been nativists, unions, business interests, ethnic and religious groups, unskilled citizen workers, nationalists, and farmers. Since most immigration statutes have been enacted through compromise among interest groups, when the church identifies with a particular policy initiative, it inevitably runs the risk of supporting some groups over others, such as migrants over legal residents, noncitizen workers over low-wage citizen workers, business interests over unions, and ethnic groups over nationalists. Given the church's universal mission,

215

aligning its interests with particular groups risks compromising spiritual authority and moral credibility.

I have written this book because I believe that Christian denominations have been excessively engaged in the particularities of immigration reform and have neglected their responsibilities to teach theological political ethics. In giving priority to policy advocacy, churches and Christian groups have neglected the more fundamental task of showing how biblical morality can be applied to the difficult task of devising an effective and just immigration system—one that advances justice for citizens and noncitizens alike. Church groups have used biblical morality to promote immigration reforms, and they have done so by justifying policy advocacy with reference to basic biblical principles, such as the universality of human dignity, the need for mercy and compassion in social relationships, and the need to welcome strangers. But usually churches have not provided a comprehensive account of biblical revelation relevant to migration; instead, they have preferred to highlight selective principles. Most important, they have failed to show how national and global justice can be advanced by nation-states in light of biblical teachings.

Believing that all human beings are entitled to dignity, churches have sought to express solidarity with migrants and to advance their rights and welfare, which has meant, fundamentally, embracing a more liberal migration policy, one that increases total immigration levels and provides a means of legalizing unauthorized aliens living in the United States. Their advocacy has been informed by a one-sided ethical assessment that has given precedence to compassion and inclusion and has de-emphasized justice and the rule of law. In addition, whereas churches have acknowledged the government's right to regulate borders, many of their declarations and studies regard states as an impediment to human migration and to poor people's right to support their families. Church reports have generally neglected important subjects such as citizenship, the rule of law, and the legitimacy of immigration rules.

In view of the shortcomings of the political engagement of Catholics, Evangelicals, and Mainline Protestants on US immigration policy, I offer suggestions in this concluding chapter that would strengthen Christian political witness on global migration, and I examine major issues that are relevant to the application of biblical ethics to the moral challenges of immigration reform.

The Challenge of Christian Political Engagement

The central dilemma in applying Christian norms to immigration issues is how to illuminate the distinctive responsibilities in the City of God and the City of Man. Christians differ on the correct way to approach these two realms from their disparate obligations and ways of life. For some Christians, government exists to provide temporal order so that the church can carry out its spiritual tasks. For others, the church not only supports the government's maintaining of social order; the church must also seek to influence the state's ordinances in order to advance communal justice. But due to human sin, the pursuit of justice and the common good is a never-ending task. Scripture does not provide specific guidance on how to reconcile the competing—at times conflicting—demands of spiritual and temporal authority. Instead, believers must follow Jesus' admonition: "Render to Caesar the things that are Caesar's, and to God the things that are God's" (Matt. 22:21).

Discerning how Christians should carry out their redemptive mission in the world will largely depend on the cultural context or environmental conditions in which they undertake action. In his classic book *Christ and Culture*, H. Richard Niebuhr describes five different approaches that Christians have used in relating Christ to culture, that is, in fulfilling the demands of following Christ at the same time as fulfilling the demands of citizenship in temporal communities. Niebuhr says that there is no single "Christian" answer to the dilemma of how to relate the demands of faith to the demands of temporal citizenship because the strategy of the church in the world is in the mind of the Creator, not in the minds of God's lieutenants.[1] Humility and tentativeness are thus essential when believers seek to influence government, whether as individuals or as a group. But this does not mean that churches and religious groups should refuse to be engaged with public affairs. Far from it. Instead, churches must be engaged in the City of Man by carrying out their temporal responsibilities and concerns with care and caution.

However, in view of the risks involved in direct political action by church members, denominations should focus on moral teaching rather than policy advocacy. Such a strategy has the advantage of using the church's comparative advantage in biblical and moral analysis and de-emphasizing its limited competence in political action. That strategy also has the advantage of giving priority to the moral education of church

---

1. H. Richard Niebuhr, *Christ and Culture* (New York: Harper Torchbooks, 1951), 2.

members rather than to lobbying government officials. At the same time, the church must acknowledge the intractability of many of the major economic, social, and political challenges in contemporary life. In addressing such problems, churches need to be reminded that moral ideals, separated from political power, are insufficient to overcome evil and advance justice.

Richard Niebuhr's brother, Reinhold, the mid-twentieth-century ethicist, offered wise advice to clergymen seeking to address temporal affairs by relying chiefly on moral ideals derived from Scripture. In *Love and Justice* he criticizes idealists who try to "substitute the law of love for the spirit of justice."[2] Although individuals should be guided by love, the state is not capable of carrying out its responsibilities based on this ethic because of sin. Instead, government—guided by love—must pursue justice by weighing the competing merits of individuals and groups while taking into account the self-interest of all human action. Since all policy initiatives to advance the common good are subject to partiality and self-love, they provide, at best, "proximate justice."

As human institutions, churches and religious groups are not immune to the power of self-interest. Consequently, the immigration studies and resolutions that I have examined in the foregoing chapters should not be viewed as divinely inspired initiatives but as partial answers to the intractable problems of human migration. The problem with political advocacy by churches emerges when they assume that their initiatives represent a more complete expression of Christian virtues. In criticizing church politics, Reinhold Niebuhr observes, "The pronouncements of church bodies and the preachments of the pulpit tend to smell of sentimentality in our day because the law of love is presented without reference to the power of the law of self-love."[3]

If denominations are to contribute to the development of a more humane world, they must set forth more than moral ideals to guide policy. Instead, they must illuminate how biblical norms apply to immigration concerns in order to ensure justice for citizens and migrants alike. At a minimum, if churches are to assist government officials and citizens alike in morally assessing immigration, they must develop teaching documents that comprehensively apply biblical morality to the moral dimensions of immigration policy.

2. Reinhold Niebuhr, *Love and Justice* (Philadelphia: Westminster, 1957), 25.
3. Niebuhr, *Love and Justice*, 26.

The Ethics of Immigration Policy

In order for churches and Christian groups to contribute to the ethical debate on immigration reform, they must first illuminate the fundamental moral elements of immigration policy. Not all immigration issues involve basic moral values. This means that Christians must differentiate between moral and nonmoral concerns. Moral elements involve right and wrong, justice and injustice; nonmoral issues are by nature instrumental and do not raise core justice issues. Examples of moral concerns in the immigration debate include deportation causing family separation; the care and status of unaccompanied children; visa preferences for family unification; and the relative status of refugees. Examples of nonmoral issues include the annual total of immigrant visas; the balance between family-based and employment-based visas; skilled versus unskilled employment visas; and geographical distribution of visas.

Key questions

If churches are to increase awareness of key moral issues of immigration policy, they must identify important policy concerns involving political morality. To illustrate some moral dimensions of the policy debate, I list below a variety of issues involving moral concerns on current US immigration.

1. Should refugees be given moral priority over regular immigrants?
2. Should the United States maintain a ceiling on the number of annual refugee admissions? Is the current level of 85,000 admissions just?
3. In setting immigration policy, should the needs of the host society take precedence over the needs and wants of people seeking admission?
4. If low-wage migrants negatively affect the employment possibilities for unskilled American citizens or depress their wages, should the number of temporary migrant workers be reduced?
5. How should the wishes of illegal aliens be reconciled with the desires of prospective immigrants who have followed the legal admissions procedures? Should unlawful aliens be "placed at the back of the line" to give precedence to those who have followed established policies?
6. Should the United States give preferential treatment to children en-

tering the country illegally? If one or more parents are with children, should the parent(s) also be given preferential treatment?

7. Should unauthorized aliens be entitled to government benefits, including medical care and welfare assistance?

8. Should unauthorized aliens be legalized? What preconditions, if any, need to be fulfilled before legalization? Is unconditional amnesty justified for aliens who have been living "in the shadows" for many years?

9. If unlawful aliens are given legal status, what should be done with future unauthorized aliens?

10. Does marriage to a citizen or legal resident justify granting an unlawful alien legal status?

11. When unauthorized alien parents have a US-born child (a citizen), does this justify granting those parents legal status?

12. Is birthright citizenship justified if the parents are unlawful aliens?

13. Is the legal stipulation (in the 1996 IIRIRA law) requiring unlawful aliens to leave the United States for three or ten years before they can apply for legal status a just rule?

14. If unlawful aliens are allowed to eventually apply for citizenship, should they be allowed to sponsor other family members under the existing family-unification priorities?

15. Should deportation be limited to aliens who commit serious crimes, or should it also include those who have violated border and visa regulations?

16. Should an unlawful alien be deported even if that deportation leads to separation from a spouse and/or child?

17. Since the United States requires workers to have legal permits, when government authorities uncover unlawful workers, who should be sanctioned—the employer, the worker, or both?

Addressing moral issues in the immigration policy debate is important because the most significant contribution that churches and religious groups can make on this issue is to illuminate and apply Christian principles. Not all immigration concerns raise important moral issues. For example, the decision concerning how many immigrants should be admitted in a given year is primarily a political decision—an action taken by elected government officials. In Myron Weiner's view, migration policy is essentially a political judgment, a decision made by elected government officials. He writes, "On matters of migration and refugees, governments will also be moved by both the generosity and the visceral anxieties of their citizens. But at the end of the day, states will not and cannot allow others to decide who will permanently live and work in their own societies."[4]

Other immigration issues, however, will involve political and moral elements, and in addressing such concerns, the integration of morality and power will be necessary. For example, both moral and political considerations will typically affect how the international community is conceived. This means that both moral ideals and political realities will affect whether a person relies on a communitarian or a cosmopolitan worldview. Those who give precedence to existing political conditions will necessarily identify with a communitarian perspective, while those who give precedence to universal moral ideals will view the world via a cosmopolitan theory. A further illustration of how moral values must be integrated with existing political realities is the need to balance citizens' claims with the universal claims of all human beings: on the one hand, people are citizens of particular political communities; on the other hand, they are also members of global society. Thus, in addressing immigration concerns, policy-makers must seek to reconcile the claims of their own citizens with the desires of noncitizens. Although the former have priority, the latter—as members of the international human community—also have legitimate claims by virtue of their inherent human dignity.

Key themes

In addition to differentiating moral from nonmoral issues, the ethical analysis of immigration must illuminate the context in which global migration occurs. Since scholars and public officials hold a variety of views on the nature of the international community, churches and religious organizations involved in the immigration policy debate should make explicit their assumptions about domestic and global political institutions. In particular, they should disclose their perspectives on the nature of global society and the role of states in advancing international peace and justice. The following are four key themes that should be a part of an ethical framework for assessing immigration concerns.

1. *The Nature of the International Community.* How should the world be understood? Should the world be viewed as "a global family under

---

4. Myron Weiner, *The Global Migration Crisis: Challenge to States and to Human Rights* (New York: HarperCollins, 1995), 222.

God," as suggested by the US Catholic Bishops, or should it be conceived of as an international society of sovereign nation-states, as specified by the United Nations Charter?[5] As I noted in chapter 4, scholars espouse a variety of approaches to the international community, of which, for our purposes, the two major theories are communitarianism and cosmopolitanism. By way of review, the former emphasizes the importance of social and cultural bonds within a particular defined territory, which assumes that people realize their social natures through participation in a political community held together by a common language, shared traditions and history, common political, economic, and social beliefs, and shared aspirations, including the desire for self-rule. According to the communitarian perspective, states are responsible for regulating migration to ensure that the rights of citizens are protected. Cosmopolitanism, by contrast, views the world as a coherent moral community based on the fundamental worth and equality of all persons. According to this perspective, nationalisms, including local and regional ties, are an impediment to global solidarity. From the cosmopolitan perspective, the rights of persons are absolute and must therefore take precedence over the rights of states. Since the cosmopolitan view sees the world as a unitary society, people have the right to move wherever they desire. Restrictions on global migration are inimical to the universality of human bonds.

In this book I have argued that a communitarian worldview provides a more satisfactory approach to the analysis of migration because it reflects the political conditions of global order. Although globalization has challenged the independent authority of nation-states and increased the porosity of borders, the structure of the international community remains decentralized. The global constitutional order, enshrined in the United Nations Charter, is rooted in the autonomy of states.

2. *The Moral Legitimacy of States.* If we accept the legitimacy of the existing system of nation-states, how should Christians view the state and the authority of government? Should believers accept or challenge the division of the world into states and the coercive authority of government? Although God has ordained government in order to sustain social order, this does not mean that the nation-state is the only form of legitimate community. Historically, political community has been expressed via a variety of institutions, including tribes, empires, kingdoms, and city-

5. US Bishops' Committee on Migration, "One Family under God" (Washington, DC: United States Catholic Conference, 1998).

states. Despite the transient nature of political organizations, the state is a divinely ordained institution that makes communal order possible.

According to Reinhold Niebuhr, the biblical stance on government involves two important dimensions: order and justice. The first element, social order, is secured through government in order to prevent anarchy. The second element, justice, is advanced through divine or "prophetic" judgment based on the fact that temporal authority is subject to God's sovereign rule.[6] The balance between order and prophetic judgment contributes to justice not only within states but also in the world community itself.

3. *The Nature of Citizenship.* As I have noted above, Christians have citizenship in the political community where they reside and also in the heavenly kingdom—as disciples of Christ. Political communities are sustained through the coercive authority of government, while the spiritual community is sustained by love—love of God and of neighbor—and nurtured through the church. Furthermore, while nation-states have distinct territorial boundaries, the scope of the church is universal. As a result, the church is a borderless society that welcomes all, while the nation-state protects its territorial borders by regulating immigration. To the extent that church groups adopt a cosmopolitan conception of the world, they are likely to support the idea of global citizenship. But such a notion is an ideal. It does not reflect the political institutions of the contemporary international system. Whereas citizens of a state are entitled to vote and to carry a passport, global citizens have no specific rights or responsibilities that are specified by governmental authority.

While the citizenships in the City of God and the City of Man are both important, there is no consensus among Christian thinkers on how the competing and conflicting responsibilities of each realm can be fulfilled and, if necessary, reconciled. For our purposes, however, it is important to recognize that the ethic of love sustaining the City of God cannot be the foundation of political community. This means that laws regulating international migration need to be developed and enforced by states. The sovereign authority of government is the primary basis for making and applying immigration policies, not the virtues of love and compassion that sustain the church.

4. *Human Rights and Migration.* Because Scripture teaches that humans bear the image of God, a basic postulate of Christian political

---

6. Reinhold Niebuhr, *The Nature and Destiny of Man*, vol. 2, *Human Destiny* (New York: Charles Scribner's Sons, 1964), 269-70, 285.

thought is the fundamental worth of persons. In the divine cosmology, people matter because they are a priority to God. The equality and universality of human dignity is expressed in the belief that people have basic (natural) individual rights. Following the adoption of the Universal Declaration of Human Rights by the United Nations General Assembly in 1948, the international community developed a large body of international law that codified and amplified conceptions of human rights. Although such conventions and treaties have expanded the breadth of human rights, international law has refused to acknowledge a human right to immigrate. People may leave their homeland, but they are not entitled to join another nation-state. The only institution with the authority to grant official entry is the receiving state.

Refugees and economic migrants present important challenges to existing international legal treaties, but these challenges do not qualify a state's power to regulate borders. According to the 1980 Refugee Convention, for example, refugees who flee war and persecution are to be granted protection by foreign states, but entry into a foreign country is an act of generosity and compassion (an exceptional *ex gratia* act), not a basic human right. Similarly, people have a right to work in order to meet basic human needs, but the right to work to provide essential needs does not entail the right to immigrate. Some church groups have used the need for basic material sustenance to justify unlawful migration. But the decision about how to respond to refugees and economic migrants is a decision only a government can make as it weighs the relative merits of other admissions claims. Although inspired by compassion, the government's fundamental task is to advance justice for all persons in its territory—citizens, noncitizens, refugees, immigrants, and irregular migrants.

Christian Ethics, Advocacy, and Immigration Reform

Christian groups and churches concerned with immigration policy have often claimed that the United States needs a more liberal and flexible immigration policy. To advance that goal, they have emphasized political advocacy rather than moral education. And they have issued studies and resolutions that highlight biblical teachings emphasizing human dignity, love, compassion to neighbors, and the need to welcome strangers. These denominational statements and studies have typically focused on biblical principles and have then drawn public-policy conclusions from them.

However, they suffer from several limitations. First, they are based on insufficient analysis of existing immigration conditions and policies. In other words, they emphasize biblical morality, but they contain little political science. For one thing, there is little appreciation for, or understanding of, the constraints that are brought to bear on government officials in devising just migration policies. As I have noted above, the political ethics of immigration should address, at a minimum, four major themes: the international community, the nature of the state, citizenship, and the basic rights of migrants. But, with few exceptions, denominational resolutions and church studies have neglected these concerns. An example of the avoidance of domestic political constraints is Daniel Carroll's book *Christians at the Border* (noted in chapter 5 above). Although the book seeks to develop a biblical perspective on migration, Carroll approaches the challenge of Hispanic migration as a social issue requiring the cultivation of proper values and attitudes toward the "other" rather than a problem of statecraft. He emphasizes attitudinal adjustments of the "majority culture," and minimizes or disregards political terms such as "nation-state," "citizenship," "rule of law," and "public justice."[7]

How can one advance a more just immigration system if one has not accurately assessed the current rules? Most church statements and studies offer little analysis of existing policies and practices. For example, the National Association of Evangelicals' "Immigration 2009" resolution identifies a number of shortcomings of the existing system under the heading "National Realities." It declares that the major weakness of the current system is that the United States is not admitting sufficient workers to meet the demands of the American economy, and as a result, migrant workers have entered the country illegally.[8] Similarly, most church statements neglect a discussion of current policies to focus almost entirely on biblical teaching. The Wesleyan Methodist Church's statement, for example, presents the church's "spiritual DNA" by setting forth eight biblical norms relevant to migration.[9] The Free Methodist Church's statement sets forth six biblical principles but neglects an analysis of the international political context in which global migration occurs.[10] Of the

7. M. Daniel Carroll R., *Christians at the Border: Immigration, the Church, and the Bible* (Grand Rapids: Baker Academic, 2008), 107–12 and 136–40.

8. NAE, "Immigration 2009." Available at: http://nae.net/immigration-2009/.

9. "A Wesleyan View of Immigration, 2008." Available at: https://www.wesleyan .org/237/a-wesleyan-view-of-immigration.

10. "Free Methodist Position on Immigration, 2013." Available at: http://fmcusa .org/files/2014/03/The-Free-Methodist-Church-on-Immigration.pdf.

church documents that I have reviewed here, only two offer some description and assessment of US policies and rules—the Catholic Church's 2003 pastoral letter and the Christian Reformed Church's 2010 Synodical Migration Report. "Strangers No Longer," the Catholic Bishops' letter, provides a short overview of some of the major shortcomings of current policies, including impediments to family unification, per-country visa ceilings, not enough visas for unskilled workers, and problematic enforcement policies.[11] The CRC study begins its analysis with a short overview of current immigration practices and their limitations, focusing on the plight of illegal immigrants.[12]

A second shortcoming of church documents on immigration is the failure to acknowledge and assess the political conditions in which global migration occurs. Just as it is necessary to have an informed view of a state's immigration laws and practices, it is also desirable to have knowledge of the international political system that establishes the context of global migration flows. It can be easily demonstrated that context matters if we contrast domestic and international migration. Moving within a country does not present legal or moral problems. There are few, if any, impediments in moving from, say, Mississippi to New Hampshire, or from a South Dakota farm to a suburb of Indianapolis. Free movement is possible because all of these areas are within the sovereign territory of the United States. But moving from one country to another is a more difficult undertaking because though emigration is generally unimpeded, immigration is carefully regulated by states.

Most church documents on immigration give little coverage to the existing international political system. Instead, they either view the world through the lens of utopian idealism (the Catholic approach) or simply neglect the topic altogether (the approach of Evangelicals and Mainline Protestants). Declarations by the Catholic Church (e.g., the Vatican and the US Conference of Catholic Bishops) view the world as an ethical community, a unitary system where the rights of persons trump state sovereignty. As I noted in chapter 6, the Catholic Church has historically been uncomfortable with the decentralized global order and has consistently regarded the world as a unified ethical family. It mostly regards

11. "Strangers No Longer: Together on the Journey of Hope," A Pastoral Letter Concern Migration from the Catholic Bishops of Mexico and the United States. Available at: http://www.usccb.org/issues-and-action/human-life-and-dignity/immigration/strangers-no-longer-together-on-the-journey-of-hope.cfm.

12. CRC, "Committee to Study the Migration of Workers." Available at: https://www.crcna.org/sites/default/files/Migration.pdf.

the nation-state system negatively, viewing it as an impediment not only to international peace and global solidarity but also to the well-being of persons in poor nations. In their 2003 pastoral letter on immigration, the Catholic Bishops claim that the root cause of economic migration is in the inequalities of the international system.[13] Ideally, the letter declares, migration should be a choice, not a necessity. Of course, Catholic bishops grudgingly acknowledge the existing decentralized political order, but their message is to call for more transnational cooperation to minimize the harms resulting from the fragmented international system. There is little appreciation among Catholic clergy of the important work of constitutional states in advancing human rights and fostering economic prosperity.

A third (and related) shortcoming of church initiatives is the conflation of church and state in addressing immigration issues. To a significant degree, Christian denominations have been influenced by a cosmopolitan perspective of the international community rather than by a more realistic communitarian perspective. Because Christians regard the bonds of faith as universal, they have tended to transpose the global affinities of the church to the social and political realities of the international system. But the church and the state, the kingdom of Christ and the kingdom of man, are not the same. To be sure, Christian norms should guide how believers define their responsibilities in the temporal realm. But since the Bible is not an international-relations manual, it does not provide ready-made answers to the difficult and complex tasks of determining the degree and the way sovereign states should regulate borders. While ideal norms are important in advancing a more just and peaceful world, the challenge in public life is not simply to articulate ideals but to advance social, economic, and political conditions in light of the prevailing realities in the world. If this is correct, the promotion of a more just US immigration system must be rooted in the existing global system (the one enshrined in the United Nations Charter), which places the responsibility for global order and the protection of human rights on sovereign nation-states.

A fourth limitation of church initiatives is the failure to develop a robust political theology of immigration. If believers are to advance immigration policies consistent with Christian principles, then they must devise a more comprehensive body of biblical teachings and integrate them with the political ethics of immigration. Morality involves values

---

13. "Strangers No Longer," paras. 59–63.

and beliefs of right and wrong, justice and injustice. Political ethics involves reflection on and application of morality. Therefore, the development of a political theology of immigration will necessarily involve both morality and ethics. The challenge is not simply to illuminate biblical morality but to show how those biblical norms relate to the competing and conflicting demands through ethical analysis. In developing a body of teachings about the applied political ethics of immigration, Christians must seek to illuminate important tensions involved in immigration policy. These include such competing claims as the wants of citizens and noncitizens, the rule of law and the need for mercy for unauthorized migrants, and the defense of territorial boundaries and the moral demands of global solidarity.

A final shortcoming of the Christian initiatives on immigration reform is the priority given to political advocacy and the neglect of moral education. Rather than developing and advancing a Christian approach to immigration by teaching political morality, churches have sought to give advice to the governing authorities. As a result, churches have de-emphasized their potential contribution as moral teachers and have sought instead to advance policy reforms. In effect, churches have pursued political advocacy—an arena in which they have comparatively limited competence—and neglected the realm of theological and political ethics, in which they have a comparative advantage.

My analysis of Catholic, Evangelical, and Mainline Protestant political engagement suggests that Christian denominations have frequently used biblical principles to justify increased immigration levels and the legalization of unlawful aliens. Church leaders, as citizens, are certainly entitled to advance policies they believe are consistent with their own concerns and moral values. But when those leaders use Scripture or the moral authority of the church to justify specific reforms, they enter the contested realm of political conflict. The use of spiritual resources to advance political goals is problematic because it can detract from the church's spiritual task of proclaiming the gospel, can foment disunity among believers, and may ultimately undermine the church's moral authority.

During the Cold War, Christian ethicist Paul Ramsey called into question the propensity of church bodies to undertake political advocacy, especially in his book *Who Speaks for the Church?* He criticized the political activism of the World Council of Churches, arguing that churches had little competence in the realm of domestic or international politics. He also suggested that the church had a moral responsibility to critique government policies when their actions conflicted with fundamental biblical teachings but that they should refrain from giving public policy advice. In that book he says,

> Christian political ethics cannot say what should or must be done but only what may be done. In politics the church is only a theoretician. The religious communities as such should be concerned with perspectives upon politics, with political doctrines, with the direction and structures of common life, not with specific directives. They should seek to clarify and keep wide open the legitimate options for choice, and thus nurture the moral and political ethics of the nation. Their task is not the determination of policy.[14]

Carl F. H. Henry also critiqued the tendency of the clergy to advance specific public policies in the name of the church. While serving as editor of *Christianity Today,* he developed a set of principles to guide Evangelical political engagement. Some of the elements of his theological framework for church-state relations had these principles: (1) the institutional church has no mandate, jurisdiction, or competence to endorse specific public policies; (2) the pursuit of a more just society is the task of all citizens, and individual Christians should be politically engaged to the limit of their competence and opportunity; and (3) Scripture limits the proper activity of both government and church for divinely stipulated objectives—the former, for the preservation of justice and order, and the latter, for the moral-spiritual task of evangelizing the world.[15]

If churches have no special wisdom in the realm of political affairs, this does not mean that they should refrain from addressing temporal concerns. After all, the gospel is not solely concerned with personal salvation; it is also called to the redemption of all aspects of God's creation. This means that the church should illuminate how biblical morality applies to the social, economic, political, and cultural domains of society and denounce government actions that are inconsistent with divine will. In carrying out the task of political and social redemption, churches may highlight problems that are contrary to God's created order and illuminate how biblical ethics can help contribute to a more just and humane world. But, following Ramsey's admonition, the task of the church is not

---

14. Paul Ramsey, *Who Speaks for the Church?* (Nashville: Abingdon, 1967), 152.
15. Richard J. Mouw, "Carl Henry Was Right," *Christianity Today,* January 2010, 31.

to advance specific public policies; rather, it is to teach political morality—to its parishioners as well as the general public.

Developing a Christian Perspective on Immigration

If Christian groups are to devise a more effective strategy of political engagement on immigration reform, they need to develop a more comprehensive theological and political analysis of immigration. Such an initiative will, at a minimum, require knowledge of biblical revelation, the existing immigration system, and a nuanced integration of biblical ethics and immigration policy. Church analyses of immigration will necessarily address a variety of immigration issues, such as the nature of the nation-state, the rights and responsibilities of citizens and migrants, and the nature of public policy. Though scholars and ethicists hold a variety of assumptions and beliefs about the political ethics of global migration, I offer below a number of fundamental principles for carrying out the task of integrating faith with the politics of global migration. Other political themes must undoubtedly be addressed in developing a political theology of migration, but this list below provides a rudimentary foundation for addressing immigration from a Christian perspective.

Nation-states

1. Since people are by nature social, the development of communal relationships is an important moral task. Social ties can be established in a variety of ways—through religion, ethnicity, tribal affinities, and so on. In the modern era, nations that are based on shared traditions and common values and aspirations within a constrained territory provide an important basis for nurturing human social bonds.
2. The international community is made up of more than 190 nation-states. States have a responsibility for caring for people within their territorial boundaries and for carrying out peaceful relations with other states.
3. States are important in promoting and protecting human rights. Without a state, there can be no authority, and without authority, there can be no just enforcement of laws.
4. Because all persons are entitled to dignity and respect, states should

seek to affirm human dignity not only within their territorial boundaries but also in the international community itself.

Citizens and migrants

1. The most fundamental claim in political ethics is the equality and universality of human worth. People are entitled to dignity because they are created in God's image.
2. The chief task of government is to protect and advance the worth and dignity of its people. In order to carry out this task, government focuses its responsibilities on advancing the security and well-being of its citizens.
3. While states are duty-bound to give preference to the needs of citizens, they must also take into account the needs of noncitizens and foreigners. Preferential treatment is morally legitimate, provided it does not disregard the basic needs of other human beings.
4. Sovereign states have the right to regulate immigration. People have an inherent right to emigrate, but they do not have a right to enter another state. That decision is the responsibility of the receiving state.
5. Because they are fleeing persecution and violence, refugees have moral precedence over regular migrants.
6. Governments must distinguish refugees from unauthorized aliens: the former are lawful migrants, while the latter are unlawful aliens.

Immigration policies

1. There are no ideal immigration policies. Policies create winners and losers. The aim is to advance proximate justice, making the system more effective and more just.
2. Immigration policy is especially difficult because the benefits of new policies are concentrated, while the costs are broadly distributed throughout society. As a result, interest groups have much to gain from advocacy.
3. Governments should ensure that immigration laws and procedures are just and applied impartially.
4. Since governments establish criteria and ceilings for immigrant admissions, this task will necessarily be rooted in prudential and political considerations of their citizens.

5. Since the international community is a society of states, states must be sensitive to the needs of peoples from disadvantaged foreign societies.

6. Actions toward unauthorized aliens need to be perceived as just, not only by citizens but also by noncitizens. In particular, actions should take into account the claims of other potential migrants, especially those currently waiting patiently for an opportunity to apply for admission legally.

7. Ethical analysis must involve more than intentions to care for strangers living in the United States; at a minimum, the goals, means, and outcomes of any action toward the irregulars must accord with justice.

8. Some Evangelicals have emphasized the need to begin the analysis of immigration with Scripture. Whether or not the moral assessment of immigration begins with the Bible, it is imperative to develop a comprehensive understanding of immigrant policy. Applied political ethics must necessarily integrate biblical and moral principles with a competent account of immigration policy.

In previous chapters I have suggested that the immigration initiatives of Catholics, Evangelicals, and Mainline Protestants have had limited influence on the moral debate over immigration policy in American society. They have had little impact because they have emphasized policy advocacy rather than developing educational resources to assist believers and the general public in morally assessing existing policies and practices toward contributing to a more just and effective immigration system. Rather than providing ethical guidance in weighing policy alternatives, churches have used their institutional credibility to call for a more flexible and compassionate immigration system based on such moral ideals as human dignity, the universality of human community, the imperative of welcoming strangers, and the need for charity and compassion for the poor and oppressed. To a significant degree, the fundamental value inspiring Christian action on migration has been the conviction that all persons, regardless of their nationality or legal status, are entitled to dignity. Protecting and enhancing human welfare is viewed as a basic requirement of a just world.

Teaching Christian Immigration Ethics

If churches are to carry out their task of illuminating and applying biblical morality to specific economic, social, or political issues in society, how should they carry out this task? What resources should the church develop, and how should it disseminate its ethical teachings? To begin with, churches should focus first on equipping their own members. The church is the body of Christ in the world, and the clergy's primary task is to proclaim the gospel and teach believers how to carry out their responsibilities as Christians while sojourning in the temporal city. But churches should also seek to influence the general public by way of proclamations and teachings. Although churches can issue pronouncements and resolutions on specific temporal concerns, the most effective instruments in educating the laity are the teaching documents that illuminate biblical morality in specific problems. Examples of such documents in the immigration debate include the joint US–Mexican Bishops' pastoral letter of 2003 ("Strangers No Longer") and the Lutheran Church Missouri Synod's study "Immigrants among Us." When undertaken with care, teaching documents not only provide moral education to parishioners but also can influence the general public and thereby help structure the public-policy debate. The extent of their influence will depend in great measure on the depth and breadth of the analysis.

What are the essential elements of effective teaching documents from the church? How should such studies integrate biblical ethics with specific political concerns? Ideally, these teaching documents will have four distinctive attributes. First, such studies will include a competent and comprehensive overview of biblical teachings relevant to the particular issue. Biblical scholars will need to illuminate teachings from the Old and New Testaments that are potentially relevant to the issue being addressed. The temptation is to identify a select number of biblical principles that support a desired policy preference. But since biblical revelation involves a complex set of teachings that is not easily reduced to a set of moral principles, the analysis should facilitate highlighting diverse and even conflicting perspectives that emerge from the interpretation and application of Scripture.

Second, church documents will highlight the political theology used in applying Scripture to the specific temporal political and social problems. Since Christians have historically viewed the relationship of church and state differently, church leaders inevitably interpret Scripture through a theological tradition, such as Lutheranism, Catholicism, or Calvinism. It is thus important that church leaders make explicit their theological presuppositions. As I observed above, though Christians have historically believed that church and state have distinct roles, they have held different theological perspectives on the responsibilities of dual citizenship in the "two kingdoms" (the City of God and the City of Man). Therefore, it is important that, in addressing immigration concerns, the denominational studies make explicit the political theologies informing their analyses and actions.

A third requirement of effective teaching documents is an evident understanding of the issue of concern. If the church study is to be taken seriously by public policy officials, it must show a sophisticated knowledge of the issue being examined. A simplistic account of a problem may gain approval from those already committed to advocacy, but it is unlikely to increase awareness of the moral dimensions of the issue and to influence the structure of the policy debate. Since most public-policy issues (e.g., climate change, global poverty, international peacekeeping) are complex, multidimensional problems, developing a thorough understanding of the issues will require time and guidance from policy experts. While specialists and scholars typically concur on the basic facts of a problem, they frequently hold divergent perspectives and explanations on the nature, causes, and possible remedies. And this is, of course, the case with the subject of immigration. In chapter 2, I outlined some of the major laws and governmental institutions regulating US immigration, and in chapter 3, I offered an assessment of the immigration system, noting some of its strengths and weaknesses. While immigration scholars will no doubt concur with the facts set forth in chapter 2, they may differ with my assessment of existing policies. Given the diverse perspectives among scholars, developing an authoritative account of US immigration policy will require significant knowledge and discernment in setting forth a succinct but compelling account of this issue.

Finally, an effective teaching document must provide a sophisticated integration of faith and politics. This integrative task will require discovering and defining the most important biblical norms relevant to the issue. Such norms are important because without moral standards, it is impossible to guide analysis or to advance political initiatives. However, while moral ideals provide motivation and direction, they do not provide guidance on how to respond to social and political problems. Biblical morality must be integrated with knowledge of public affairs. Just as a medical doctor must have knowledge of patients' health if he or she is to foster their healing, church leaders must have a competent understanding of the domestic and international political conditions that give rise to existing immigration problems and then provide a strategy for ameliorating those conditions. To undertake the latter task will require knowledge and application of political ethics, which involves the prudential weighing of different alternatives to advance the good and minimize the harm. Assessing conditions and developing policy recommendations must be mediated through ethical analysis weighing alternatives based on anticipated outcomes. Competent church documents will thus offer a moral assessment of the specific political issue based on the integration of biblical norms with the specific issues at hand. If policy recommendations are advanced, they will be advanced in light of the policy's goals, methods, and potential outcomes.[16]

Perhaps the most sophisticated public policy document ever produced by an American church is the 1983 US Bishops' pastoral letter on nuclear arms. When the report was released, Rev. Theodore Hesburgh, a leading public figure in American public life and the president of the University of Notre Dame, called it the finest document that the American Catholic hierarchy had ever produced. McGeorge Bundy, the former national security advisor for Presidents Kennedy and Johnson, similarly offered praise for the bishops' report, declaring the letter a landmark study in the application of religious and moral principles to ethical challenges posed by nuclear weapons. The pastoral letter is noteworthy because by highlighting the morality of nuclear deterrence, it influenced the thinking of government decision-makers and national security advisors and scholars. The letter's social and political impact derived from its authoritative account of nuclear policy and the moral analysis of deterrence. In drafting the letter, the bishops took their time (three years) and relied on the contributions of many arms control specialists, government officials, theologians, and scholars. Indeed, the project was regarded as a major achievement that received broad media coverage. For example, *The New York Times* gave significant coverage to the preliminary drafts released in 1981 and 1982, and when the final report came out, the paper published a significant portion of the document itself.

The letter, titled "The Challenge of Peace: God's Promise and Our Response," had four major parts: (1) theological, biblical, and moral perspectives on peacekeeping, including an assessment of the just-war

---

16. For a discussion of this issue, see Mark R. Amstutz, *International Ethics: Concepts, Theories, and Cases in Global Politics*, 4th ed. (Boulder, CO: Rowman and Littlefield, 2014), chap. 4.

tradition; (2) the problem of peacekeeping through nuclear deterrence; (3) proposals and policies for promoting peace in the nuclear age; and (4) a pastoral challenge to the church and selected constituencies.[17] For our purposes, the most important sections of the letter—the ones that gave it credibility and authority—are the first part, which sets forth a biblical and moral account of the task of peacekeeping in the nuclear age, and the second part, which describes and assesses the role of nuclear arms as part of the national security strategy of the United States.

To address the complex issues involved in assessing nuclear strategy, the letter offers a moral assessment of two key issues: the use of such weapons and the ethics of nuclear deterrence. The bishops argue that unlike conventional arms, whose destructive power can be controlled and limited, the power of nuclear weapons is so great that the key moral priority must be prevention. As a result, the bishops declare, "Our 'no' to nuclear war must in the end be definitive and decisive." The letter's central argument about the morality of deterrence is based on four principles: first, nuclear war is unacceptable; second, the first use of nuclear arms, whether strategic or tactical, must be prohibited; third, deterrence (the threat of nuclear retaliation) is conditionally justified while the United States and the Soviet Union work toward mutual disarmament; and fourth, the declaratory policy on deterrence must be consistent with the just-war principles of discrimination and proportionality.

The bishops offer a number of recommendations they believe will contribute to peacekeeping. These include support for a freeze on the testing and production of new nuclear weapons, support for significant reductions in the number of strategic weapons, and support for a comprehensive ban of nuclear tests. These suggestions, however, are less important than the moral assessment of nuclear strategy. The bishops themselves acknowledge that fundamental moral principles are much more important than the specific prudential recommendations they offer. The bishops declare,

> When making applications of these principles we realize . . . that prudential judgments are involved based on specific circumstances which can change or which can be interpreted differently by people of good will. . . . The moral judgments that we make in specific cases, while not binding in conscience, are to be given serious attention and consider-

17. US Catholic Bishops, "The Challenge of Peace: God's Promise and Our Response," Pastoral Letter on War and Peace, *Origins*, May 19, 1983.

ations by Catholics as they determine whether their moral judgments are consistent with the Gospel.

The letter admonishes Christians "to enlighten one another through honest discussion, preserving mutual charity and caring above all for the common good." The bishops declare, "Not only conviction and commitment are needed in the church but also civility and charity."[18]

This pastoral letter is noteworthy because it provides a model of how a church can carry out the task of teaching biblical political ethics on a difficult public-policy concern. Had the Catholic bishops emphasized specific public policies to advance global peace, they would have contributed little to the moral debate on nuclear deterrence and would not have enriched their own parishioners' understanding of the grave problems posed by the United States' reliance on nuclear weapons for national security. By bringing biblical, theological, and moral principles to bear on a complex public-policy concern, the Roman Catholic Church contributed to a deeper understanding of the threats and challenges posed by nuclear deterrence.

Some Christians may conclude that the current problems in the US immigration system require more than a campaign of moral education. For them, the church must be directly engaged in the design and implementation of policy reform. For those believers, coming to the aid of refugees and migrant workers is a necessary expression of their commitment to Christ. In this book I have argued that churches should be cautious in offering public-policy advice on complex issues like international migration. Given the multidimensional nature of global migration, churches should avoid providing simplistic analyses and policy recommendations on US immigration policy. A lack of careful, sophisticated analysis will contribute little to the policy debate and has the potential to undermine the credibility of Christian witness.

In conclusion, while the Christian faith does not offer answers to specific policy concerns, it does provide perspectives, dispositions, and moral principles that can assist in addressing thorny moral challenges. It can best carry out this task by championing moral education, as was illustrated by the bishops' pastoral letter on nuclear deterrence. If Christian groups and churches were to undertake a serious campaign of teaching Christian immigration ethics, they would illuminate biblical principles and apply them to the conflicting demands of immigration policy. In particular, churches should develop studies in the political theology of

18. US Bishops, "Challenge of Peace," 3.

immigration. Ideally, such comprehensive documents would include a succinct account of current immigration policies, a description of key moral dimensions of migration policy, an overview of biblical teachings relevant to migration, and, finally, an integrational theological reflection with policy analysis. The goal of such a document would not be to recommend public policies but rather to help structure moral analysis.

The current US immigration system has numerous shortcomings. To a significant degree, many of these shortcomings are the direct result of competing and conflicting political demands: the desire for more migrants versus the desire to decrease their number; the demand for more low-wage migrant workers versus the desire to restrict such labor in order to bolster the wages of unskilled citizens; the desire to facilitate family unification versus the desire to cap total annual migrant admissions; and the desire to give unauthorized aliens a road to citizenship versus the desire to first hold them legally accountable for disregarding US laws. Because of these and other conflicting national impulses, it is not surprising that the US immigration system is fraught with contradictions, ambiguities, and inconsistencies. Some of the ambivalences and contradictions are the result of inconsistent or ambivalent policy implementation. Other shortcomings are the result of failure to provide the means to achieve the desired policy goals. Still others are the byproduct of unintended consequences of laws designed to address existing problems. Given the deep polarization concerning immigration concerns, political leaders and citizens—as well as Christians themselves—remain divided on the fundamental problems and injustices of the US immigration system and how best to improve it.

It may be easier for religious idealists to simply consider a utopian world where sovereignty is replaced by global governance. But simply moralizing about the injustices of contemporary migration is insufficient. A credible analysis of immigration policy must begin with a careful assessment of the strengths and limitations of the existing US system. It must also begin with the recognition that the current international political order is a loose society of sovereign states. Religious actors wishing to create more just migration practices may wish for more open borders or a more liberal immigration policy. Or they may call for the transformation of the global political order. But churches and Christian groups can make their most important contribution to the strengthening of immigration policies by illuminating political morality that is relevant to migration. In effect, the church should describe how Christian perspectives apply to the challenges of global migration.

Because immigration is a complex public-policy issue, it does not lend itself to categorical moral verdicts. Rather, public officials must make and enforce rules that reflect a balance of competing interests and moral values. Christians can contribute to the task of helping develop and implement immigration policies that advance "proximate justice." But rather than telling public officials what policies to pursue, the task of the church is to help structure the ethical analysis of international migration.

Bibliography

General

Alden, Edward. *The Closing of the American Border: Terrorism, Immigration and Security Since 9/11*. New York: HarperCollins, 2008.

———. *Visa Overstay Tracking: Progress, Prospect and Pitfalls*, prepared statement before the Committee on Homeland Security, 111th Cong., 2nd sess. New York: Council on Foreign Relations, 2010.

Amstutz, Mark R. *Evangelicals and American Foreign Policy*. New York: Oxford University Press, 2014.

———. *International Ethics: Concepts, Theories, and Cases in Global Politics*. 4th ed. Boulder: Rowman & Littlefield, 2013.

———. "Two Theories of Immigration." *First Things*, December 2015.

Amstutz, Mark R., and Peter Meilaender. "Public Policy & the Church: Spiritual Priorities." *The City* 4 (Spring 2011): 4-17.

Andreas, Peter. *Border Games: Policing the U.S.-Mexico Divide*. 2nd ed. Ithaca: Cornell University Press, 2009.

Bacon, David. *The Right to Stay Home: How U.S. Policy Drives Mexican Migration*. Boston: Beacon, 2013.

Barber, Benjamin R. "Constitutional Faith." In *For Love of Country: Debating the Limits of Patriotism*, edited by Joshua Cohen, 30-37. Boston: Beacon, 1996.

Barry, Brian. "The Quest for Consistency: A Skeptical View." In *Free Movement: Ethical Issues in the Transnational Migration of People and of Money*, edited by Brian Barry and Robert E. Goodin, 279-87. University Park: Pennsylvania State University Press, 1992.

Beitz, Charles. *Political Theory and International Relations*. Princeton: Princeton University Press, 1979.

Bennett, John C. *Foreign Policy in Christian Perspective*. New York: Charles Scribner's Sons, 1966.

Borjas, George J. *Heaven's Door: Immigration Policy and the American Economy*. Princeton: Princeton University Press, 1999.

Bibliography

Bosniak, Linda. *The Citizen and the Alien: Dilemmas of Contemporary Membership.* Princeton: Princeton University Press, 2006.

Bottum, Joseph. "The Death of Protestant America: A Political Theory of the Protestant Mainline." *First Things,* August/September 2008.

Bouman, Stephen, and Ralston Deffenbaugh. *They Are Us: Lutherans and Immigration.* Minneapolis: Augsburg Fortress, 2009.

Brotherton, David C., and Philip Kretsedemas, eds. *Keeping Out the Other: A Critical Introduction to Immigration Enforcement Today.* New York: Columbia University Press, 2008.

Budziszewski, J. *Evangelicals in the Public Square: Four Formative Voices on Political Thought and Action.* Grand Rapids: Baker Academic, 2006.

Bush, Jeb, and Clint Bolick. *Immigration Wars: Forging an American Solution.* New York: Threshold Editions, 2013.

Cafaro, Philip. *How Many Is Too Many?: The Progressive Argument for Reducing Immigration into the United States.* Chicago: University of Chicago Press, 2015.

Calavita, Kitty. *Inside the State: The Bracero Program, Immigration and the I.N.S.* New York: Routledge, 1992.

Carens, Joseph H. *The Ethics of Immigration.* New York: Oxford University Press, 2013.

―――. "The Rights of Irregular Migrants." *Ethics & International Affairs* 2 (Summer 2008): 163–86.

Carroll R., M Daniel. *Christians at the Border: Immigration, the Church, and the Bible.* Grand Rapids: Baker Academic, 2008.

Chacón, Jennifer M. "Immigration Detention: No Turning Back?" *The South Atlantic Quarterly* 113 (Summer 2014): 621–28.

Chaput, Charles J. *Render unto Caesar: Serving the Nation by Living Our Catholic Beliefs in Political Life.* New York: Doubleday, 2008.

Chomsky, Aviva. *Undocumented: How Immigration Became Illegal.* Boston: Beacon, 2014.

Christiansen, Drew, SJ. "Movement, Asylum, Borders: Christian Perspectives." *International Migration Review* 30 (Spring 1996): 7–17.

―――. "Sacrament of Unity: Ethical Issues in Pastoral Care of Migrants and Refugees." In *Today's Immigrants and Refugees: A Christian Understanding,* Bishops' Committee on Migration, U.S. Conference of Catholic Bishops. Washington, DC: USCCB, 1988.

"Citizenship, Values, and Cultural Concerns: What Americans Want from Immigration Reform." *Public Religion Research Institute,* March 2013. http://public religion.org/research/2013/03/2013-religion-values-immigration-survey /#.Vobu9Fc8Dww.

Collier, Paul. *Exodus: How Migration Is Changing Our World.* New York: Oxford University Press, 2013.

Cornelius, Wayne A., Philip L. Martin, and James F. Hollifield. "Introduction: The Ambivalent Quest for Immigration Control." In *Controlling Immigration: A*

Global Perspective, edited by Wayne A. Cornelius et al., 3–42. Palo Alto: Stanford University Press, 1994.

Daniels, Roger. *Guarding the Golden Door: American Immigration Policy and Immigrants Since 1882*. New York: Hill and Wang, 2004.

Dear, Michael. *Why Walls Won't Work: Repairing the US-Mexico Divide*. New York: Oxford University Press, 2013.

Dowty, Alan. *Closed Borders: The Contemporary Assault on Freedom of Movement*. New Haven: Yale University Press, 1987.

Dulles, Avery Cardinal, SJ. *Magisterium: Teacher and Guardian of the Faith*. Naples, FL: Sapientia, 2007.

Ensalaco, Mark. "Illegal Immigration, the Bishops, and the Laity: 'Strangers No Longer.'" In *On "Strangers No Longer": Perspectives on the Historic U.S.-Mexican Catholic Bishops' Pastoral Letter on Migration*, edited by Todd Scribner and J. Kevin Appleby, 251–80. New York: Paulist Press, 2013.

"Few Say Religion Shapes Immigration, Environment Views." *Pew Research Center*, September 17, 2010.

"Five Facts about Illegal Immigration in the U.S." *Pew Research Center*, November 18, 2014.

Gerken, Christina. *Model Immigrants and Undesirable Aliens: The Cost of Immigration Reform in the 1990s*. Minneapolis: University of Minnesota Press, 2013.

Gibney, Matthew J. *The Ethics and Politics of Asylum: Liberal Democracy and the Response to Refugees*. Cambridge: Cambridge University Press, 2004.

Gimpel, James G., and James R. Edwards Jr. *The Congressional Politics of Immigration Reform*. Boston: Allyn and Bacon, 1999.

Gonzales, Alberto R., and David N. Strange. *A Conservative and Compassionate Approach to Immigration Reform: Perspectives from a Former US Attorney General*. Lubbock: Texas Tech University Press, 2014.

Goodhart, David. *The British Dream: Successes and Failures of Post-War Immigration*. London: Atlantic Books, 2013.

Graham, Otis L. Jr. *Unguarded Gates: A History of America's Immigration Crisis*. Lanham, MD: Rowman & Littlefield, 2004.

Green, Emma. "The Catholic Church Isn't Doing So Well with Hispanic-Americans." *The Atlantic*, May 7, 2014.

Groody, Daniel G., and Gioacchino Campese, eds. *A Promised Land, A Perilous Journey: Theological Perspectives on Migration*. Notre Dame, IN: University of Notre Dame Press, 2008.

Hanson, Gordon H. *The Economic Logic of Illegal Immigration*. New York: Council on Foreign Relations, 2007.

Hauerwas, Stanley. *After Christendom? How the Church Is to Behave if Freedom, Justice, and a Christian Nation Are Bad Ideas*. Nashville: Abingdon, 1991.

Henkin, Louis. *The Age of Rights*. New York: Columbia University Press, 1990.

Heyer, Kristin E. *Kinship across Borders: A Christian Ethic of Immigration*. Washington, DC: Georgetown University Press, 2012.

Bibliography

Himmelfarb, Gertrude. "The Illusions of Cosmopolitanism." In *For Love of Country: Debating the Limits of Patriotism*, edited by Joshua Cohen, 72–77. Boston: Beacon, 1996.

Hoffmeier, James K. *The Immigration Crisis: Immigrants, Aliens, and the Bible.* Wheaton: Crossway, 2009.

Hornsby-Smith, Michael P. *An Introduction to Catholic Social Thought.* Cambridge: Cambridge University Press, 2006.

Huntington, Samuel P. *Who Are We? The Challenges to America's National Identity.* New York: Simon & Schuster, 2004.

Hylton, Wil S. "The Shame of America's Family Detention Camps." *The New York Times Magazine*, February 4, 2015.

Joppke, Christian, ed. *Challenge to the Nation-State: Immigration in Western Europe and the United States.* Oxford: Oxford University Press, 1998.

———. "Why Liberal States Accept Unwanted Immigration." *World Politics* 50 (January 1998): 266–93.

Kanstroom, Daniel. *Aftermath: Deportation Law and the New American Diaspora.* New York: Oxford University Press, 2012.

Kellstedt, Lyman A., and Ruth Melkonian-Hoover. "White Evangelicals and Immigration Reform." *The Christian Post*, April 19, 2015.

Kerwin, Donald M. "Rights, the Common Good, and Sovereignty in Service of the Human Person." In *And You Welcomed Me: Migration and Catholic Social Teaching*, edited by Donald Kerwin and Jill Marie Gerschutz, 93–122. Boulder: Rowman & Littlefield, 2009.

———. "Catholic Church and Immigration." In *Debates on U.S. Immigration*, edited by Judith Gans, Elaine M. Replogle, and Daniel J. Tichnor, 429–42. Los Angeles: Sage Reference, 2012.

Kretsedemas, Philip. *The Immigration Crucible: Transforming Race, Nation, and the Limits of the Law.* New York: Columbia University Press, 2012.

Land, Richard. "God and Immigration Reform." *USA Today*, August 15, 2010.

Levin, Yuval, and Reihan Salam. "The Immigrant Middle Ground." *National Review Online*, August 14, 2014. http://www.nationalreview.com/article/385258/immigration-middle-ground-yuval-levin-reihan-salam.

Lipka, Michael. "Catholic Leaders Urge Immigration Reform." *Pew Research Center*, September 6, 2013.

Masci, David. "Compared with Other Christian Groups, Evangelicals' Dropoff Is Less Steep." *Pew Research Center*, May 15, 2015.

Markoe, Lauren. "Evangelicals See 8-point Drop in Support for Immigration Reform." *Religion News Service*, June 11, 2014.

McGrath, Alister E. *Christianity: An Introduction.* Oxford: Blackwell, 1997.

Mead, Walter Russell. "God's Country?" *Foreign Affairs*, September/October 2006.

Meilaender, Peter C. "Ethics without Political Science." *Journal of Lutheran Ethics* 10 (April 2010). Available at: https://www.elca.org/JLE/Articles/311.

———. "Immigration: Citizens & Strangers." *First Things*, May 2007.

———. *Toward a Theory of Immigration.* New York: Palgrave, 2001.

Merritt, Jonathan. "Evangelicals and Immigration: Crunching the Numbers." *Religion News Service,* August 1, 2013.

———. "Why Evangelicals' Push for Immigration Reform Isn't Working." *Religion News Service,* July 23, 2013.

Miller, David. "Irregular Migrants: An Alternative Perspective." *Ethics & International Affairs* 2 (Summer 2008): 193–203.

Moloney, Deidre M. *National Insecurities: Immigrants and U.S. Deportation Policy Since 1982.* Chapel Hill: University of North Carolina Press, 2012.

Motomura, Hiroshi. *Immigration outside the Law.* New York: Oxford University Press, 2014.

Mouw, Richard J. *Abraham Kuyper: A Short and Personal Introduction.* Grand Rapids: Eerdmans, 2011.

———. "Carl Henry Was Right." *Christianity Today,* January 2010.

"National Poll of Evangelical Voters' Biblical Views and Moral Priorities on Immigration Policy." Pulse Opinion Research, February 2014. https://www.numbersusa.com/content/files/PulseSurvey_Evangelicals.pdf.

Nevins, Joseph. *Operation Gatekeeper: The Rise of the 'Illegal Alien' and the Making of the U.S.-Mexico Boundary.* New York: Routledge, 2002.

Ngai, Mae M. *Impossible Subjects: Illegal Aliens and the Making of Modern America.* Princeton: Princeton University Press, 2004.

Niebuhr, H. Richard. *Christ and Culture.* New York: Harper Torchbooks, 1951.

Niebuhr, Reinhold. *The Children of Light and the Children of Darkness.* New York: Charles Scribner's Sons, 1944.

———. *Love and Justice.* Philadelphia: Westminster, 1957.

———. *The Nature and Destiny of Man.* Vol. 1, *On Human Nature.* New York: Charles Scribner's Sons, 1964.

———. *The Nature and Destiny of Man.* Vol. 2, *Human Destiny.* New York: Charles Scribner's Sons, 1964.

———. "Why the Christian Church Is Not Pacifist." In *The Essential Reinhold Niebuhr: Selected Essays and Addresses,* edited by Robert McAfee Brown, 102–19. New Haven: Yale University Press, 1986.

Nussbaum, Martha C. "Patriotism and Cosmopolitanism." In *For Love of Country: Debating the Limits of Patriotism,* edited by Joshua Cohen, 2–17. Boston: Beacon, 1996.

Orrenius, Pia M., and Madeline Zavodny. *Beside the Golden Door: U.S. Immigration Reform in a New Era of Globalization.* Washington, DC: AEI Press, 2010.

Palazzolo, Jose. "Can Illegal Immigrants Practice Law?" *The Wall Street Journal,* September 3, 2013.

Pevnick, Ryan. *Immigration and the Constraints of Justice: Between Open Borders and Absolute Sovereignty.* Cambridge: Cambridge University Press, 2011.

Philpott, Daniel. *Revolutions in Sovereignty: How Ideas Shaped Modern International Relations.* Princeton: Princeton University Press, 2001.

Plaut, W. Gunther. *Asylum: A Moral Dilemma*. Westport, CT: Praeger, 1995.

Preston, Julia. "Judge Orders Immigrant Children and Mothers Released from Detention." *The New York Times*, July 26, 2015.

———. "Murder Case Exposes Lapses in Immigration Enforcement." *The New York Times*, July 8, 2015.

———. "States Are Divided by the Lines They Draw on Immigration." *The New York Times*, March 29, 2015.

Price, Bob. "Immigration Courts' Backlog Creates Virtual Amnesty." *Breibart*, August 29, 2014. http://www.breitbart.com/texas/2014/08/29/immigration-court-backlog-creates-virtual-amnesty/.

Putnam, Robert E., and David E. Campbell. *American Grace: How Religion Divides and Unites Us*. New York: Simon & Schuster, 2010.

Ramsey, Paul. *Who Speaks for the Church?* Nashville: Abingdon, 1967.

Rawls, John. *The Law of Peoples*. Cambridge: Harvard University Press, 1999.

Renshon, Stanley A. *The 50% American: Immigration and National Identity in an Age of Terror*. Washington, DC: Georgetown University Press, 2005.

Roberts, Bryan, Edward Alden, and John Whitley. *Managing Illegal Immigration in the United States: How Effective Is Enforcement?* New York: Council on Foreign Relations, 2013.

Rose, Amanda. *Showdown in the Sonoran Desert: Religion, Law, and the Immigration Controversy*. New York: Oxford University Press, 2012.

Schain, Martin A. *The Politics of Immigration in France, Britain, and the United States*. New York: Palgrave Macmillan, 2008.

Schuck, Peter H. *Citizens, Strangers, and In-Betweens: Essays on Immigration and Citizenship*. Boulder: Westview, 1998.

Schuck, Peter H., and Rogers M. Smith. *Citizenship without Consent: Illegal Aliens in the American Polity*. New Haven: Yale University Press, 1985.

———. "The Disconnect between Public Attitudes and Policy Outcomes in Immigration." In *Debating Immigration*, edited by Carol M. Swain, 17-31. Cambridge: Cambridge University Press, 2007.

Schueths, April, and Jodie Lawston, eds. *Living Together, Living Apart*. Seattle: University of Washington Press, 2015.

Shapiro, Jeffrey Scott. "The Evolution of Evangelicals on Immigration." *Washington Times*, June 20, 2013.

Shanks, Cheryl. *Immigration and the Politics of American Sovereignty, 1890-1990*. Ann Arbor: University of Michigan Press, 2001.

Shoichet, Catherine, and Tom Watkins. "No Green Card? No Problem—Undocumented Immigrant Can Practice Law, Court Says." *CNN*, January 3, 2014. http://www.cnn.com/2014/01/02/justice/california-immigrant-lawyer/index.html.

Sider, Ronald J. *The Scandal of Evangelical Politics: Why Are Christians Missing the Chance to Really Change the World?* Grand Rapids: Baker Books, 2008.

Singer, Peter. *The Life You Can Save*. New York: Random House, 2010.

————. *One World: The Ethics of Globalization*. 2nd ed. New Haven: Yale University Press, 2002.

Singer, Peter, and Renata Singer. "The Ethics of Refugee Policy." In *Open Borders? Closed Societies? The Ethical and Political Issues*, edited by Mark Gibney, 111–30. New York: Greenwood, 1988.

Singh, Manmeet. "Lament of a Legal Alien." *The Wall Street Journal*, August 12, 2014.

Skerry, Peter. "Splitting the Difference on Illegal Immigration." *National Affairs* 14 (Winter 2013): 3–26.

————. "Why 'Comprehensive Immigration Reform' Is Not Comprehensive." *The Forum* 7 (2009): Art. 5, 1–11.

Smietana, Bob. "Evangelicals Say It Is Time for Congress to Tackle Immigration." *LifeWay Research*, March 2015. http://lifewayresearch.com/2015/03/11/evangelicals-say-it-is-time-for-congress-to-tackle-immigration/.

Soerens, Matthew, and Jenny Hwang Yang. *Welcoming the Stranger: Justice, Compassion and Truth in the Immigration Debate*. Downers Grove, IL: IVP Books, 2009.

"Statement of Leith Anderson, President, National Association of Evangelicals." *Hearing on Faith-Based Community Perspectives on Comprehensive Immigration Reform before Senate Judiciary Subcommittee on Immigration, Border Security, and Refugees*, October 8, 2009. http://www.judiciary.senate.gov/imo/media/doc/10-08-09%20Anderson%20testimony.pdf.

Suro, Robert. *Watching America's Door: The Immigration Backlash and the New Policy Debate*. New York: Twentieth Century Fund, 1996.

Thomas, Andrea. "Germany Took in 1.1 Million Migrants in 2015." *The Wall Street Journal*, January 7, 2016.

Tichenor, Daniel J. "Navigating an American Minefield: The Politics of Illegal Immigration." *The Forum* 7 (2009): Art. 1, 1–21.

Tinder, Glenn. "Can We Be Good without God?" *The Atlantic Monthly*, December 1989.

Tooley, Mark. "Evangelical Grassroots versus 'Grasstops.'" *The American Spectator*, July 31, 2013.

Wallis, Jim. "The Bible's Case for Immigration Reform." *Los Angeles Times*, August 8, 2013.

Walters, Mary C., and Reed Ueda, eds. *The New Americans: A Guide to Immigration Since 1965*. Cambridge: Harvard University Press, 2007.

Walzer, Michael. *Spheres of Justice: A Defense of Pluralism and Equality*. New York: Basic Books, 1983.

Weiner, Myron. "Ethics, National Sovereignty, and the Control of Immigration." *International Migration Review* 30 (Spring 1996).

————. *The Global Migration Crisis: Challenge to States and to Human Rights*. New York: HarperCollins, 1995.

Weissbrodt, David, and Laura Danielson. *Immigration Law and Procedure in a Nutshell*. 6th ed. Minneapolis: West Publishing Co., 2011.

Bibliography

Welch, Michael. *Detained: Immigration Laws and the Expanding I.N.S. Jail Complex.* Philadelphia: Temple University Press, 2002.

Wellman, Christopher Heath, and Phillip Cole. *Debating the Ethics of Immigration: Is There a Right to Exclude?* New York: Oxford University Press, 2011.

Wilbanks, Dana W. *Re-creating America: The Ethics of U.S. Immigration and Refugee Policy in a Christian Perspective.* Nashville: Abingdon, 1996.

Wildavsky, Aaron. *Speaking Truth to Power: The Art and Craft of Policy Analysis.* New Brunswick, NJ: Transaction, 1987.

Wilsher, Daniel. *Immigration Detention Law, History, Politics.* Cambridge: Cambridge University Press, 2012.

Wogaman, J. Philip. *Christian Ethics: A Historical Introduction.* Louisville: Westminster/John Knox, 1993.

Wolterstorff, Nicholas. "Theological Foundations for an Evangelical Political Philosophy." In *Toward an Evangelical Public Policy,* edited by Ronald J. Sider and Diane Knippers, 140–62. Grand Rapids: Baker Books, 2005.

———. *Until Justice and Peace Embrace.* Grand Rapids: Eerdmans, 1983.

Woodward, Kenneth L. "Dead End for the Mainline? The Mightiest Protestants Are Running Out of Money, Members and Meaning." *Newsweek,* August 9, 1993.

Worthen, Molly. "Love Thy Stranger as Thyself." *The New York Times,* May 11, 2013.

Zolberg, Aristide R. *A Nation by Design: Immigration Policy and the Fashioning of America.* Cambridge, MA: Harvard University Press, 2006.

Government Documents

Baker, Bryan, and Nancy Rytina. "Estimates of Legal Permanent Resident Population in the United States: January 2013." Office of Immigration Statistics, Department of Homeland Security, September 2014.

———. "Estimates of the Unauthorized Immigrant Population Residing in the United States: January 2012." Office of Immigration Statistics, Department of Homeland Security, March 2013.

Executive Office for Immigration Review. *FY 2014: Statistics Yearbook.* U.S. Department of Justice, Office of Planning, Analysis, and Technology, March 2015.

Foreman, Katie, and Randall Monger. "Nonimmigrant Admissions to the United States: 2013." Office of Immigration Statistics, Department of Homeland Security, July 2014.

Kandel, William A. "U.S. Family-Based Immigration Policy." *Congressional Research Service,* November 19, 2014.

———. "U.S. Immigration Policy: Chart Book of Key Trends." *Congressional Research Service,* December 17, 2014.

Martin, Daniel C., and James E. Yankay. "Refugees and Asylees: 2013." Office of Immigration Statistics, Department of Homeland Security, August 2014.

Monger, Randall, and James E. Yankay. "U.S. Lawful Permanent Residents: 2013." Office of Immigration Statistics, Department of Homeland Security, May 2014.

Simanski, John F. "Immigration Enforcement Actions: 2013." Annual Report, Office of Immigration Statistics, Department of Homeland Security, September 2014.

Siskin, Alison. "Alien Removals and Returns: Overview and Trends." *Congressional Research Service*, February 3, 2015.

2013 *Yearbook of Immigration Statistics*. Office of Immigration Statistics, Department of Homeland Security, August 2014.

United States Commission on Immigration Reform. *Becoming an American: Immigration and Immigration Policy*. Final Report submitted to Congress, 1997.

———. *Legal Immigration: Setting Priorities*. Interim Report submitted to Congress, 1995.

———. *U.S. Immigration Policy: Restoring Credibility*. Interim Report submitted to Congress, 1994.

———. *U.S. Refugee Policy: Taking Leadership*. Final Report submitted to Congress, 1997.

U.S. Immigration and Customs Enforcement. "ICE Enforcement and Removal Operations Report, Fiscal Year 2014." Department of Homeland Security, December 19, 2014.

U.S. Select Commission on Immigration and Refugee Policy. "U.S. Immigration Policy and the National Interest." Submitted to Congress and the President of the United States, March 1, 1981.

Wasem, Ruth Ellen. "U.S. Immigration Policy on Permanent Admissions." *Congressional Research Service*, March 13, 2012.

Church Documents

Christian Reformed Church. "Committee to Study the Migration of Workers, 2010." www.crcna.org/sites/default/files/Migration.pdf.

The Episcopal Church. "The Alien among You." General Convention, 2006. http://madreanna.org/immref/alien.pdf.

———. "The Nation and the Common Good: Reflections on Immigration Reform." A Pastoral Letter from the House of Bishops, September 21, 2010. http://www.episcopalchurch.org/notice/house-bishops-issues-pastoral-letter-along-theological-resource-%C2%93-nation-and-common-good-refl.

Evangelical Covenant Church. "2014 Resolution on Immigration." http://www.covchurch.org/wp-content/uploads/sites/65/2013/03/2014-Resolution-on-Immigration-FINAL-without-Resource.pdf.

Evangelical Lutheran Church in America. "A Message on . . . Immigration." Division for Church in Society, 1998. http://download.elca.org/ELCA%20Resource%20Repository/ImmigrationSM.pdf.

————. "Toward Compassionate, Just, and Wise Immigration Reform," 2009. http://lirs.org/wp-content/uploads/2012/05/ELCA.STATEMENTELCA TOWARDCOMPASSIONATEJUSTWISEIMMIGRATIONREFORM.pdf.

"Family Beyond Borders." An Open Letter from the Bishops of the Border Region of Mexico, Texas, and New Mexico, November 28, 2013. http://www.justice forimmigrants.org/documents/Family-Beyond-Borders.pdf.

"Forming Consciences for Faithful Citizenship: A Call to Political Responsibility from the Catholic Bishops of the United States." Washington, DC: United States Conference of Catholic Bishops, 2007.

Free Methodist Church. "The Free Methodist Position on Immigration." Study Commission on Doctrine, 2013. http://fmcusa.org/files/2014/03 /The-Free-Methodist-Church-on-Immigration.pdf.

"Immigration and Our Nation's Future: A Pastoral Letter on Immigration." Archdiocese of Denver, October 2, 2013. http://archden.org/wp-content /uploads/2014/09/Immigration-and-future-bilingual.pdf.

Lutheran Church Missouri Synod. "Immigrants among Us: A Lutheran Framework for Addressing Immigration Issues." A Report of the Commission on Theology and Church Relations, November 2012. http://www.lcms.org/?pid=675.

National Association of Evangelicals. "Immigration 2009." http://www.nae.net /immigraton-2009/.

Presbyterian Church (USA). "Comprehensive Legalization Program for Immigrants Living and Working in the United States With Study Guide." General Assembly, 2004. http://www.pcusa.org/site_media/media/uploads/_resolutions /immigrant-legal.pdf.

————. "Transformation of Churches and Society through Encounter with New Neighbors." General Assembly, 1999. https://www.pcusa.org/site_media /media/uploads/_resolutions/encounter-with-new-neighbors-1999.pdf.

Sutton, Eugene Taylor, and John L. Rabb. "Welcoming the Stranger: A Pastoral Letter Addressing the Need for Comprehensive Immigration Reform." The Episcopal Diocese of Maryland, 2010. http://www.collegeforbishops.org /assets/1145/2010-09-02-pastoral-ltr-immig-english.pdf.

Southern Baptist Convention. "On Immigration and the Gospel." SBC Resolution, 2011. www.sbc.net/resolutions/1213.

Taylor, Bishop Anthony B. "I Was a Stranger and You Welcomed Me . . ." A Pastoral Letter on the Human Rights of Immigrants, Catholic Diocese of Little Rock, November 5, 2008. http://www.stlukerc.org/PDF/pastoralimmigration _english.pdf.

"Traveling Together in Hope." A Pastoral Letter on Immigration from the Catholic Bishops of Wisconsin, December 12, 2011. http://www.wisconsincatholic.org /WCC%20Immigration%20Letter--ENGLISH.pdf.

United States Catholic Bishops. "The Challenge of Peace: God's Promise and Our Response." The Pastoral Letter on War and Peace. *Origins*, May 19, 1983.

United States Conference of Catholic Bishops. "Strangers No Longer: Together on the Journey of Hope." A Pastoral Letter Concerning Migration from the Catholic Bishops of Mexico and the United States, 2003. http://www.usccb .org/issues-and-action/human-life-and-dignity/immigration/strangers-no -longer-together-on-the-journey-of-hope.cfm.

The Wesleyan Church. "A Wesleyan View of Immigration, 2008." https://www .wesleyan.org/237/a-wesleyan-view-of-immigration.

"You Welcomed Me." A Pastoral Letter on Migration Released on the Feast of Our Lady of Guadalupe. Arizona Catholic Conference and the Byzantine Catholic Eparchy of Van Nuys, December 12, 2005. http://www.justiceforimmigrants .org/documents/you-welcomed-me.pdf.

Index

Bush, George W., 4, 47, 64, 167–68
Bush, Jeb, 71
Burma, 27
B visa, 21

caesar, 157, 185
California Proposition, 51, 67, 77, 79, 187
Campbell, David, 163
Canada, 17, 176
"cancellation of removal," 28
Carens, Joseph, 92–95
Carroll, M. Daniel, 99, 128, 131, 225
catch-and-release program, 32, 38
Catholic bishops, 222; and immigration
    reform, 146–60; pastoral letter on
    immigration, 146–55; pastoral letter
    on nuclear deterrence, 235–37; view
    of the world, 136–40, 226–27
Catholic Church, 110, 112–13, 125,
    134–40, 226; and democracy, 140
Catholic Social Thought (CST), 111, 135,
    140–44, 139
chain migration, 60–61
Chaput, Archbishop Charles, 157
charity, 210, 237
China, 9, 23, 27, 56, 60, 61
Chinese Exclusion Act, 10
Chomsky, Aviva, 1, 2
Christian ethics, xi, 97, 124, 229; and
    approach to immigration, 12–15,
    97–102, 109
Christian Reformed Church, 125, 176–78
Christiansen, Drew, 97, 144, 154
Christian worldview, 97
church, 122, 152–53, 167, 198, 202, 215,
    227
citizen, 7, 14, 16, 17, 41, 90, 91, 102, 178,
    219; birthright of, 220
citizenship, 23, 88, 106, 110, 121, 132,
    157, 158, 159, 175, 180, 195, 199, 217,
    223, 225; dual nature of, 121–23, 127;
    global, 223
Citizenship and Immigration Services
    (CIS), 9, 20, 28
"City of God," 110, 121, 123, 145n19, 194,
    215, 217, 223, 234

"City of Man," 110, 121, 123, 145n19, 194,
    215, 217, 223, 234
civility, 237
Civil Law, 209, 210
client politics, 70, 72, 74–76
Cold War, 115, 135, 155, 171, 228
collective action problem, 74
Collier, Paul, 23, 68, 75, 91, 105
Colson, Charles, 166
common good, 72, 102, 113–14, 120, 140,
    141, 143, 155, 205, 217, 237
communitarianism, 13, 80–84, 106, 129,
    221, 223; contribution of, 100–102
compassion, 155, 171, 173, 175, 177, 179,
    180, 185, 186, 202, 205, 206, 214, 216,
    224, 232
"Compendium of the Social Doctrine of
    the Church," 136–40
compliance, 215. See also Obedience to
    government
Conference of Latin American Bishops
    (CELAM), 142
Constantine, Emperor, 136; influence on
    the church, 136–38
cooperation, 91, 109
cosmopolitanism, 13, 80–81, 84–86, 129,
    144, 221, 223
Cuba, 27
Customs and Border Protection (CBP),
    20, 28
cynics, 84

Deferred Action for Childhood Arrivals
    (DACA), 49, 50, 76; eligibility criteria
    for, 49n1
Deferred Action for Parents Act (DAPA),
    60, 64, 76
democratic government, 93, 106, 156,
    166
Denmark, 3
Department of Health and Human Ser-
    vices (HHS), 30, 36, 46, 54, 55
Department of Homeland Security
    (DHS), 27, 29, 32, 62–63, 77
Department of Justice (DOJ), 28, 77
Department of Labor, 28, 37
Department of State, 26, 35–36, 63

Index

Iran, 26

Iraq, 3, 27

irregular migrants, xii, 39, 94. *See also* illegal aliens and unauthorized aliens

Japan, 17

Jesus, 157, 162, 163, 175, 177, 187, 197, 202

Johnson, Jeh, 47

Joppke, Christian, 70

Jordan Commission, 60, 62

Jordan, Rep. Barbara, 39

justice, 2, 82, 83, 91, 109, 123, 129, 148, 158, 160, 168, 179, 186, 195, 196, 198, 210, 213, 216, 218, 223; types of, 86–87, 130. *See also* "proximate justice"

just immigration, 2, 15, 100, 130, 152, 205, 216

just-war principles, 236

Kellstedt, Lyman, 184

Kerwin, Donald, 145

Kretsedemas, Philip, 11

Kuwait, 17

Kuyper, Abraham, 116

labor, 1, 143

labor unions, 75

Land, Richard, 168, 186

legal compliance, 41

legal enforcement, 37–41

legalization of immigrants, 70, 150, 158, 170, 175, 200

legal permanent resident (LPR), xii, 4, 23, 24, 25, 28, 29, 53, 71

Levin, Yuval, 12, 73

Lewis, C. S., 160–61

liberation theology, 142

liberty, 190. *See also* freedom

Libya, 3

lottery, 25, 26

love, 100, 117, 119, 120, 123, 177, 179, 185, 194, 197, 202, 205, 212, 215, 218; divine love, 124, 194; impediments to, 119

low-wage workers, 5, 10, 37, 67, 74, 90, 169, 201, 215. *See also* guest workers

Luther, Martin, 114

Lutheran Church Missouri Synod (LCMS), 204; approach to immigration, 207–14

Lutheranism, 204, 233

Macedo, Stephen, 90, 105

Macedonia, 3

magisterium, 126, 135

Mainline Protestant churches, 115, 184, 191, 192–94; political ethics of, 194–97

Mariel boatlift, 78

McCarran-Walter Act. *See* Immigration and Nationality Act of 1952

McGrath, Alister, 162

Meilaender, Peter, 98, 156, 172, 206, 207

Melkonian-Hoover, Ruth, 184

mercy, 174–75, 183, 210

Merritt, Jonathan, 181, 183

Mexico, 3, 23, 45, 46, 56, 60, 61, 65, 67, 98, 104, 150, 153, 154

migration, 14, 16, 160, 218, 220, 225, 231; Christian perspectives on, 97–102; communitarian view of, 87–91; cosmopolitan view of, 92–96; regulation of, 109, 145; right to, 145, 147, 160

misdemeanor, 7, 44, 95

"mixed-status" families, 68

Monroe Kullberg, Kelly, 127, 184

Moore, Russell, 168, 180

moral analysis: of immigration policy, xi, 152, 157, 217, 219, 238; of state system, 92–93

"moral hazard," 187

moral claims: conflict of, 174, 189, 199

moral education, 152, 189, 217, 224, 228, 233, 237

moral ideals, 234

morality, 157, 227; of nuclear deterrence, 235

moral obligations, 90

moral principles, 14, 112, 160

moral teaching, 153, 157–58, 159, 213, 217, 228

Motomura, Hiroshi, 40n42, 78

Mouw, Richard, 117, 164